Systemic Therapy and Attachment Narratives

CW00540206

Professional interest in the clinical applications of attachment theory continues to grow and evolve, and at the same time narrative approaches are also gaining ground. This book explores how attachment-based ideas can be used in clinical practice by offering a practical and sophisticated exposition of clinical approaches.

Bringing together three main systems of thought and psychotherapeutic practice – systemic theory, attachment theory and narrative theory – practitioners are shown how to use these ideas in their work through the integrated approach of 'attachment narrative therapy'.

Using clinical examples, the authors provide guidance on how to use attachment narrative therapy in different clinical contexts and with various client groups, including working with:

- addictions: alcohol dependency and eating distress
- loss and grief
- trauma and dissociation
- love and sexuality: applications with couples.

Systemic Therapy and Attachment Narratives provides practical guidance for a range of mental health professionals including family therapists, child, adolescent and adult psychotherapists, clinical psychologists and social workers, enabling them to apply this approach in a range of contexts.

Rudi Dallos is the Programme Director of the Plymouth University Doctorate in Clinical Psychology. He also works as a clinical psychologist specialising in work with adolescents and their families.

Arlene Vetere is Deputy Director of Clinical Psychology Doctorate training at Surrey University and a family therapist, registered with the UKCP. She is also President of the European Family Therapy Association.

Systemic Therapy and Attachment Narratives

Applications in a range of clinical settings

Rudi Dallos and Arlene Vetere

Routledge
Taylor & Francis Group

LONDON AND NEW YORK

First published 2009
by Routledge
27 Church Road, Hove, East Sussex BN3 2FA

Simultaneously published in the USA and Canada
by Routledge
711 Third Avenue, New York, NY 10017, USA

Routledge is an imprint of the Taylor & Francis Group, an Informa business

Typeset in Times by
RefineCatch Limited, Bungay, Suffolk

Paperback cover design by Design Deluxe
Paperback cover painting by Ben Healey (benhealey@live.co.uk)

British Library Cataloguing in Publication Data
A catalogue record for this book is available from the British Library

Library of Congress Cataloging-in-Publication Data
Dallos, Rudi, 1948–
   Systemic therapy and attachment narratives : applications in a range of clinical settings / Rudi Dallos & Arlene Vetere.
      p. ; cm.
   Includes bibliographical references and index.
   1. Attachment Behaviour. 2. Narrative therapy. 3. Systemic therapy (Family therapy) I. Vetere, Arlene. II. Title.
   [DNLM: 1. Psychotherapy—methods. 2. Object Attachment.
WM 420 D147s 2009]
   RC455.4.A84D35 2009
   616.89'14—dc22   2008036298

ISBN: 978–0–415–41657–3 (hbk)
ISBN: 978–0–415–41658–0 (pbk)

Contents

List of figures and tables

FIGURES

TABLES

Foreword

This book, in association with Dallos's (2006a) book, provides a comprehensive and excellent picture of family therapeutic practice covering and connecting all the dimensions of attachment and narrative into a systemic framework. It represents a landmark in the unfolding integration of family attachments into the heart of family therapy.

After the Second World War, Bowlby wrote about attachment and the consequences of evacuation, which separated children from their families. Later, in 1949, he wrote about his work with whole families as part of therapy with children (see Bowlby, 1988). His ideas about family work spread to the United States and helped to initiate family therapy there. It can be claimed that he started family therapy, and if so, he was a founder of both family therapy and attachment theory. He went to the early lectures in the United States, presenting systems theory, which was then incorporated into family systems. He supported family therapy from the beginning, knowing that the original research had to start with mother and child, and then extending it to family attachments. This book incorporates the results. Bowlby would have been delighted.

In terms of developing his ideas, Bowlby gained much from his own clinical work. He knew that working with clients was vital to develop ideas about attachment and techniques. He had regular seminars with clinicians of various orientations and with researchers. I was privileged to be part of that group.

Specific attachment approaches have now been introduced to the field of therapy, and family therapy. In this book the authors, Dallos and Vetere, go further with their systemic model, which integrates attachment with other suitable family therapy approaches. Their model also incorporates various aspects of narrative. The links between attachment and narrative have been well researched. To apply this the authors have illustrated the clinical relevance of the links between secure attachments and healthy relationships. They discuss how insecure attachments lead to incoherent narrative of three kinds – dismissive, ambivalent and disorganised – which are linked to various problems.

Using this interlinking model, the authors incorporate many strands of family life; for instance, affect, which they emphasise is an important aspect of attachment, and other driving forces in human behaviour such as love and sexuality and life cycles. There are links to the various behaviours associated with each of these phenomena. All this points to useful family techniques and strategies.

This book describes in comprehensive detail the many dimensions within the model and its applications. It is fascinating and informative and took me on a journey to a wider perspective. My own attempt has been to help family therapists to add attachment to their own approach. Dallos and Vetere take the field to a significant new level that encompasses a comprehensive range of therapeutic practices. They provide an approach to family therapy that incorporates various suitable family therapy techniques. Their book also describes how to collaborate with other professionals involved in tackling particular situations and problems.

The authors discuss the process of mutual exploration, which is made possible through establishing a secure therapeutic base that enables the family to create a secure family base, which then enables change to evolve. This can be applied to a series of contexts and techniques such as exploring feelings involved in attachment, emotional sculpting, communication using genograms, scripts and exploring patterns of comforting. The authors describe reflective team discussion, reflective conversation and addressing attachment injury.

There is a discussion about therapists' own needs and how the exploration involved in the writing of this book led to new ideas. The authors describe their own attachment histories relevant to their work. Their collaboration together could be called a secure base in intra-professional working, and they suggest that family therapists should also collaborate in this way.

This book is a treasure and will benefit all family therapists, researchers and trainees. I learned a lot that has widened my perspectives of the field.

John Byng-Hall

Chapter 1

Introduction

Emotion is a leading element in the system that organises interaction between intimates.

(Johnson, 1998, p. 3)

Both of us in our respective clinical therapeutic contexts have felt the need to be able to draw on models that have a better fit with our experiences of working with couples and families. Family members have often showed intense feelings in our sessions: people have broken into tears, have felt deep shame, have become agitated and have shouted and mutually accused each other, and sometimes people have even gotten up and walked out. In our earlier days we sometimes wondered what we might be doing wrong to have aroused or aggravated their feelings. RD was trained initially in the ethos of the rather 'cool' strategic and then Milan therapies in which it seemed that family therapy was about being rather clever and engaging in a sort of jousting with families. The early Milan approaches were developed to work with extreme problems, such as longstanding eating disorders and longstanding problems with psychosis, and were based on the assumption of family members' over-involvement. At the same time, these approaches, especially in the sophisticated hands of the originators, such as Paul Watzlawick *et al.* (1967), the Milan team (Palazzoli *et al.*, 1978), Jay Haley (1987) and John Weakland (1982), also frequently revealed a deep sense of hopefulness, acceptance, fun, benign teasing and sympathy for families and their problems. Paulo Bertrando (2007) nicely captures this, describing what is often untold, especially in the written descriptions of the ways in which therapists work in the different family therapy models:

[A]n expert Milan-style therapist would never forget the concrete life experiences and the *emotional tones* of the client's situation and would have calibrated herself to these, but such a sensibility is difficult to convey and teach purely through writing, where ideological infatuation becomes easier.

(Bertrando, 2007: 11)

We are not claiming to be free of 'ideological infatuation' but we do take heed of Betrando's observations and hope to consider in this book some of what has been untold, especially in relation to the role of emotions and attachment in family and other forms of psychotherapy.

AV was initially trained in the structural approach, which was developed to help families struggling with emotional disconnection and parental authority. Both of us have retained an interest in structural theory and the methods where feelings and their expression in sessions were not only more accepted but some of the techniques, such as enactment and intensification, were specifically directed at eliciting strong feelings in order to help provoke and promote change. However, these more directive and emotional ways of working seemed to go out of fashion in the UK, although arguably they are showing signs of a renaissance. Interestingly, the structural approach also connects with something very important that we have experienced over the years in working with families: the situations where family members try not to and do not show feelings; more precisely, where they seem to be attempting to conceal, hide, deny or camouflage their feelings although we, the therapists, may feel in our bodies some intense but unstated tensions in the room.

Interestingly, what is said less frequently is that the early pioneers of various schools were great storytellers. Arguably, narrative therapy was not invented in the 1990s but maybe all good therapists become skilled in listening to and weaving healing stories with individuals and families.

This book is based around our integration of ideas from systemic family therapy, narrative therapies and attachment theory (Vetere and Dallos, 2003; Vetere and Dowling, 2005; Dallos, 2006a). In the next chapter we will review the attempt we have made to forge these approaches together and also some developments that we have made in this evolving journey. But an important point of focus for us in this chapter is the consideration of ourselves in the therapeutic process – what we might call a reflexive position. The feelings that we experience in our work with families might be referred to in psychodynamic theories in terms of transferences or projections and identifications. In our use of attachment theory, we wish to think about our own attachment experiences and how these shape how we respond to couples and families both emotionally and cognitively. Although a reflexive stance has not been at the forefront of attachment theory, in our attempts to apply it to therapy we want to argue that it is very compatible with the approach. Some therapists, for example Johnson (2004), regard emotions and their expression as the central dynamic in couples and family therapy. In order to experience, recognise and act on these feelings we need to be personally present in the room and able to engage with, touch and connect with the emotions in the room – not to be overwhelmed by them but neither deny nor distance ourselves from them. This positioning has profound implications for how we train couples therapists and family therapists. Sometimes we observe a trainee therapist's discomfort with strong feelings, leading them to seek to calm, soothe and gloss over strong feelings too soon, thus denying family members a chance to expand and illuminate their own responding.

We have decided to write this book to complement *Attachment Narrative Therapy*, which was published in 2006 (Dallos, 2006a). This was an attempt to draw together ideas from systemic and narrative therapies with ideas from attachment theory. Although the title of the book suggests a 'new' form of therapy, the intention was less to do this than to outline an emerging integration of ideas from these various approaches. In the start of the 2006 book, a set of clinical and theoretical issues was outlined as the prompts to the development of the attachment narrative therapy (ANT) approach:

Systemic theory and therapy

- Risks neglecting individual emotional experience.
- Lacks a developmental perspective.
- Recent family therapy and narrative approaches neglect patterns of interaction and communication.
- Related to the above there has been less interest in considering how particular patterns or styles of family interaction may relate to different kinds of problems.

Arguably the revolution in thinking that systemic therapy presented (Vetere and Dallos, 2003; Dallos and Draper, 2005) perhaps moved us to place such a great emphasis on patterns and processes that we started to overlook the nature of individual emotional experiences in couples and families and how different identities and personalities developed. The person risks becoming lost in the complexity of discussion about context, processes and patterns.

Narrative theory and therapy approaches

As with systemic theory, some nagging questions arise regarding the narrative therapy approaches:

- How do narratives develop in couples and families?
- Do people have developmental differences in their narrative abilities/ 'skills'
- What are the links between narratives, emotions, life events and family patterns?
- How are relationships conceptualised?

We have raised some questions of concern for these approaches, such as: Does the emphasis on language and narrative presuppose the extent to which being able to place our experiences into narratives is a sophisticated skill, which develops gradually through childhood and needs to be fostered and nurtured, and for some people may be developmentally constrained? We can also see a need for an understanding of the learning processes and experiences that foster or alternatively hinder the development of narrative abilities or styles, for example the impact of continuous trauma on a child's developing ability to narrate their experiences is important for us to consider. As therapists we need to recognise how and why family members have come to develop narrative styles that exclude the contribution of feelings, attachments and relationships to problems. Such recognition may help us in our ability to talk with them in order to construct more open narratives and retain our focus on the importance of relationships.

Attachment theory

- Overly biological and deterministic research-based descriptive categories.
- Mother-blaming or blaming of the primary carer?
- Is a dyadic focus too simple and somehow decontextualised?
- Neglect of intergenerational processes and transmission of attachment responding.

Attachment theory can be seen as over-narrow in its emphasis on the dyadic process between a parent and a child, or between two intimate partners. Worse, this has predominantly been a focus on mother–child patterns with some implications of mother-blaming for the development of insecurity in their infants. Attachment theory is a developmental theory of the social regulation of emotion, but it has perhaps adopted an overly biological view of the basis of attachments rather than considering sociocultural processes that shape what is regarded as appropriate and good parenting, appropriate levels of bonding, the role of mothers and fathers, economic pressures on families and so on.

For us, these questions are much more than predominantly theoretical concerns. They connect with our clinical experiences and also with our own clinical and personal identities.

RD: For me, the pathway to the integrated approach was through a period of involvement in systemic family therapy spanning over 30 years. Initially, my immersion was more in constructivist approaches that emphasised an exploration of family beliefs and understandings (Bateson, 1972; Watzlawick et al., 1974; Palazzoli et al., 1978; Haley, 1987). Arguably, these early approaches, though differing in many ways, shared an emphasis on the reconstruction of meaning in families as a central component of change. The idea of 'reframing' was pivotal in this search to help families find new ways of seeing problems to help them move out of unhelpful or 'stuck' ways of seeing their relationships and difficulties. At the same time, I also experienced the impact of the structural family therapy movement (Satir, 1964; Minuchin *et al.*, 1978), which had a greater emphasis on working with feelings and actions in the room with families.

In retrospect I can now see that, along with many colleagues, I was weaving together aspects of the different models. For example, in the supposedly 'cooler' Milan models it was not infrequent that people could become very emotional on receiving a positive connotation or paradoxical task. Of course we responded to their feelings but it might be fair to say that often we had less of a language to think about these experiences. Looking back on this period of my early training I sometimes squirm at how naïve we were at the time regarding people's feelings, for example in suggesting 'paradoxical tasks' such as deliberately increasing a symptom.

AV: My professional pathway to a synthesis of attachment theory with systemic psychotherapy was through an early training in structural family therapy, cognitive behaviour therapy and brief focal psychodynamic therapy (Malan, 1979) and the opportunity over the years to work with couples. My training in structural family therapy introduced me to ways of working with couples and families that enabled emotional expression and the development of supported risk taking in communication, which led to changes in family members' felt experiences in relation to each other. My training in cognitive behaviour therapy taught me the importance of beliefs in governing behavioural choices, and the interconnected nature of thought, feeling and action. At that time, neither of these approaches paid much attention to developmental pathways in the formation of cognitive schema, or the patterns of communication in families. Both were oriented to working in the here and now of people's lived experiences. I turned to object relations theories, and in particular attachment theory, to help me understand and formulate with family members how things had come to be, so to speak. I have always believed that working with felt emotional experience facilitates change through a trusting therapeutic relationship. Thus, I trained in Malan's brief focal psychodynamic therapy to develop further my own comfort in working therapeutically with strong negative feelings of anger, grief, shame, hostility, contempt and disgust.

Through this early period it was clear that Minuchin (1974) was much less naïve about possible feelings that might be evoked and more able to evoke feelings deliberately in families. His techniques included *enactment* – in which family members were requested to play out difficult and emotionally distressing patterns in their lives in the room, thus creating an opportunity to experiment with different responses in the safety of the therapeutic encounter – and *intensification* – which involved a deliberate intensification of feelings designed to disrupt the pattern whereby difficult feelings had been repeatedly avoided. As an example, anxiety and conflict in a couple could be seen to be 'detoured' by a change of topic to a child's problems or misbehaviours. The emphasis was on supporting action in the room, rather than talking about action, in the belief that most people had the necessary interpersonal resources to take risks and go beyond their usual response patterns, in the safety of a therapeutic alliance.

We are not trying to say that emotions have been absent in the field of family therapy; more that they were like 'ideas that kept knocking on the door' but never quite joined the dinner party. One reason for this might be that systemic family therapy developed as a contrast and counter to the intra-psychic excesses of Freudian psychodynamic models. However, these models also were the dominant models of emotional life but offered a highly indi-vidualistic view. In addition, through Freud's abandonment of the detec-tion of the destructive impact of actual sexual abuse occurring in families, an important bridge between internal emotional states and family experiences was destroyed. Of course, one of the key arguments that we wish to make in this book is that attachment theory was a much stronger contender as a model on which systemic family could have drawn. This seems to have hap-pened rather sporadically and we can perhaps only guess at why this was the case. One reason might be that it was over-identified with psychodynamic theories as predominantly another version. In retrospect, we can see that this was a great pity and perhaps based on misunderstandings of attachment theory. Bowlby (1988) was eclectic and drew on systemic theory, as well as ideas from evolutionary theory, cognitive psychology as well as, but certainly not exclusively, object relations theories.

This, of course, is moving into the professional story of RD and AV's journeys towards the development of the ANT approach. Another more personal story is to do with RD's own family history and early attachment experiences. RD: I came out of Hungary as a refugee in the Hungarian revolution in 1956. This was an emotionally disruptive time and involved considerable upheaval, some danger and anxiety. One of the ways that I learnt to cope was to hold my feelings back and in addition, being the oldest son, I had to take on a role of being responsible and caring for my mother and younger siblings at a very early age. This role reversal and position as a parental child (Byng-Hall, 2008a) has been well documented and possibly is one that many of us in the helping professions occupy (Crittenden, 1997). It is also involves a survival strategy in which we may distance ourselves from our own feelings and may well contribute to an interest in therapeutic approaches that are relatively exclusive of emotions. Arguably, the strategic and Milan family therapies nicely fit this profile and of course the all-pervasive cognitive behaviour therapy even more. Interestingly, my early interests were precisely in strategic systemic approaches combined with personal construct theory – an elegant but essentially semantic approach. Gradually, as my own life circumstances developed – I married, had children, got divorced, got married again and separated again – my abilities, or more precisely lack of them, to deal with my emotions became increasingly clear. It also became clear that my beloved systemic family therapy models were not helping me to make sense of my own life as much as I had hoped!

Here we meet an important question: to what extent is it relevant or important that we are able to utilise the therapeutic models we are choosing to employ with clients to help negotiate our own lives? We want to argue here that if we advocate a reflexive approach to therapy and clinical practice, the answer needs to be that the approach we choose does need to make personal sense (Simon, 1995). So, in my own life, trying to be strategic, talking about being stuck in circularities and patterns, and looking at underlying beliefs, although of some help, was not quite getting at why, for example, my partner was blazingly angry with me, or me with her! However, ideas such as replaying childhood insecurities, behaving emotionally like my parents did, being unreasonably jealous and so on were closer to what I was experiencing. So, eventually, attachment theory started to make increasing sense of my own internal experiences. At the same time, my systemic training helped me to feel slightly less guilty and responsible – it's the two of us, not just *my* fault!

AV: My personal story is one of inter-continental migration, loss and resilience. My father was killed in a road traffic accident when I was 11 years old. I learned about grief, and watched how it changed my mother and affected our lives at home. My wish to help my mother gave me a chance to learn how to be a listener and to carefully attune myself to how someone else was feeling. In later life I lost my beloved husband Graham to cancer. I hope I have never underestimated the impact of loss, of the fear of loss, and the capacity for resilience, strength and change. For me, attachment theory speaks strongly to my own experiences, and makes sense of my belief that accessibility and responsiveness in relationships is the building block of attachment security. Attachment theory does not pathologise dependency in relationships, rather, it sees dependency as an active act of integration. I think one of the reasons our field tended to minimise emotion and emotional experience was an unanticipated consequence of the feminist critiques of family therapy theories and practices. In our wish to elucidate the importance of power in relationships and gender inequalities in social roles and opportunities, we deconstructed the accusation that women use 'emotional power' to get their own way in unequal power relationships, and somehow left emotion behind as well. In my work with couples I work with the fear of loss, rejection and abandonment, which often finds its expression in anger, blame and jealousy. Speaking personally, many is the time I have self-righteously demanded an apology from Graham, when all I really wanted was a cuddle and reassurance that all was well. Over 30 years of couples' therapy experience, you may well say, and still struggling to change! I am happy to say that humour often came to the rescue!

Chapter 2

Systemic therapy and attachment narratives

Guiding framework for formulation and therapy

Attachment narrative therapy model

The approach we describe in this book draws on the attachment narrative therapy (ANT) model described in a previous book by Dallos (2006a), which details how concepts from attachment theory and systemic and narrative therapies can be brought together in ways that offer some potential for extensions of each of the three approaches. Although offering some new ways of thinking about work with families, we also want to emphasise that ANT and the developments and applications described in this book are offered, not as a new set of 'techniques', but as a framework with some new ways of seeing what we already do – an alternative lens with which to look at systemic and narrative therapies. To take a few examples, we think that externalising and discussing unique outcomes is effective not just, or even predominantly, because it helps to challenge problem-saturated stories but because it helps to create a sense of acceptance, safety and a secure base with and for families. The systemic concept of 'both/and – and more' perhaps captures this sense of how what we do with families may be seen to operate in multiple ways. However, how we describe what we do has very important implications in shaping what areas we decide to explore with families. A re-examination or a re-cognition of the potential effects of the techniques that systemic and narrative therapies employ can free us to explore further some of the emotional domains of experience in families that have become somewhat neglected in our conceptualisation and training. We are not suggesting that family sessions should become a relentless discussion or exploration of families' feelings and attachments, but we are suggesting that it can be helpful to be aware of the emergence of feelings, at times to be able to comment and identify these, and walk around in the experience with families. In our view, these discussions are likely to emerge in the process of the systemic work we are engaged in already. We do not need to force attachment-related emotions to emerge any more than we should not ignore them when they do!

Our starting point is the view that the stories that we create about our lives are a key component in how we live and also how we develop problems and difficulties in our relationships. We create narratives about what has happened to us in our lives and these help shape how we think of our past and importantly how we view and embark on the future. The ANT approach focuses on an important set of stories that we develop about our connections, namely our emotional and sexually intimate relationships, our attachments with others, such as our parents and children, and our dependencies, experiences and expectations of trust in our relationships. Attachment theory emphasises that we have a fundamental need, which appears to be based on an evolutionary survival instinct, to engage in intimate relationships fuelled by our need, starting in infancy, to seek safety and protection with our parents/carers when faced with threats of danger, loss and adversity. These early interactions between the parent and the child produce the experiences that form the material of our developing narratives about ourselves and others. These early experiences subsequently come to be shaped into broader narratives and sets of expectations that we generalise to other relationships outside our families.

However, narratives are not a passive recording of the past but constitute an active process of continual construction, reconstruction and review. We tell our stories to others and their questions, reactions, comments, additions, revisions and corrections serve to reshape our stories with each telling. As we tell our stories, powerful feelings are evoked, even when we muse to ourselves, which shape how and when we tell our stories – for example: who we tell, what we leave out, forget or defend ourselves from remembering, alter, adjust and edit – and, of course, why we tell. We may also alter our stories according to whom we are telling and thus how safe we feel we are to be honest, straightforward, open and able to access our memories. Our framework approach therefore shares much with the narrative therapies in our emphasis on working with people's narratives and relationships to foster change, liberation and release from their interpersonal problems. However, we add an emphasis on the emotional content of people's stories, and as yet unstoried experiences, such as trauma, and in particular on how they manage their feelings and attachments, for example how they comfort themselves and others in times of anxiety, distress and difficulties. We are interested in how children learn to narrate their experiences and what assists them in developing the skills for open, consistent and coherent communication of their emotional experiences. In addition, we focus on the *process* of the telling of the narratives to consider what types of self-protective strategies or defences people are employing as painful, uncomfortable and anxiety-provoking memories are evoked in the telling. This shares some similarities with psychodynamic models in recognising the need to elicit both what is explicit and also what is implicit – what we find harder to articulate. This does not involve adopting an 'expert' position of knowing better than the families we see but of finding ways to help them to articulate the more hidden, subjugated aspects of their emotional experiences in their relationships and the self-protective strategies that they may have been employing. Central to this is the creation of a context of safety and trust for families that can help such material to be accessed, illuminated, expanded, expressed and processed.

Stages of therapy in the ANT approach

The ANT approach broadly conceptualises the process of change and therapeutic work as consisting of four stages (Dallos, 2006a):

Creating a secure base

The central feature of the first stage of therapy is to create a situation of emotional safety and trust for families. The prospect of therapy can be experienced by families as a threatening and anxiety-provoking situation and they may approach this situation by employing their characteristic family patterns. For example, some family members may be extremely guarded and suspicious whereas others may see it as an opportunity to quickly vent their feelings. Likewise, the initial meeting can provoke anxiety for the therapist, as can any new encounter. The therapist (and team) and the family need to be able to jointly create a sense of safety and mutual trust. Below we list some components to this process and also how some of the existing techniques of family therapy, for example holding a non-blaming position, externalising the problems, validating people's experiences, proceeding cautiously and so on, can all contribute to building this sense of safety. For some family members, this could be their first experience of taking emotional risks in a long time. The therapist often acts as a bridge, helping people reorient to other people as a source of comfort and security, rather than seeing all people as a source of emotional threat and danger. Above all, there is a need for the therapist to be able to offer a sense of containment and empathy through attuned interaction. This is similar to the ideas of intersubjectivity in infant–parent interactions whereby we are able to show that we understand the pain and difficulties that they are experiencing but also to communicate that we are not overwhelmed by this. This process can also involve subjugating our own needs in order to stay engaged and attuned. For the infant, the parent offers comfort and soothing when they are distressed, and helps them learn to comfort and soothe themselves, and to turn to others for support. The parallel in therapeutic work is for the therapist to be able both to feel some of the pain and frustrations that family members may be feeling and to communicate back to them an awareness of this along with a sense of hope and belief in the potential for change. One client put this elegantly as 'being able to borrow the therapist's belief in my ability to change'.

- Clarify the context – aims, goals, expectations.
- Containment – convey a reassuring stance that we can manage painful, feared, difficult and warded-off feelings – therapist/s as secure enough.

- Empathetic reflection, listening and communication – show our empathy with understanding and illumination of feelings.
- Map the family, their resources, support systems, professional systems.
- Convey an accepting stance, no blame, slow pace.
- Focus on competencies, externalise problems.
- Talk about talk – what it is OK to talk about, explore families' rules and feelings – what it is not safe to talk about.

Exploring attachment and narratives within a systemic framework

The primary intention of this stage is to gather together material to provide the content for some modifications or for the development of alternative stories. By analogy it is like a builder or an artist assembling the materials that they will employ to create their work. This stage is also associated with risks, for example uncomfortable feelings may be evoked as families are asked to remember forgotten or suppressed memories and experiences. Sometimes, sad and painful feelings can even be evoked by positive and happy memories, which may lead families to mourn for the lost opportunities and times they could have had and serve to remind them of 'how bad things are now'. It is important in this stage to encourage material from the various representational systems, for example to ask for memories from the past including images, sensations, feelings, past actions and family members' reflections about these. Often families focus on the semantic or verbal mode, for example with lists of generalisations and labels, such as Johnny has attention deficit hyperactivity disorder (ADHD), is attention seeking, dishonest, selfish and aggressive. It can be helpful to make use of drawings or sculpting, bring in photos, engage in visual or metaphorical descriptions and so on to offer material that can help reduce the constraint and constriction of the verbal generalisations. Many of the family therapy techniques, such as the use of genograms, timelines and depicting and tracking patterns of interactions, can be helpful. Additionally, our ANT approach here also pays attention to families' stories of how feelings are managed and how comfort may be provided at times of distress and difficulty, and what happens when it is not.

- Look at relational patterns and attachment processes in the family.
- Explore beliefs about the problems and ideas about how to overcome them.
- Explore, expand, validate and process positive and negative feelings.
- Encourage reflection in different representational systems – embodied and procedural, visual and sensory memories, episodes and reflections.
- Affect regulation – explore how comfort and soothing is offered and received.

- Explore transgenerational patterns of relating and attachment, genograms.
- Reflect on feelings and the processing of feelings in the process of therapy.

Considering alternatives

The central task at this stage is to combine the materials that have been gathered in the earlier stages into altered or new stories. Potentially, this represents one of the most challenging parts of therapy since challenges and changes to long-held beliefs, explanations, expectations, sensitivity to interpersonal threat, such as perceived rejection and abandonment, and self-protective strategies can provoke extreme anxiety. We see this even when self-protective strategies have been holding families in painful or difficult positions, for example a pattern of employing narratives that emphasise the necessity of avoiding relational issues of emotional confrontation. Narratives that have been central to shaping and managing people's experiences may be difficult to alter since our defences have evolved over time and may not be fully part of our conscious awareness. Thus, to be asked to try different ways of thinking, feeling and acting may seem very dangerous and potentially or actually overwhelming. As a part of this we as therapists can consider plans and attempted solutions to look at what has worked and what the limitations have been. This can allow families to see these changes as modifications, or achievable steps, rather than extreme changes to what they have been doing. For example, a discussion of exceptions to the problems or 'unique outcomes' can helpfully point to past successes that can be built on and hence ease the move to reorganising our narratives.

An important focus in this stage is on a discussion of corrective and replicative scripts (Byng-Hall, 1995). These are concerned with exploring what people have learnt from their own childhood experiences and what they wish to retain or repeat as opposed to alter or reject in their current relationships with their children or intimate partners.

- Explore corrective and replicative scripts.
- Discuss attachments in a relational framework – working 'within' and 'between'.
- Consider alternative explanations and narratives.
- Consider and enact open and consistent attachment communication – building more secure connections.
- Hypothetical – explore future-oriented attachment narratives.
- Reflect on and process feelings in the process of therapy.

Consolidating change and maintaining the therapeutic base

This stage is concerned with ending or altering the relationship that has been developed and maintaining what has been gained. A central feature of this is a consideration of what the family will be able to take with them in terms of what they will be able to hold onto from the sessions. Just as a child comes to internalise the advice, comfort and sense of felt security that his/her parents have been able to provide, so too in therapy the family needs to be able to remember to hold onto and call on when necessary the conversation and experiences they have had with the therapist and the team. Minuchin (1974) refers to this as the 'ghost of the therapist'. Hence, the final stage of therapy can involve some discussions about what has been learnt, what the experience has been like and what the family thinks they will remember from the sessions for the future. One family described that they would remember being able to address difficult topics in the sessions and talking about them in a way that made them feel proud that they could do so and that they could carry the memory of this with them into the future. Some of the risks for the family at this stage can be that they come to see the work as another example of professionals becoming involved but then abandoning them. We are not encouraging the construction of unhelpful dependencies but it is possible to find ways of keeping in touch or letting the family know that we as therapists will hold them in mind. Occasional contact can be helpful, for example the possibility of telephone contact if they wish or other forms of correspondence. It is also important that the family is encouraged to reflect openly on what was helpful, less than helpful and be open about how they felt during the process. One family described how they were extremely suspicious of the therapy to start with but gradually came to see it as helpful and to be able to trust the process. It can be helpful both to reflect on their needs in the future, continuing to weigh up situations carefully, but also to be able to trust others and to be able to use help and discuss issues more openly when they need to. In short, to be able to make discriminating judgements about how and when they may need support and to whom they will turn for it.

- Reflect on, consolidate and integrate the therapy experience.
- Anticipate relapse and planning aftercare.
- Reflect on future support.
- Negotiate future contact – separation from the therapy.
- Encourage listening and reflection – experience of the therapy.
- Reflect on feelings in the process of therapy.

Theory of change

Core ideas of change

In the following we state briefly some of the core premises of how we think change occurs and is fostered in therapy:

1   Change occurs through alterations in the nature of the relationships within the system of intimate relationships in which people are involved and accompanying changes within and for the members involved. This process is circular such that individual family members both influence and are influenced by the dynamics of the family. An obvious implication for this is that therapy should involve the participation of family or other intimate members although it may also involve therapeutic work with individuals or subsystems of a family (Vetere and Dallos, 2003).

2   Change occurs through helping people and their families to shift from narratives that view problems as residing essentially within individuals to narratives that view them also as relational problems. Helping to make connections between individual experience and relational processes and *vice versa* can contribute to positive changes. Narratives are seen as the central way in which people are able to make sense of their lives and their experiences. Narratives can consist of procedural, episodic, sensory and semantic memories, and although expressed verbally, rely on non-verbal process to communicate a coherent and consistent account. At the same time they look into the future and hold implications for what we see as our potential and the choices we are able to make. Families can be seen as composed of individuals who hold unique narratives but also as sharing and holding narratives in common. In particular, problems appear to be associated with situations where the shared narratives in a family become 'problem saturated' or excessively focused on what is going wrong and often also focused on attributing the problems to one person as the 'cause'. Similarly, relational distress can be expressed as the fault of one person, and repeated and reinforced in the telling.

3   Change is facilitated when people feel emotionally safe and secure so that their abilities to think, reflect and attempt new ways of acting and relating are liberated and facilitated (Byng-Hall, 2008b; Johnson, 2008). The idea that our thoughts, actions and feelings are interconnected has support from many areas of psychology. We draw in particular here from attachment theory, which emphasises that, similar to young toddlers who are able to play freely and explore when they feel safe, people in families are also freed up to be able to think creatively and to reflect on their own and each other's actions more effectively when they feel safe. Hence, a central feature of therapy is to help to build a secure base with the therapist and the context/setting of therapy for their creativity and

problem solving to re-emerge. Also, it is important that therapy assists the family to transfer this sense of safety to their home context so that it can continue and generalise to the rest of their lives.

4 Change occurs through shifts in how family members think, feel and act towards each other. Shifts in only one of these areas is often not sufficient for substantial change to occur and to be maintained. More specifically, attachment theory and contemporary cognitive neuroscience emphasise that these different aspects of human experience are inextricably interconnected. Hence, therapy should not simply focus on words and semantic processes, nor just predominantly on emotions or on behaviours. Therapy needs to address all of these areas and help people to be able to use information from all of them and to be able to integrate and reflect on all of them. Specifically, it is important that family members are able to recognise and deal with contradictions between these different areas of experience.

5 Change occurs through the development of open communication in families or other important relationships, namely, when it becomes emotionally safer to talk about feelings, ideas, actions and intentions that had previously been difficult to acknowledge or discuss. In order for people to be able to develop coherent, elaborated, reflective and relatively *undistorted* narratives in families they need to be able to communicate about both positive and negative feelings. They also need to be able to share and communicate about events without feeling that they have to hide, distort, conceal, fabricate, deny and generally distort their memory of events. This in itself is a circular process since in families where such distortion is present and openness is felt to be dangerous, the process can become so embedded that people are increasingly unable to experience events in an undistorted way such that, over time, important aspects of events may be ignored or go unnoticed.

6 Change occurs through a revision of the ways that we have learnt to deal with a wide variety of feelings, distress, threat, anxiety and loss through our early childhood experiences. The nature of our early and continuing attachment experiences lays down patterns for how we learn to manage difficult feelings and these come to shape our expectations of our relationships. Therapy needs to explore what these patterns are, for example how people comfort themselves and each other in families, how they respond when their feelings are hurt, how they seek reassurance when they are afraid and so on. This involves both an exploration of their experiences and an understanding of how they manage their feelings, but also commenting on these as they arise in sessions, exploring what works and considering and experimenting with some new ways of managing their feelings and attachments (Hill *et al.*, 2003; Byng-Hall, 2008b).

7 Change occurs when we are able to reflect on and utilise the patterns of behaviour from our attachment scripts to cope with difficult feelings

and relationship issues (Fonagy *et al.*, 1991a; Crittenden, 2006). These patterns can be seen as reaching across the generations and consideration of them through, for example, family genograms, can be constructive (Byng-Hall, 2008). Again, the focus in therapy can be in retrospective discussions of the past and patterns across the generations as well as those currently played out. It is important to recognise these patterns in sessions, for example, moments in a session where a rapid pattern of feelings, such as anger, shame and distress, is triggered by a particular comment from a family member.

8 Change occurs by working alongside people to help them to be able to develop their skills in constructing open, coherent, integrated and reflective narratives that effectively communicate their wishes, feelings and intentions in their intimate relationships. Research and clinical practice from attachment theory, especially with instruments such as the Adult Attachment Interview, the Story Stems, and the Separation Anxiety tests, indicate that people acquire habitual ways of processing the events in their lives and, in particular, ways of managing the more difficult and distressing interpersonal experiences in their lives. These are related to their attachment experiences and the profound feelings that have been evoked by the experience of the ways in which their attachment needs were dealt with. The self-protective attachment strategies are the fabric of their narrative styles, such that some people develop narratives that exclude feelings and others develop narratives that are saturated with feelings. Therapy needs to involve points of reflection and increased awareness about the styles and defences that people employ. However, it also needs to include an experiential component, such that any dangerous and frightening feelings are evoked, illuminated and reprocessed, so that people gain confidence and an ability to utilise the full range of information that is available and assimilate these experiences into their narratives.

Identifying core attachment patterns and the attachment significance of interactional events

A central feature of an ANT formulation is to identify and describe patterns of actions and beliefs in relationships that are fuelled by core attachment processes (Dallos, 2006a; Vetere and Dallos, 2007, 2008). Attachment emotions, needs, anxieties and patterns are seen as the central driving energy of relational systems, and what we sometimes see as the rigidity of the patterns in families and couples is seen to be maintained by the attachment fears and anxieties of each partner or family member. The core of a family is the relationship between the couple – the parents – and what learning and expectancies each partner brings to the relationship from their own attachment histories in their families and previous relationships. Johnson and Best

(2003) similarly emphasise that emotions and attachment-related feelings are at the heart of relational dynamics – they are the furnace that drives the relationship dynamics.

Debbie aged 8 was referred to the Child and Adolescent Mental Health Services (CAMHS) due to her feelings of anger, which tended to be directed at her stepmother (Sarah) or her older sister Jill. She suffered with diabetes and on occasion would refuse to comply with taking her medication, leading her to become 'hypo' glycaemic – out of control, moody and aggressive. She and her older sister were living with their father (George) and stepmother. Their father had gained custody because their birth mother (Jane) was seen as unreliable and irresponsible at times. A story of Jane's inadequacies featured predominantly in our first session with the family. A transcript from the first session is shown below:

SARAH: ... She [Jane – Debbie's mother], her behaviour is not beneficial at all – it was suggested that perhaps Debbie go to counselling, that we do family therapy and she be included as well ... she turned it down ... also said that Debbie doesn't have problems. She won't get involved ... she has her own problems ... she has a problem with alcohol. ...

DEBBIE: No she doesn't, she never used to. ...

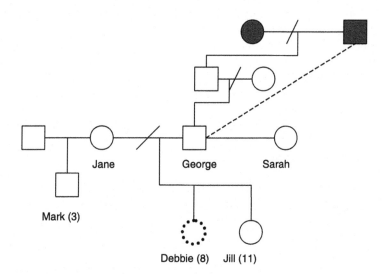

Debbie – angry, diabetes
Jane – excess alcohol use
George – diabetes, brought up by his grandfather

Figure 2.1 ANT formulation: Debbie and her family.

GEORGE: When she drinks . . . alcohol, her personality changes, so she's been advised not to . . . that's all Debbie. . . .

JILL: When she looks after us she'll often make us stay up late and drink quite a lot, it's quite scary. . . .

DEBBIE: Yeah it's scary but you can't. . . .

RD: *If you don't mind me making a comment. Often we see that one child takes on the part of being loyal to the parents, that sounds like you Debbie. . . . Every time we talk about Jane you say kind of positive things about her, defend her. That's a very nice quality isn't it? I would really appreciate it if my children did that. Does that put you in a bit of a difficult position trying to stick up for her?*

DEBBIE: Yeah.

RD: *Do you feel that she lets you down sometimes?*

DEBBIE: No.

RD: *You try not to feel that she lets you down?*

DEBBIE: Yeah.

RD: *But do other people feel that she lets you down?*

DEBBIE: Yeah.

RD: *So what does that feel like? When other people say she lets you down and you don't want. . . .*

DEBBIE: It makes me feel quite sad sometimes 'cos people say, hmhmm, 'cos people say things like . . . mmhm, it's hard to explain.

RD: *What happens to that sadness? Does it turn into something else, does it turn into other feelings?*

DEBBIE: It turns into anger.

RD: *It turns into anger?*

DEBBIE: Sometimes if I get angry it turns into . . . like last few times I have been in my room and I get a bit claustrophobic sometimes . . . I'm not really a room girl.

RD: *What helps you sort those feelings out, can Sarah help, can Dad help, can Jill help?*

DEBBIE: Jill can help.

SARAH: Actually, sometimes when she's like that if you go near her she just says it's your fault, she's quite violent towards her, towards Jill . . . if she's feeing, she's feeling that Jill doesn't care and it's partly my fault 'cos I'm here and I'm not her Mum. She'll never say anything down the phone to her Mum, she will just take it . . . and come off the phone and then go mad. . . .

RD: *It must be really hard for you. I've been a step-parent as well and it can be a no-win situation because you're not Mum and if you try and be Mum . . . and which ever way you try to do it you can get pushed away?*

SARAH: In circumstances like that.

RD: *What do you think she would like you to be able to do as parents?*

SARAH: Take her over to Jane [her mother's] to change things.

RD: *Is it a bit like that Debbie, that you get a bit angry because you think why can't the grown-ups in my life just sort it out and make things alright?*

DEBBIE: I was going to Jane . . . but Jill hated it.

SARAH: There have been times when Jill was forced to go . . . we agreed to pay on instalments to a Germany trip and she [Jane] didn't even give us petrol money and she gave us a cheque and lied about it and it bounced . . . so we don't trust her . . . hasn't been near since.

GEORGE: Never asked her for money for me . . . I said if you want to contribute, pay for the kids, pay for the school, give them money . . . and she agrees but never goes through with it, lots, a lot of false promise, she gets. . . .

SARAH: Then she gets, she won't come on the bus to pick them up. It's an hour and half, she says that it's not fair on Marcus [the child of Jane's new partner Joe] to sit on the bus for three-and-a-half hours.

GEORGE: She blames me and Sarah for her not seeing the children.

SARAH: Demands that we drive them over and things, our relationship isn't. . . .

RD: *One of the things I'm thinking as you are talking, and again speaking partly from my own experience as a parent, God almighty it would be easier for everyone if there was no contact. It's more hassle than it's worth. But for the kids it's difficult to face that, maybe when they get older?*

GEORGE: That's why I'm leaving it to, I think Jill has already come to that decision. . . .

RD: *Have either of you two been through anything like that, have you been in stepfamilies?*

SARAH: No I haven't.

GEORGE: I have . . . yeah.

RD: *What was it like, can you say a little bit about your family background?*

GEORGE: Nasty . . . with these children I've always wanted to be a full-on parent because I never got it. . . . My parents were never interested in anything I did. . . .

RD: *So what happened, your parents split up?*

GEORGE: Yeah, my Mum and Dad just fell out . . . I can't remember, I was about seven years old. . . .

SARAH: You went to one parent.

GEORGE: I went to live with my Dad.

RD: *So that's a bit similar to what happened to your children?*

GEORGE: Yeah, but then my Dad just dropped me at my grandparents and my grandparents brought me up. . . .

DEBBIE: That's not very nice [gently touching her Dad's leg].

GEORGE: I don't think my Dad was very interested in me . . . then he got a stepmum and she just hated me, she was jealous of me and what Dad gave me and she was nasty.

RD: *And what about your Mum?*

GEORGE: I errh, I left, when I was about Jill's age I left to go and live with my
    Mum again. . . .
SARAH: You weren't. . . . Dad properly.
JILL: Was that Judith? . . . Judith was the stepmum.

Formulation within the ANT framework attempts to weave together core
elements of systemic, attachment and narrative perspectives (see Figure 2.2).
In effect this equates, first, to a consideration of systemic patterns and
relational processes, and second, to an exploration of the understandings and
narratives that family members are employing, particularly in relation to
attachment. Finally, the formulation includes a consideration of the attachment needs, attachment significance of events, and patterns of emotional
connections in the family.

    In the short extract from the session it is possible to see a repeating pattern
whereby Sarah and George criticise Debbie's mother Jane. This pattern
appears to happen about three times despite the therapist's (RD) discussion
with Debbie about how the criticisms about her birth mother can be upsetting
for her. Part of the intention here was to indicate to the family that this is a
difficult issue for Debbie and might have been contributing to her anger and
sadness. However, it seems that it is a powerful pattern in the current family
dynamics and Debbie's sister Jill appears to side with George and Sarah in
this criticism of Jane, leaving Debbie rather caught in between attempting to
stay loyal to both her mother and her father. A related dynamic appears to be

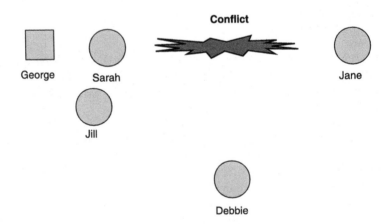

- Debbie – triangulated between the two families.
- George and Sarah critical of birth mother Jane, escalating conflict.
- Conflict is escalated by George's insecure childhood attachment and corrective
  scripts – need to do it better than his own childhood, need to be a 'good' parent.

Figure 2.2 Systemic processes.

that Debbie is not able to be angry towards her mother but takes out her difficult feelings, such as feeling abandoned by her mother, on Jill or Sarah, for example when she returns from her mother's or after she has been speaking on the telephone with her.

Attachment needs

With regard to attachment patterns within this family, possible needs and anxieties are as follows:

- Debbie and Jill – attachment loss of their birth mother Jane
- George and Sarah – new couple relationship – attachment needs regarding insecurities about their relationship
- George – insecure childhood experiences, trying to meet his daughter's attachment needs
- Sarah – need to be a 'good' mother, anxious to do it better than Jane?
- Jill – cut off, avoidant regarding her attachment needs for her mother
- Debbie – diabetes (illness), sense of loss about her childhood, loss of her health.

A primary attachment need in this family can be seen to be the connection between Debbie, Jill and their birth mother Jane. Often, the mother is a child's primary attachment figure and in this family we can see that both girls may be experiencing a loss of this important figure in their lives. Their parents have separated and in turn this can represent a loss of their family and a secure family base. The sisters appear to be attempting to deal with this in different ways such that Debbie is attempting to maintain a relationship with her mother while Jill is attempting to distance herself from her mother and perhaps start to attach to her stepmother Sarah. We can see this in the ways in which Debbie attempts to defend her mother whereas Jill supports the criticism of her mother in stating that she can be scary when she is drunk. There is also an attachment process in relation to illness – diabetes. Debbie has in effect 'lost' her childhood in that she is not able to be free and easy-going like her friends. Instead, she has to adhere to a regime of insulin medication and observation of her diabetes. This requires support from her parents and possibly this is made more difficult by the fact that her father George has also recently discovered that he has the illness, which is anxiety provoking for him. It may help him to sympathise with Debbie's needs but may also make it harder for him to attend to and comfort her when he is also anxious about his own health.

There are also important attachment issues between the adults, for example George and Sarah have a relatively new relationship and Sarah may have some anxieties about whether George has any remaining feelings for his ex-partner. Connected with this, Debbie seems close to her father, she physically comforts him and it may be that she resembles, physically and/or emotionally, her birth mother Jane. Children who are the most loyal to the absent parent may see themselves, and be seen, as similar to this parent. This may be a source of some anxiety for Sarah. She also has no children of her own and may feel a pressure to prove herself as a mother and also to help George to provide the 'good' family environment that he described having missed out on. George for his part explains this in terms of his troubled and painful childhood and appears to have a need to provide a good family and avoid the conflictual marital relationships that his parents had.

Attachment narratives/themes

Connected to the attachment needs of the family members it is possible also to see how these are contained within a number of important narratives or themes that emerge during the conversation with the family in the above extract from the session. Some of these are presented in Table 2.1 together with suggestions about the kinds of emotions that may be associated with each theme.

A very strong narrative at the start of the above extract of the session with the family is that Jane, the girls' birth mother, is irresponsible, cannot be trusted and might even be somewhat dangerous and unsafe to the girls at times. This narrative is repeated elsewhere in the extract and in the session as a whole. In contrast, there appears to be a story from George and Sarah that they are 'good' parents and trying to do their best but that Jane makes things very difficult for them. This story connects with others regarding the role of step-parents and Sarah's sense of unfairness that, despite her efforts, Debbie takes her angry feelings out on her. This is developed in conversation with the therapist as a more general story of how being a step-parent can be a frustrating and emotionally unrewarding experience at times. There is also a

Table 2.1 Attachment themes and emotions

Themes	Emotions
(Sarah re: Debbie)	
Irresponsible mother	sadness, anger, loss, fear
Step-parent	frustration, sadness, loss
Loyalty	anger, sadness, loss, frustration
Failure	sadness, shame
Personality	anger, sadness
Illness (diabetes)	anger, sadness, loss
Takes it out on me	anger, frustration, not fair
(Dad as a child)	
Painful childhood, ignored, parents not interested in me	sadness, loss, hope, failure

narrative of 'personality' in a suggestion that Debbie can be difficult and perhaps an implication that she is rather wilful and unreasonable alongside an appreciation that this might be aggravated by her mother's irresponsible behaviour. Especially important here is that Jane is seen as letting the girls down and this aggravates Debbie's way of responding to things.

Combining the three perspectives

Transgenerational patterns and narratives

The extract ends with a very powerful story from George regarding his own childhood. He describes poignantly how his parents used to argue and had little time for him or interest in him. He was then fobbed off to his grand-parents who in turn had little time for him so he eventually returned to his mother. George goes on to state that it is his intention to do things differently with his own girls – to be a 'full-on' father. The family's narratives or scripts therefore connect events in the family over time and across generations. It is significant, though, that in fact some aspects of childhood appear to be repeating themselves here in that George's girls are also not living with their mother and have experienced a painful divorce and conflict between their parents.

Attachment theory suggests that we parent our children in terms of how we were parented ourselves. It is suggested that this transmission is through our internal working models, for example (Fonagy *et al.*, 1991a) found that the attachment styles of expectant mothers in the Adult Attachment Inter-view (AAI) is predictive of the patterns of how their infants will be attached to them two or so years after the birth. This is not to suggest that we are simply blind victims of the patterns that we have acquired from our child-hoods; rather that we hold these experiences in our narratives about ourselves and others. The experiences are held in terms of how we see others and ourselves, what we expect emotionally from others and how worthy we feel ourselves to be of love and affection. Formulation in ANT therefore attempts to explore how the expectations that people hold and the stories that they have about their childhood experiences are being played out in their current relationships. This can allow for a position of therapeutic neutrality in that we can recognise the patterns across the generations rather than becoming caught up in inadvertently blaming or finding fault in what the parents are doing.

Organisation of narratives

An ANT formulation includes a consideration of not only the content of people's narratives but also how these are organised. This adds to the narra-tive perspective, which can be overly cognitive, overlook structural features of stories and not pay sufficient attention to how narrative skill develops. A focal point is the idea of 'narrative competence' in that the formulation takes account of what experience people may have had in placing the past events in their lives into coherent narratives. With families we can look for what the current patterns are in terms of how family members talk with each other and try to find explanations for their problems and how these are connected with their relationships and emotional processes. At the broadest level we can describe this as thinking about the extent to which their communication is open, but more specifically in terms of how it is organised around the two main attachment dimensions: restriction of feelings and restriction of cognition. For some families, talking about feelings may be a difficult activity, for others, forming structured cognitions may be difficult, or in extreme and abusive circumstances, it may be too difficult to contemplate that someone who looks after you also holds mal intent towards you. Typically, there may be considerable differences in emotional styles of relating within a family. Families may vary in the extent to which openness is possible. In our case illustration, although George and Sarah appear to be attempting to explore their situation, it does seem difficult for Debbie to be able to say that she misses her mother and feels both sad and angry about the situation. In fact, George's attempts to do things differently may be making it hard for him to hear Debbie's feelings and though he himself complains that his parents were not interested in him, it does appear hard for him to listen to what Debbie has to say. Instead, the conversation repeatedly focuses on blaming Debbie's mother, which Debbie has indicated is hard for her to hear.

Representations and unresolved experiences

This formulation can be developed further by a consideration of memory systems and how defensive processes may appear to be operating. Especially in more severe problems, it may be the case that different experiences are held in different memory systems, with a lack of integration between them. For example, painful or traumatic memories may be held in sensory and procedural memory systems, with intense imagery at times or repetitive patterns emerging or intruding. These may not be connected with a semantic or episodic memory system in which events are forgotten or where defended versions of events prevail. A possible process for George here is that his childhood memories are still very vivid for him, possibly even traumatic. As he talked of these memories in the session he became hunched over, rubbed his legs and eventually Debbie reached over and stroked her father's knee, commenting that 'that wasn't very nice' for him. It is possible that such unresolved feelings combine with a corrective script in such a way that the intentions, although positive, become somewhat inflexible and shape George's feelings so strongly that he loses sight of what his daughters are actually feeling in the present, with a lack of experienced emotional attunement.

Guiding formulations for intervention

Regulating emotions and providing/seeking comfort

Throughout our lives we need to turn to others to help us manage difficult feelings, problems, conflicts, distress, humiliations and anxieties. It is typical in family therapy sessions that members recount the problems they are experiencing, for example extended descriptions of what a child is doing wrong. In some cases, as in self-harming behaviours, there are dramatic descriptions of the details of the problems. It is clear in many such conversations that family members can feel hopeless and helpless in the face of the problems. Frequently, the problems have come to be seen as some essential quality, inside one member of the family, for example a 'difficult', or unmanageable child. An attachment perspective focuses on how family members have come to feel that they cannot turn to, depend on or comfort each other. Such a discussion is often difficult because moving too quickly towards it can result in the parents further describing how all their efforts to help have been useless or have been dismissed. One helpful approach can be to trace patterns of comforting transgenerationally to discuss what the parents' experience of it has been themselves, what they have learnt from their own experiences. Often this reveals that the parents have themselves had little experience of having been comforted. Or, there are unconvincing statements that what they had was fine but there is very little evidence to support what this might have involved. Similarly, talking to the parents in role, and asking them future-oriented questions, about what they hope for their children in their future relationships, brings forth positive aspirations. Such discussion requires that there is already a good therapeutic relationship in place or the family members are likely to withdraw into a sense of being accused that they are inadequate because of their own upbringing. Alongside a transgenerational exploration it can be helpful to explore experiences in the current family, such as how they comforted a child or, for couples, each other, early on in the relationship. This fits with a 'unique outcomes' or 'solution focused' approach, which looks for previous examples of successes. It becomes clear in this exploration that many families have had to construct, or to piece together, some ideas about what it might feel like to be comforted.

In some families, for example where parents have been brought up in institutions, we have held conversations with them about how they have acquired ideas about how parents comfort children. This can reveal idealised versions of how this happens but also allow a sympathetic appreciation with parents of how hard such an activity is if you are having to assemble such skills from books, magazines, films, television or what you have observed friends and others doing. This can lead to a helpful discussion about how such learning needs to happen at an emotional and experiential level and offers a sympathetic position to parents about their good intentions and understandable distress when they do not understand why things are not working in the way they hoped. In part the therapeutic relationship can itself be explored as part of this process, for example for the family members to be able to comment on what the therapist does and what is or is not supportive, comforting and reassuring for them. This involves understanding what emotional safety in the therapeutic relationship might feel like, and how this contributes to a growing sense of trust that others can be responsive and accessible around you. This can help to model and give opportunities to practice engaging in a similar process at home, for example parents can check with their children what is helpful, in a way that probably nobody did for them. These discussions can raise powerful feelings for parents as they remember their own attachment hurts. In one case a parent commented that just at the point where she felt close to her child and able to offer her comfort she remembered her own abusive childhood. This set off painful memories for her, so her behaviour towards the child changed, she withdrew and grew cold, which confused her child and led to distress and anger. This reaction then fuelled the mother's feelings that she was inadequate and failing, leading her in turn to a further angry withdrawal from her child. This is illustrated in Figure 2.3.

Returning to Debbie and her family it appeared to us that although George wanted to be a better parent this was a hard task for him. He held this as an intention at a semantic level but had not himself experienced being comforted, looked after or emotionally contained when he was sad or angry as a young boy. Hence, to attempt to do this with his own children was difficult,

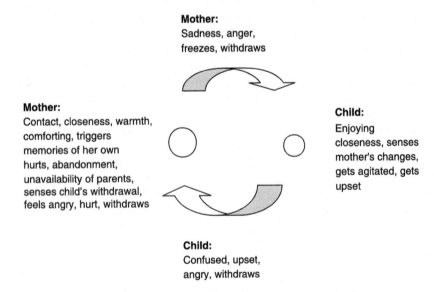

Figure 2.3 Intrusion of traumatic memories in a mother–child relationship.

since he did not have memories to draw on to help him from an embodied, visual and emotional level. Possibly he attempted to turn to Sarah to help since she appeared to say that her childhood had been secure. However, this also placed pressure on *her* to succeed and the fact that Debbie was being difficult perhaps belied her assertion that she had these skills to draw on. We have seen many parents in these circumstances turn to their partner to offer the emotional support for their children. However, this is a complex scenario. Debbie and Jill also have loyalties to their own mother and despite Sarah's best intentions may not wish or be able to respond to her since this may imply being disloyal to their mother and perhaps also running the risk of losing her due to some 'disloyalty'. Also Debbie may feel all the more anxious fearing that she has been displaced by her mother's new child Mark.

Identifying key emotional moments

Johnson and Best (2003) dramatically refer to this as 'catching the emotional bullet'. In work with couples and families, and also when individuals are recounting their stories of events, it is possible to identify processes where emotional changes are being attempted. For example, in work with a couple – Louise and Martin – we spent part of a session where Louise discussed with the female therapist how she had felt about her relationship and their problems, while Martin and the male therapist listened. She went on to describe how his insistence on sexual contact, even when she had been ill, had started to feel for her like a kind of rape. After listening, Martin and RD discussed his thoughts and feelings and he became tearful and apologetic that she had felt that he was acting in an abusive way. Although this felt like an important turning point and a possible point of forgiveness, Louise responded by saying that she was not sure that he would ever really change his ways. Frequently when remorse is expressed it is not always acknowledged, as if the person who is hurt wants to hurt back. This can be a dangerous point emotionally since the temptation can be for Martin in this situation to think and feel rejected and perhaps to feel hurt and retaliate with 'see what she does, she never forgives – oh what's the point in coming here'. Johnson and Best describe how it is important to catch a moment like this and explore its attachment significance by helping people to discuss what the feelings are, what sense of rejection, abandonment or maltreatment is operating, how hard it can be to forgive and that this will take time to happen. Small first steps can be taken to help them begin to listen to each other, to soften a position of blame, and to stay accessible, responsive and engaged. Connection with their own childhood attachments can also be helpfully woven in to discuss what of their own anxieties are activated in such interactions. Specifically, it can be helpful to locate what events are perceived as having led to the anger, loss of trust and feelings for each other – 'the attachment injuries'.

Encouraging coherence and integration

In the formulation with a family or couple we include a consideration of their narrative styles and, as discussed above, as a starting point we might consider whether their style is to organise in terms of a dismissing strategy – dismissing emotions and emphasising cognition – or a preoccupied strategy – dismissing cognition and emphasising emotions. This is not a rigid typology or 'diagnosis' but a helpful starting point that can allow us to adopt a compassionate approach that acknowledges the difficulties and strengths that the family may have in developing coherent and integrated attachment narratives. Recognising the difficulties that people may have arising from their own family patterns can help to adopt a more compassionate stance but also indicates some possible initial orientations that we may adopt. Broadly, the therapeutic orientation can focus on approaches to foster emotional expression or cognitive structuring, as shown in Table 2.2.

The broad aim of encouraging the expression of feelings is to help people get nearer to their feelings rather than the distancing position that they have learnt is safer and more protective, albeit constraining the development of trust and intimacy. The following extract illustrates a dismissing approach to emotion, where Mark talks of his early childhood experiences:

Mark:

Mark: I think tears were very frequent, but I probably ran to my mother, but I am guessing but I cannot remember. I remember cutting my hand badly on a shard of glass and screaming my head off and possibly running back home.
Int: *Running back home to your mom?*
Mark: Possibly, I can't remember.

(Crittenden, 2004)

Table 2.2 Therapeutic approaches and attachment styles

Dismissing	Preoccupied
Encouraging expression of feelings	*Encouraging cognitive processes*
Enactment	Genograms
Role play	Life story lines
Reflective functioning questions	Tracking circularities
Internalised other interviewing	Mapping beliefs and actions cycles
Exploring areas of conflicts	Scaling questions
Managing conflict	Circular questions
Caring and comforting	Shared family beliefs
←Reflecting teams→	

As we can see, for Mark his memories of comforting are vague and hypothetical. Part of a therapeutic orientation to help him develop a more coherent narrative would be to access information about feelings. More generally, for people with a dismissing style and living in emotionally avoidant patterns, it may be helpful to broadly adopt a more experiential orientation, using role play, suggesting enactments or demonstrations of emotional process, asking empathetic questions (how others might be feeling) and internalised other interviewing (Tomm, 1988). There can be an emphasis on exploring the emotional issues, such as how conflict is managed and how caring and comforting is given and received. The aim is to help them to develop narratives that incorporate feelings and emotion and do not involve such a shutdown of sensory and episodic memory systems.

In contrast, encouraging an expression of cognitions aims to assist people to gain some distance from the immediacy of their feelings and the potential to be unhelpfully overwhelmed by emotion, such as fear and shame, and to be able to reflect on and develop narratives that can locate experiences in causal and temporal connections. Lillian, in the following extract, offers a flavour of what the narrative style might be like for people with a preoccupied pattern of emotional responding:

Lillian:
When you were upset as a child what did you do?
I don't know, I can't remember, I used to run away apparently, hum . . . So it used to get quite bad, so I would have a tantrum, and I still have tantrums, yes I still do it, but (Laugh) . . . yes, I used to throw things, you know like a psychic child, but that's all I can remember, . . . remember once being, I used to run away but I always came back, run away through the back garden because I was very tiny and it was a small hole in the fence where the cats used to go out and I went through there, . . . *(Do you remember how old you were?)* yes, and my expedition always ended up somewhere (Laugh), *(so, How old were you?)* . . . yes, I was probably about three or so, and I remember once I rolled and rolled and could not stop because I was so tiny and it was very windy and I ended up at the bottom of the hill, that was one of my expeditions out, running away angry.

(Crittenden, 2004)

For people with a more preoccupied attachment style the emphasis in therapy is on strengthening semantic processes. This can include a variety of structured therapeutic approaches, such as the use of genograms and life story lines that ask people to locate key events in their lives in terms of time and place. This can help to build more temporal order to their stories so that they are less disconnected in terms of timing of events. Tracking circularities and mapping cycles of beliefs and actions can help to foster causal and temporal relations between events in their narratives. Also, questions can be asked that encourage semantic descriptions about how other people see events, their own beliefs and cognitions and circular questions can be asked that attempt to identify patterns of responding in their systems (Dallos and Draper, 2005).

It is interesting to note that this sort of shaping of our therapeutic style and response to people's attachment patterns seems to occur almost intuitively. A typical response is to seek to introduce some sense of order. We can see the interviewer in the extract above perhaps attempting to introduce some cognitive coherence to Lillian's account by asking repeatedly how old she was when the incident she is describing took place! With regard to Mark, he inspires strong feelings in us of wanting to help him to express what he feels, to help him move beyond this painful defence. However, the emotional processes can be very powerful and we can become caught up in unhelpfully engaging with such patterns. For example, without noticing it we may become over-rational and lacking affect in a session with Mark. In fact, it is quite easy to start to think that things are quite all right, 'there is no problem at all and no need to worry'! Or, feeling overly animated and emotional or feeling chaotic and out of control with Lillian. This framework is not meant to be a rigid prescription for our responses and our collective sense of 'fit', but there may be times when it is important to validate both Mark and Lillian's styles and not engender anxiety by deliberately or inadvertently challenging their coping styles. However, a recognition of these styles can help us to be more flexible and creative in assisting them to develop fuller and clearer, more coherent narratives about their lives and relationships. In the following chapters we develop these ideas further, by looking at their applications in diverse settings and relationships.

Chapter 3

Life-cycle transitions and attachment narratives

Individual theories of emotional and social development

The development of systemic theory and practice has led to a significant shift in how we regard the nature and development of psychological and relational problems. Early systemic theory emphasised that individual experience was fundamentally related to the nature of the interpersonal context within which a child and other family members developed. In this it is also implied that development could be seen not just in terms of individual stages but also as intimately connected to the interpersonal processes and developmental transitions in families. In psychology, there has been a variety of individual developmental models that propose a trajectory or pathway of development from infancy, childhood and adolescence into adulthood. Clinical psychology and psychiatry also contain a number of developmental, stage models that detail a variety of progressive stages and the resultant potential for the onset of psychological problems if tasks and goals are constrained and/or interrupted. For example, Freud's (1922) psychodynamic model suggests that a child progresses through the oral, anal, genital and phallic stages of psychological development. Inability to resolve the demands at any of these stages leads to associated difficulties, such as obsessive compulsive disorders if the anal stage is disrupted, or an angry, attacking personality if difficulties are experienced at the phallic stage. Freud and subsequent psychodynamic theorists suggested that the progression through these stages was influenced by the child's social and emotional world and key critical events in their lives.

Although clearly aware of the relevance of family factors, the emphasis was on the nature of the child's developing inner world rather than on an analysis of the dynamics of the family. Later the object relations theorists (Fairbairn, 1952; Mitchell, 1986) came to give increasing attention to the importance of social contexts in shaping the child's inner world, such as the behaviours of the parents and family dynamics. For example, Winnicott (1965) developed concepts such as 'good enough' parenting to describe the quality of the relationship that a mother had with her child. Specifically, he argued that this consisted of a realistic balance between, on the one hand, attentiveness and care towards the infant and, on the other, the mother meeting her own needs and at times being unavailable. In fact, dealing with the frustration of mother's sometime unavailability was seen as an important feature of a child's emotional development.

An interesting and subsequently influential developmental approach was formulated by Erik Erikson (1980) in his model of psychosocial developmental stages. He proposed that as the child develops they experience a sequence of tensions or emotional and maturational dilemmas that have to be negotiated in order to be able to develop and progress. In this he elaborated further that there was an important relationship between the child's internal development and conflicts and dilemmas inherent in their relational world. His much-quoted model contains eight stages, inspired by Freud's stages of development, but he attempted to place these in a broader interpersonal context. The first two stages are:

- *Trust v mistrust:* The infant is seen to develop a healthy balance between trust and mistrust if fed and cared for and not over-indulged or over-protected. Abuse or neglect or cruelty will destroy trust and foster mistrust, leading to reluctance to take risks or to explore. On the other hand, if the infant is over-indulged or insulated from risk this may lead to a failure to appreciate reality. Infants who grow up to trust are more able to hope and have faith that 'things will generally be okay'.
- *Autonomy v shame and doubt:* Self-reliance and independence of thought are seen as related reactions, and encouragement and patience play an important role in shaping the young child's experience and successful progression through this period. Parental reaction to potty training, which features at this stage, and to all aspects of toddler exploration and discovery while small children struggle to find their feet as little people in their own right is significant (see below). The 'terrible twos' and 'toddler tantrums' are a couple of obvious analogies that represent the internal struggles and parental battles. The parental balancing act is a challenging one, especially since parents themselves are having to deal with their own particular psychosocial crisis of taking on parental responsibility.

Erickson's model offers us observations about the types of parent–child interactions that may at each stage inhibit or foster development. For example, in Western cultures, a young child starts to experience a social demand for toilet training at about 18 months. The ability to manage this requires the child to move towards some independence of action from the parents. How the parents respond is thought to be crucial, for example they may focus on and encourage achievements and play down failures and 'accidents', leading the child to feel an increasing sense of independence and confidence. In contrast, an excessive focus on the failures and criticism can foster a sense of shame and failure for the child.

Thus, Erickson's model potentially offers some interesting ideas about possible connections between systemic models and internal emotional processes. However, a useful way of developing this line of thinking is to look at the connections between attachment theory and systemic family therapy in terms of the notion of the family life cycle. Namely, how the internal and external demands for reorganisation of the family system over time involve intense demands for emotional change and adjustment – this offers the potential for a positive revision or reorganisation of attachments as well as the potential for people to move towards less secure and more defended strategies.

Family life-cycle models of change and development

The concept of the family life cycle has played an important role in the development of systemic family therapy. The concept was first articulated by Erik Erickson (1980) and subsequently developed further by Carter and McGoldrick (1988). They suggested that families encounter a number of predictable and unpredictable significant periods in their lives when they are faced with increased demands for change and reorganisation. These significant periods may make different demands on family members and involve them in different tasks, both within and outside the family. For example, if you are looking after children as a lone parent, or as a step-parent or as a birth parent, the demands may differ, and you may have to face other demands and tasks during retirement. Erickson (1980) observed that various relational problems, emotional distress and the major forms of psychiatric disturbance were associated with points of transition in a family's development. This idea of a link between the onset of psychological problems and upheaval, and demand for change and readjustment was well established in individual models of psychopathology. The early term for schizophrenia was dementia praecox (Morel, 1857), which suggested that the early onset of 'madness or dementia' in young people was seen to occur in late adolescence. There was thought to be a link between the stresses of adolescence and entry into adulthood and associated problems. The significance of the family life-cycle model was in revealing the interpersonal and especially the family context as influencing the development of problems manifest both in the family and in the individual members. Early family life-cycle models articulated that most families (defined at least as a two generational system, but more usually a three- to four-generational system) proceed through a number of key transitional stages: marriage and coupling, arrival of a child for a couple, children starting school, children leaving home, mid marriage, retirement and bereavement and loss. These stages contain accumulations of demands for change and reorganisation of tasks and relationships in the family. These demands are seen to be driven by a mixture of biological, maturational, relational and cultural factors.

Erik Erickson (1980) argued that these changes in the family life cycle are also based on 'taken-for-granted' cultural values about what is normal, acceptable and when things are supposed to happen. These expectations can be seen as embodied in a variety of cultural rituals and ceremonies, such as traditions of stag and hen parties before a marriage, christening and naming ceremonies, retirement ceremonies, graduations from school and, more recently, divorce ceremonies. These examples of broadly Western European rites of passage can be seen to embrace culturally shared expectations and values that in turn shape our lives. This has important implications for attachment theory in that these expectations importantly relate to the progress and shift in the nature of our relationships and attachments. For example, a Western European young adult may be expected to shift the intensity of their emotional connections from their parents/carers/siblings to an adult intimate partner. This also reveals that our attachment experiences are subject to social comparisons as we compare the progress of our own lives with that of others: Should I still be living at home with my parents? Should I be married by now as my friends are? Is it time to start to have a family like the rest of my friends? This is not to assume that the family life-cycle model needs to be prescriptive and normative but to consider that these subcultural comparisons do also shape what we expect and think we (and others) might need and want.

Criticisms and revisions of the Western European family life-cycle models have recognised that family life is varied and complex, with many family groups living through periods of marriage or coupling, with or without children, periods of lone parenting and the formation of stepfamilies. Rather than simply increase the number of potential life-cycle stages to accommodate the multiplicity of family living arrangements, the focus is more on the family's transitional stage, the internal and external demands for change, and the combined resources and resilience of family members in rising to the challenges posed by maturational and other life changes. Family life-cycle theories recognise that many of us live in nested three- or four-generational kin systems, who may or may not be living in the same household. Thus, cohort differences in terms of lived experience, educational opportunities, diet and medical care may influence our available resources and approach to coping, attitudes to change and so on. Furthermore, since many couples are gay and lesbian, the entry of children into the household may happen in some different and possibly even more complex ways.

In our link with attachment theory, we want to use the concept of the family life cycle as a sort of meta-concept, not as rigidly indicating key transitional stages but in drawing attention to the important emotional processes involved when the demands for change in a family system come to a head. Associated with each of these transitions are changes that can be seen as operating at a variety of levels. These are listed below, using an example of a couple going through pregnancy and childbirth.

- *Organisational* – for example, a couple has to make major modifications in how their lives are organised in their preparation for becoming parents and then massive adjustments once the baby arrives. To start with their social activities may need to alter, they will be less able to socialise, go to parties, engage in drinking alcohol and may need to be more careful about what they eat and so on. In the case of adoption, the couple may not have the time of pregnancy to begin to adjust to the idea of becoming a 'three-person system'.
- *Roles* – a couple needs to make important decisions about their respective roles, for example decisions about how they will manage at home, and with paid work and career demands. Moreover, if the woman takes on the primary task of caring, she may become more dependent on her partner for help with a range of physical tasks as well as emotional support; or the couple may try to manage a shared care arrangement. These decisions are likely to be influenced by gender discourses about what men and women should do at these times of adjustment and change.
- *Identities* – along with these changes there will be an important shift in self-concept from being an adult to becoming a parent, thus changing their position in a generational system. This involves a sense of responsibility for the care of a dependent infant and also a recognition by the couple of the need to be able to work together or with other relatives, such as a grandparent, to care for the child. This importantly involves the couple shifting from a dyad to a triad and 'making room for the baby' both physically and emotionally.
- *Emotions and attachments* – key to this stage are powerful emotional changes. Not least, until relatively recently in Western cultures childbirth was very dangerous and still is in most parts of the world. Many women still die in childbirth and many children die during it or soon after. Also, it involves pain and discomfort, which can be frightening. Furthermore, a couple may experience anxieties about how they will cope with the changes, whether they will know what to do with the baby, whether they will be adequate parents, and how their relationship will change and so on. Their intimacy may alter, including sexual intimacy, which can lead to a sense of separation, resentment and loss of the freedom and closeness they once had. At the same time, there are powerful biological changes, such as hormonal shifts, which can lead to emotional lability and increasing emotional demands on each other. All these changes of course also occur in the context of increasing discomfort, pain, sleep deprivation and so on, which places a strain on all our capacities to cope with emotional changes!

Thus, central to the concept of the family life cycle is the idea that different stages and transitions require a number of tasks to be accomplished, according to our roles and responsibilities, such as a reorganisation of relationships and expectations. Importantly, family members develop attempted solutions or ways of trying to enable these changes to happen. In some cases, though, the solution may in effect abort or delay the transition since it is too emotionally threatening to established relationships or even overwhelming for the family and their resources to manage and cope with change. The above example of the young couple going through pregnancy and childbirth offered some ideas of the potential tasks involved for a family. These in short involve a demand to make changes in terms of patterns of actions/organisation of the family and beliefs about each other and expectations of what family life should be like. We can also see that a central demand or task is also to make emotional changes and shifts and that each of these changes have an emotional and relational impact.

Attempted solutions and working models

Faced with these internal and external demands for change and reorganisation, family members need to develop ways of managing these changes. These have been referred to as 'attempted solutions' – ways of attempting to adapt to make the necessary changes. For example, a young couple may decide to curtail their social activities dramatically and focus on being very health conscious and careful in their activities for the 'sake of the baby'. Such dedication, though, has consequences, such that they may start to feel that they are missing out on life too rapidly and that things are getting a bit dull. Alternatively, some couples attempt to cope by a sort of 'business as usual' strategy – that there is no reason why a baby should interrupt anything and they will continue to enjoy themselves. This strategy also has consequences, for example finding that they are over-tired, have feelings of guilt that they are not being considerate enough about the baby and are subject to criticism from relatives and so on. Such attempted solutions are not simply or predominantly conscious strategies. Furthermore, a couple may be influenced by the responses of family members, such as parents giving advice, being critical, disapproving, supporting one partner against the other and so on. In many senses, the young couple in the above example is pioneering – they have not met this situation before, and although they may be guided by family customs, scripts and other intergenerational legacies for thought, feeling and action, they are most helped if they can learn from their, and others', experiences.

Thus, we see a potentially extremely fruitful integration here with concepts from attachment theory. On the one hand, the solutions that people adopt can be seen to be based on their working models but also we co-construct attempted solutions that lead to patterns of interactions, which in turn shape our internal working models. Periods of transition can be seen to involve a demand for revisions of our attachment strategies and relationships and consequently embody powerful currents of emotions that can be exhilarating, supportive, challenging and even overwhelming.

Attachment theory is a developmental account of the social regulation of emotion in family groups. Safety and protection are key. The fundamental ideas of attachment theory suggest that we come to develop predictable patterns or internal working models regarding how we attempt to deal with threat, distress, danger, anxiety and uncertainty. The dismissive strategy is to go into ourselves and take the position that we cannot rely on others and need to turn to ourselves to resolve problems – we are on our own. This may mean that we physically try to find time alone and try to remove our self from the situation and relationship, which can be problematic. The preoccupied strategy is that we become increasingly emotionally aroused and continually involve others in our attempt to deal with the problems. Our use of others is to both be fearful and depend on them and also critical and attacking and finding their faults. The so-called secure strategy is that we are able to employ aspects of either strategy in a balanced way so that we are able to cut off and able to involve others in ways that help us to resolve the problems and changes required. A sense of felt security in our key emotional relationships enables effective problem solving, and this can be challenged unexpectedly by the course of life events.

Family life-cycle stages and attachment reorganisations

In outlining the stages we will broadly follow those depicted by Jay Haley (1973, 1987) but add divorce and separation and repartnership as stages since these are now so common in Western Europe. We will explore each of these stages in terms of the relational reorganisations and changes required but also in terms of the attachment needs and capacities of the individuals involved.

Adolescence to young adulthood – sexuality and courtship

For some families, adolescence can stereotypically represent a time of some conflict and anguish. The young person is changing in their identity from a child to an adult and may demand more independence, rights and equality in decision-making with their parents. An important part of this process is that young adults are also turning increasingly to their friendship groups as a source of emotional support, intimacy and attachment. It is important to note that most young adults still want their parents to think well of them, to be proud of them, and wish to please their parents. The nature of the connection to parents is shifting, not that the connection is severed. Having embarked on this shift in attachment figures towards peers, young people at this stage also experience that their friends start to couple up and may for periods of time become less emotionally available to them. There may be a sense of abandonment and betrayal as a friend falls head over heels in love for a period of time. At the same time there may be competition and rivalries for particularly admired or desired potential mates. Hence, relationships may be quite volatile and the young person may feel an erosion in, or a growth of, their ability to trust their friends and others, to learn who their 'real friends are'. Coupled with this, the young person may oscillate between intense dependencies on their friends and turning back to their parents for support. Not infrequently the parents can feel blamed for whatever happens and hence the ability to provide comfort and reassurance can be a difficult balance to achieve at this stage.

An important feature of this stage for young people is the exploration of sexual intimacy and potentially some progression towards finding a relatively permanent partner. This exploration raises a wide range of family issues, for example the moral and religious views of chastity within the generations, the young person's connections may disrupt intimacies and closeness with one or the other parent. In some cases the parents' relationship may be emotionally distant and the young person has served to fulfil one parent's needs for emotional intimacy and a confiding connection. The young person may therefore perceive some indications of sadness from their parents and feel torn in their feelings of closeness to their girlfriend or boyfriend and a sense of abandoning their parent. Similarly, parents may find the young person's blossoming of sexuality disconcerting, especially if their own has waned. Of course, the reverse can also be possible where the parents, delighted at the child's new independence, grab the opportunity to go off for romantic holidays and leave the young person feeling somewhat abandoned or embarrassed by their parents' sexuality.

The young person faces complex attachment issues at this stage. They need to be able to choose suitable partners and take relational and emotional risks. This needs to be guided by their ability to draw on information about their potential partners, such that they do not experience excessive emotional hurt or physical danger. In making decisions the young person draws on their internal working models acquired through their childhood with their parents and others. In Chapter 4 we outline some of the consequences for children and young people raised in households where domestic violence is a concern, where care has been provided by parents who are frightened, frightening, or both. Central to the attachment model are our expectations of the availability and responsiveness of others but also our use of different strategies to distort information in various ways. This means that young people with dismissive patterns may be less able to use information about other's feelings and their own feelings. They may try to manage their relationship in a logical manner or at more extremes always put the other's needs first, perhaps entering into relationships where they come to be exploited or a carer for the other. Alternatively, the preoccupied patterns may involve an excessive focus on emotions but a failure to be able to use cognitive information effectively. For example, a sensitivity to 'seeing' the threat of abandonment and rejection, based on past experience, sometimes expressed as jealousy, may involve scenarios of accusations of others based on their own anxieties and an inability to see patterns and predict sequences in their relationship so that remedial action might be taken. The cycle can be of triggering intense arguments, tears, fights, with frequent break-ups, and equally intense 'making up', which can serve to powerfully reinforce the cycle of behaviour, so that it becomes patterned over time. Thus, the capacity to reflect on the pattern, and see the pattern as the 'enemy', rather than the partner, to use cognitive information as a way of learning from experience becomes a crucial task of any therapy or 'corrective' life experience.

The wish for a sexually intimate connection as well as the subcultural social expectation that young adults should find a partner at this stage may potentially trigger challenges and the possibility of a revision or a deterioration of attachment resources. For example, for a young person who has learnt to employ a characteristically dismissive attachment strategy they may be propelled to take a risk and enter into an intimate relationship. If this goes well and their partner shows warmth and care, there is a potential for a revision to become more trusting and achieve a sense of felt security and be able to reduce over-reliance on defensive strategies. This may require a partner who has experienced relatively secure attachments in the past and is able to understand their partner's emotional history and position and be patient in expecting them to change. Alternatively, the partner may respond with a similar defensiveness such that the relationship becomes somewhat distant and perhaps focuses on sex as one of the few sources of contact, holding and comfort, or alternatively that intimacy decreases and the relationship becomes platonic. In contrast again, if the partner shows a preoccupied pattern then their extreme emotions may become confusing and overwhelming for both of them.

Young adults are increasingly able to reflect on their experiences and their coping strategies. This in itself can offer a vehicle for reorganisation, for example, a recognition that 'I tend to cut off my feelings and need now to think about when I still need to do this – and ponder on whether I may in some situations be able to be less defended'. One young man we worked with stated that he was aware of this and disappointed that 'People think I have no feelings about anything. I do, but for now I am deciding not to show them'. This increased mental ability to engage in self-reflection means that young people also become aware that a relationship with someone different is what they need to help them overcome some of their defences. This can lead to a certain choice, for example as indicated by the pattern of dismissive–preoccupied pairings. This is a common one that may appear to work for a while since each feels they have found in the other the parts that they feel are missing. For the dismissive partner the other provides emotions and immediacy of feelings, for the preoccupied partner the other may offer some regularity and containment of their feelings. However, over time they may actually come to feel that rather than offering one another the potential for attachment change they have started to become interpersonally locked into these attachment positions in the relationship.

This stage also clearly overlaps with the leaving home stage, as identified in Haley's (1973, 1987) work, and the nature of the attachment relationships and emotional connections can be complex and ambivalent. In courtship the young adult is typically transferring their primary attachment relationship to that of their new partner. In an arranged marriage, the courtship process and period may be governed by certain strictures on getting to know one another, but the tasks remain the same from an attachment perspective. The family context has in a sense laid down the basic pattern of influence for the young person's internal working models of relationship security and continues to have an influence. Yet at the same time there is some need for separation and detachment from the parents for without this the partner may feel that the emotional hold of the parents is too strong and come to resent the potential in-laws. Furthermore, the couple need to start to draw up some sense of balance in terms of equity about how they are both still attached to their parents. In our experience, the young couple is helped to bond when both sides of the extended family approve of their union and support their relationship. Involved in these are ideas about what is normal and appropriate, which involves a cultural and social comparison to their friends, kin, media representations and so on – the dominant culturally shared narratives or discourses.

However, courtship can also be a stormy period and the young person may go through several attachment losses or events that they may even experience as emotionally gruelling. In particular the end of the first 'big love affair' can be an extremely distressing experience for many young people. For example, if the young person has been somewhat defended in showing their feelings to others they may feel extremely betrayed, rejected and abandoned when they are left alone by the partner they love and desire. At this point they may need the support of their parents to help them through this crisis. However, this is complicated since the young person has predominantly developed their attachment strategy in relation to their parents/carers and hence may feel, as they have done throughout their childhood, that there is no point trying since the parents will not understand, or be available for support and comfort. One possible solution here might appear to become promiscuous and engage in sex without commitment, for risk of being hurt again, or to, 'reject others quickly before they get a chance to reject me'. There are always possibilities though for individual and systemic reorganisation. The parents may realise that this is a chance for them to change and become closer to their child,

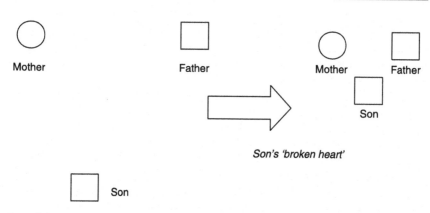

Figure 3.1 Potential increase of closeness following child's relationship loss.

having felt that the distance was becoming too great for them. A danger might be that the young person becomes too entangled with his parents especially if they side with him too much rather than helping him to prepare for future relationships (Figure 3.1).

Another possibility for reorganisation is that young people become attachment figures for their friends. This might be stretching the original intentions of Bowlby, but given the longlasting and often very intense and confiding friendships that some people make, which may or may not be sexual, but most certainly can be affectionate, involve care taking, and hold emotional meaning, we include this particular set of relationships in our discussion here. Friendships can repeat patterns of caring and demanding care but alternatively can also offer opportunities to experience being cared for by friends, or alternatively of caring for others. Parents frequently describe that they come to see qualities, for example of unselfishness, in their children at this stage, which they knew were potentially there but had not witnessed previously. This can be a source of pride for the parents. The depth of the connections that may occur at this stage perhaps underline why young people may at this period become very attached to youth movements, bands and cults. It is possible, for example, that by becoming a member of a cult the young person gains a form of secure base – an acceptance through belonging to this that helps transcend the more immediate sense of failure or rejection by an actual person or a family group. They can stay accepted by the 'movement' – a transitional object (Winnicott, 1965) even if rejected by the last lover.

Marriage/partnership and its consequences

Although some young people decide on a partner fairly rapidly, for others courtship can be a period of 'sowing one's wild oats'. There are subcultural variations but in Western cultures there is a dominant discourse that it is best to engage in some exploration somewhat in order that the person finds a suitable partner rather than makes a bad mistake. Parents are likely to offer some advice about choices of potential partners but again the nature of the attachment relationships will shape this. For example, if the relationship with the parents is a dismissive one the young person may try to keep their anxieties and concerns hidden from their parents. However, at the same time some of these young people will also try to please their parents and may even be influenced to find a partner who their parents like, and perhaps not being very aware of their own feelings they may even welcome this guidance. Alternatively, young people who have preoccupied styles with their parents may engage in bouts of angrily rejecting their parents' opinions but then returning to them in tears for help to mop them up. This can also involve seeking the parents' help but then also angrily turning on them and blaming them for all the troubles in their relationships!

A central attachment issue for young people is the ability to form an emotional commitment to being in a stable, long-term relationship with another person. This is in itself not just a given or a prescription since there are wide cultural variations in the forms of such commitments. For example, some cultures allow polygamy such that men may have several wives (various African cultures) and also the reverse, polyandry where several men share a wife (e.g. Tibetan cultures). In Western cultures there is a general belief that people will cohabit with one partner whether this is an opposite-sex or same-sex partnership. However, within this broad agreement to cohabitation and monogamy there are considerable variations. For many couples, despite the overt commitment to monogamy, there may be occasional or even frequent sexual liaisons with others outside the marriage. In attachment terms, these extra-marital liaisons can be signals of relationship distress, and in turn become attachment injuries within the relationship. In some cases there may also be a more explicit commitment to having an 'open' marriage where each partner is free to engage in sexual relationships with others. Bowlby (1988) observed that attachment and our wish for intimate connection was a lifelong process. Hazan and Shaver (1987) conceptualised attachment as adult romantic attachment and attempted to develop measures of adult romantic attachment style. Their research has suggested that partners become attachment figures for each other and that their existing attachment patterns from childhood will play a significant part in shaping these adult relationships. Some of the issues revolve around feelings of trust, jealousy, possessiveness and emotional rights. As the couple commit to each other they also have to draw up some agreements (implicit and explicit?) about emotional commitments to others including potential sexual partners and also friends. This can involve some rituals whereby each partner agrees to decrease contact and discard mementos, pictures and gifts from previous partners. For some couples this can involve considerable insecurities and jealous feelings, whereas for others they may be able to feel relaxed and confident in their partner's commitment to them and their distancing from previous relationships.

The forming of this committed and intimate relationship in marriage or partnership can prompt reorganisations of attachment patterns. Partners bring to their relationship not just their attachment strategies from their childhood but also the legacy of previous intimate relationships through courtship. As we saw earlier, there may have been opportunities for some positive revision of attachment strategies through the experiences of intimacy at this stage, but at the same time there is the reverse possibility that relationships had been problematic and have aggravated previous strategies or even rendered some people with secure patterns more insecure. One possibility at this stage is that partners find solace and refuge from previous hostile partners in each other, for example choosing someone 'safe and dependable' in contrast to a previously more exciting but ultimately rejecting and unreliable partner. Such choices may have a temporary viability but this might be at the cost of being able to be open and free about expressing positive and negative feelings. A frequent discourse here is the difference between selecting a more 'solid' and reliable partner for marriage as opposed to more 'exciting' partners for sexual flings. Here attachment theory needs to interface with social constructionist perspectives regarding how such dominant discourses may operate to shape our choices of partners and emotional expectations. Arguably, such a discourse contains assumptions that privilege an avoidant or dismissive attachment orientation, which attempts to distance sex from feelings of emotional intimacy and potential vulnerability. For some young people it can be an eventual surprise that high levels of sexual excitement and fulfilment are better accompanied and deepened by feelings of intimacy and closeness. Furthermore, because secure relationships are able to contain the opportunity for expressing both positive and negative feelings, they can allow a sense of excitement and passionate emotional engagement to continue. On the other hand, relationships where one feels abused and misused by the other, or alternatively over-indulged and smothered emotionally, are ultimately more likely to become boring, unsatisfactory, unacceptable and unrewarding.

Birth of children

The arrival of a first child for a couple changes their attachment dynamics from a pair to a threesome. Of course there is a period preceding the arrival of a child, and with a planned pregnancy, a decision to enter into parenthood. Adoption, with or without existing birth children, provides another context for the development of attachments, and perhaps the revision of coping strategies and expectations of trust. Couples vary widely in how the decision to have children is made. For example, for some there is a joint agreement, for others one partner may make the choice and decide to go ahead hoping that their more reluctant partner will come to accept and be committed to the child. The arrival of a child involves major attachment adjustments not only in terms of the couple's relationship with each other and with their own parents, but also in terms of each partner's relationship to the child. For come couples their relationship may already be in some difficulty and the child can be seen as what they need to resolve their difficulties, that in effect the child will bring them closer together. For other couples there may be a view that it is what is expected of them, even a response to subtle pressures from their in-laws that it is time they produced a grandchild.

At workshops for professionals in the health and social care services we have asked participants to articulate their reasons for having children and this sense of obligation or cultural expectation featured for many of them as their initial responses. Typically, it took some prompting to move to a consideration of their emotional needs, for example hopes that a child could meet some of their own attachment needs. A stark example of this is sometimes seen with very young women who have been in the looked-after services and have had a series of abusive, neglectful and rejecting experiences with their own mothers and fathers, and sometimes transient and temporary relationships with carers. Many of them seek to have a baby to provide a source of unconditional love and also to give them a sense of self-respect and adult status.

The birth or arrival of a child can signal significant attachment changes for each partner. An infant demands attachment responses in terms of being comforted, cared for, attended to, and with emotional attunement. For a mother who has coped with relationship demands in her family and with peers by using an avoidant strategy this can be a dramatic challenge. She may feel trapped in being unable to avoid or cut off from her child's emotional demands, leaving her to feel overwhelmed, confused and possibly angry. At the same time these demands may offer a point of reorganisation such that she gradually becomes comfortable with this new experience of intimacy and caring. However, this may in turn depend on the support that she has available, for example whether her partner, parents and friends are able to offer some support with these changes. Alternatively, a significant danger can be that she feels a failure, attempts to withdraw and the baby experiences emotional neglect and becomes increasingly fretful and demanding. This cycle can lead to the typical problems of neglect and child abuse. Contributing to this process is the input from her own parents if this is available. In some cases her own mother may take over and be able to comfort and deal with the baby, making the younger mother feel increasingly incompetent and inadequate. Her partner may assist in offering a buttress against such over-involvement from her mother or alternatively he may feel relieved that the pressure to contribute is taken off him (Figure 3.2).

The potential ways of attachment organisation and reorganisation through

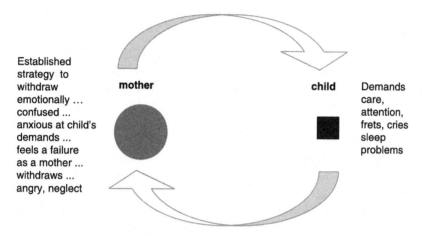

Established
strategy to
withdraw
emotionally ...
confused ...
anxious at child's
demands ...
feels a failure
as a mother ...
withdraws ...
angry, neglect

mother

child

Demands
care,
attention,
frets, cries
sleep
problems

Figure 3.2 Development of problematic mother–infant attachment processes.

this period are myriad and fathers may experience a variety of attachment issues. The baby may be less immediately emotionally and physically impacting on them and some men may resent the reduced access they feel they have to their partner. For example, sexual intimacy may cease for a while and the baby may come to occupy a much greater part of their partner's life. On the other hand, fathers may intend to be involved and the couple may have planned for shared care, but how they do this may be experienced as either supportive or interfering and unhelpful. If the latter, some fathers may withdraw emotionally and/or physically and leave it to the mother, thus starting a path whereby they come to regard themselves as peripheral to the mother. Of course, these demands are also occurring in the context of the parents being physically drained, often losing sleep and possibly having trouble coping at work.

In our experience, most couples navigate these demands, tasks and changes well and with resilience – with more or less support from extended family and friends.

But when this transition to parenthood and its associated demands overwhelm the couple, we focus first on physical resources and aids to coping, and then gently explore their attachment styles, responses and expectations of each other pre childbirth and subsequently. Sometimes when working with older couples, we trace sources of unhappiness and dissatisfaction with their relationship back to this time, and how the transition was managed. We often find that misunderstandings and disappointed expectations developed at this time and were not discussed and resolved. Such disappointments seem to have the capacity to stay hidden (but alive!) in the relationship between the couple, until perhaps a therapeutic conversation enables a process of discovery, illumination and reprocessing.

Case example: Marsha and Doug

We worked with a couple where the mother was bilingual and the father was monolingual and unfamiliar with the mother's first language. The mother had a grown-up daughter from her first marriage who moved in with her and her new husband to help with childcare. The mother and her older daughter spoke to the baby in their first language, which left the father feeling left out – unable to understand, feeling unwanted and unsure how to contribute. The father's sense of isolation and rejection grew and was not voiced, culminating in a terrible row one evening, in which the mother felt frightened and intimidated by the father's fury. Therapy established a safe context for practice and then explored the felt experience of abandonment, from both partners, as it happened – the mother had missed the father and wanted his nurturance and support at this time, and the father wanted to feel he had something to offer his wife and child.

For the couple there is also an important shift in the nature of their relationship – with, for many couples, the woman experiencing a period of physical and economic dependence on her partner, if it is agreed that she remains at home to care for their baby (Dallos and Dallos, 1997). This can offer some further potential for building a sense of trust and intimacy with each other. On the other hand, and it can produce convoluted feelings, for example for a woman a resentment at having to be dependent when she has avoided being so previously, or a loss of role and status within her career. It can also contain complex layers of obligations and expectations, such as 'I have looked after you'. In some cases it can also produce a deep sense of anxiety about the 'no turning back' aspect of becoming a parent in that the responsibility can seem overwhelming and anxiety provoking as to whether they will be able to look after the child properly and successfully. Couples are also faced with complex decisions abut whether one of them will partly or fully 'give up' their career or work to look after the children. Issues of power and control in the relationship, their kin systems and local cultural context will bear on the decision-making process, or lead to automatic assumptions regarding role changes. Again this can be a source of emotional fulfilment in terms of developing intimacy and trust between them but also the potential for feelings of loss at giving up one's paid job for a while and along with it possible friendships at work, status, adult roles and so on.

In all of the life-cycle stages it is possible to see the influence of childhood experiences and what Byng-Hall (1995) calls corrective and replicative scripts. However, it is possible that we see some of the most powerful examples of the influence of these scripts at childbirth. The birth or arrival of a child is likely to trigger in parents memories of their experiences with their own parents or carers and they are likely to use these, and their reflections on them, to guide their actions with their baby. So parents may decide that they want to be more involved, affectionate and tactile with their child than their parents had been with them. However, the couple may not have the same content in their corrective scripts. For example one parent may want to set clear rules and have more routines than occurred in the chaotic family life they experienced. The other parent, if they felt they were treated harshly as a child, may veer towards eschewing all routines for fear of being cruel. The ability to actively reflect on and process these differences in a supportive and understanding context cannot be underestimated. Furthermore, they may both not have corrective scripts, such that one parent is convinced that their own parents did a very good job and wants to do the same with the child. This configuration of 'my parents were awful' and 'yours were great' may appear to be workable to start with, but may lead to one parent assuming a moral high ground which in the longer term can deskill or disempower the other. Likewise, the parents may look to their own parents to think about who stayed at work and who was closer to the children emotionally and whether they wish to repeat or change these patterns. Consideration of gendered and other cultural expectations may or may not play a role in their thinking and decision making. In our work with couples, we find that they may have 'slipped' into parenthood roles of carer and provider without much active thought, and with hindsight are surprised at the longer-term impact on their felt intimacy.

Above all, the attachment issues for the couple at this stage can be seen to become increasingly complex. Possibly this is a change from a period where there has been a move towards attachment issues becoming less complex with their needs for security and emotional fulfilment focused on each other. Now they have a child to look after and the complexity of the child's attachment relationships within the rest of the family to consider. This is in addition to the relationships that are also in place with professionals, such as healthcare personnel. For example, the experience of a young mother who is struggling with intimacy and attachment to her child may be aggravated if she feels that a professional is critical of her or makes her feel incompetent. Of course this is not usually the intention but 'parenting' classes, for example, may convey the message that the parent has 'got it wrong' and needs to be educated. With adoption there may be an elongated process of others 'looking in' to the family relationships, so to speak, to enable a process of settling in, or with the birth of a child with an identifiable disabling condition, there may be a lifelong sharing of parental decision making with professional staff. Parents may notice the impact of sharing the care of one of their children, but not of their other children, on their bonding experiences and often say to us that with hindsight they are less sure they 'did things right'.

Marriage and family dilemmas

Following the arrival of children, and for some families there may be a decision not to have children, there can be a considerable number of transition points where revisions in attachment organisations may be required. These may include children starting school, adoption, children moving into adolescence, divorce and separation, death of family members, and possibly remarriage or new partnerships. Families become organised during this period of their lives so that the parents start to adapt to and develop their roles and also work out ways of relating with their in-laws, including cooperating over the care of the children. This can mean that the children also develop important attachments to their grandparents. In some cases these attachments can be a buffer against less secure attachments for the children with their own parents. In some of our therapeutic work, we have noticed that the birth of grandchildren can offer an opportunity for grandparents to revise their scripts as parents, with a 'second chance' to parent again. The parents may come to find the grandparents helpful and reorganise their own attachments with them to become closer, less conflictual and generally more secure.

Starting school

A significant attachment event in this period may be when children start school or nursery. Many of us report that this as a particularly painful and anxiety-arousing attachment memory as children. Others remember it as a great day when they were able to have lots of fun with new children. If the child has become very central to one parent's emotional well-being, for example where a mother is rather lonely and dissatisfied, and reliant on the child for company, the child starting school can indicate a loss and a reminder that she has lost opportunities at work and so on. A child may feel her mother's distress and loneliness and develop various means or 'symptoms' to avoid the separation and thus protect them both from the anxiety of separation. Consistent with this, the attachment relationship between the child and the parent may have developed a pre-occupied style such that separation becomes difficult and anxiety provoking. In some cases a child in such a role with the parent may be seen by peers at school as a 'mummy's boy or girl' and be ridiculed or teased. This can lead to some revision of their attachment such that with help and support they become somewhat more independent, or alternatively start to stay off school and become entangled in an angry–anxious dependent relationship with their parent. The parents at this stage both need to be able to encourage growing autonomy and independence in the young child but at the same time maintain closeness and connection and convey the message that they too miss the closeness that they had. The parents therefore have to be able to partly disguise or contain their own feelings of loss and anxiety that the child will cope but not so much that the child feels rejected and unwanted. This set of demands can also obtain when children physically move out of the parental home.

A central issue is how the parents are able to work together to assist the child and each other during this stage. Similarly, lone parents may rely on the help of a relative, a friend or a non-residential partner. For example, it may be that the parents engage in some reorganisation of their relationship so this is some compensation for them as they start to do more things together, or if the parent has been at home full time, they may start to prepare for a return to work either part or full time. Again these possibilities also require changes in their own relationship and dependencies. Also many parents do not hold this so much as a choice but as a financial necessity but with anxieties that they are becoming distant from their child too soon and perhaps a related sense of not being adequate or good enough parents for them.

Adolescence

Although much has been written from a Western perspective about adolescence as a time of upheaval and crisis, this is not invariably the case (Rutter, 1980). Some children are able to be clear with the expression of feelings, both positive and negative, with their parents and to resolve conflicts. Others may feel very anxious about their parents or intimidated and fearful so that they do not express their feelings at all. However, generally children are moving the intensity of their attachment at this stage away from their parents and increasingly towards their friends and possible dating partners. We would note that, for most young people, this is a shift, rather than a severing of attachment to parents. They may also be increasingly engaged in adult pursuits, such as starting to drink, smoke, go out on their own, find paid employment, take drugs and engage in sexual relationships. This shift can leave a parent who has stayed at home for the children now in a position of feeling somewhat redundant, or as some parents say, feeling like 'they treat the place like a hotel'. Alternatively, parents may also worry if their child is remaining too engaged with them and appears not to be making close friends and developing independence of action outside the home. Subcultural ideas about what is expected from young people at different times may be subject to variation, but attachment thinking would suggest that whatever the cultural or religious discourses on relationships with parents and adoption of adult roles, our emotional need for connection, safety and support is constant if not more fluidly and multiply interpreted as we age.

One of the core attachment processes during adolescence is that there is a simultaneous detachment of attachment support from the parents towards peers but at the same time periods of intense attachment support from the parents. When relationships go wrong, such as fallings out with friends, first loves going awry and so on, the adolescent needs their parents to be able to help them to regulate their often very intense feelings. The parents have been required to help the child developmentally manage or regulate their affect throughout their childhood but arguably at this point this task becomes more difficult since the adolescent may at the same time be more critical of their parents. The parents may struggle to cope with their own feelings of being hurt, rejected and stung by the child's criticism and having to remain relatively calm and able to help their child manage their feelings. Again this period can lead to positive reorganisations in that the parents may discover a new intimacy with their child in being able to assist them. Alternatively, for some parents there may be a crisis as they discover that they are thrown back to memories of their own childhoods where their parents were unavailable or neglectful. Attempts at corrective scripts may break down because of the whirlpool of negative emotions, the lack of successful experience with these kinds of dilemmas, the sense of being criticised and so on from their adolescents, such that the parents return, despite their very best intentions, to repeat what their parents did during their own adolescence! This is a poignant moment in therapeutic work when parents acknowledge their promise to themselves never to do this. Parents who have experienced insecure childhood attachments will hold coercive scripts in a largely semantic domain since they do not have the procedural, visual and episodic memories from their own childhoods to support them in revising scripts under duress. When their children were younger and smaller it may have been more possible to contain and support them emotionally. However, faced with the greater intellectual power of adolescents to criticise parents, not just in terms of their behaviour, but also to weaken the semantic foundation on which parents' corrective scripts are based, it can be harder for parents to support them emotionally.

Adolescence may also be the period where a child who has played a central role in the family of providing for the emotional needs of their parents may start to react against this position. The expectations of their peers, sexual urges and their comparisons to the lives of their peers may mean that they attempt to dislodge themselves from the position of tangled, emotional triangulation between parents who communicate with each other through the child. For example, Kathy (17 years old) says of her parents:

> The only thing I ever hear them talking about is me and if I didn't have this [anorexia] it's kind of like . . . would everything fall apart? At least it's keeping them talking, and they won't argue while I've got this because it might make me worse. So, um . . . that's kind of like, I'm not in control as such but I've got more control over the situation that way.
>
> (Kathy)

A danger for a young person in Kathy's position is that by remaining triangulated with the parents she is unable to practise and learn about relationships with her peers. This can mean that she becomes separated from her peers and increasingly emotionally entangled with her parents.

Leaving home

Some of the most serious emotional difficulties appear to be associated with the leaving home stage (Rutter, 1980). If and when young people leave home varies across different societies. In the UK, and largely for economic reasons, there has been a gradual increase in the ages to which children stay at home with their families. However, for many families in Western societies, children physically leave home in their late teens or early to late twenties. Even where they continue to live at home, some significant changes usually occur in how family life is organised. Dowling *et al.* (2005) write about the changes in family life concurrent upon one or more grown-up children continuing to live at home with their older parents, and comment that much less is written about this set of circumstances than, say, leaving home itself. For families the physical exit of children marks an important punctuation of the attachment relationships in the family. Especially for parents who have grown emotionally distant from each other, this can represent a crisis since they now have to face the fact of their own distance and that they can no longer rely on the child to meet their emotional needs. Children, such as Kathy, mentioned earlier, may have become very entangled in their parents' relationship and hence leaving home may be very difficult. One risk is that the attempt at leaving home may be aborted, for example by the child developing a serious emotional disorder. In Kathy's case this was a form of eating distress – anorexia nervosa – which meant that she was both emotionally and physically very vulnerable.

A key task for the parents is to both encourage and prepare the young person for their increasing independence as adult citizens but also to convey that they are not being prematurely pushed out. Attachment thinking clearly identifies autonomy and dependence as different sides of the same attachment coin – the life cycle, developmental issue is how we collectively balance these needs, requirements and obligations in ways that allow young people to take up their place in society. Haley (1973) evocatively used the expression 'weaning parents from children' to underlie the issues for some parents at this stage. There may also be a deep sense of loss for some parents that this part of their lives is over, perhaps with regrets that they had not spent as much time with their children as they would have liked. We meet parents who start to regret how much time was taken up by work at the expense of time with their children. On the other hand, there may be anxieties for the parent who has remained at home abut how they will now spend their life, as usefully and productively. This can offer creative opportunities for further education, retraining and new activities, including continuing the role of carer with older relatives or grandchildren, as much as it can be a source of anxiety about purpose in the future. Also, some parents, again as in Kathy's example earlier, may say that they have only really stayed together for the sake of the children but nevertheless continue to stay together, sometimes leading to the children feeling that they have been needlessly used in the parents' conflicts. Another possibility is that the parents do separate and the children respond to their parents' distress and loneliness by becoming more involved or even moving back in with one of the parents to look after their attachment needs.

Older age and retirement from paid employment

We discuss issues of bereavement and loss in Chapter 7. However, retirement can also represent significant attachment changes for families. The couple may have organised their lives around work with one or both of them usually spending a significant part of their life in a work setting. Retirement may mean an ending of many of these work-related relationships, and change of role, or even loss of status, which in some cases may be a relief but can also involve a sense of loss and sadness at the sense of an end to one's meaningful contribution to work. For the couple it is likely to involve spending an increasing amount of time together. Strategies of managing emotional closeness and distance, and coping, will now need to be re-examined and possibly readjusted in the light of changed circumstances. For some couples this can mean that they become closer or return to the intimacy they had in earlier years. The role of grandchildren may also be important such that they spend more time with them and in assisting their own children to have some relief and time to themselves. Hence, an increased attachment to grandchildren can have benefits for all. At the same time, couples may differ in how much they are prepared for this and to do this. For example, one grandparent may wish to spend time with the grandchildren as a way of avoiding having to spend so much time with the other grandparent! Alternatively, one grandparent may want the other to spend more time with them, for example spending time on romantic holidays rather than childminding activities. These amorous invitations can be a source of delight or dread and also a source of pleasure, some amusement or even embarrassment to the grown-up children!

Families in transition: separation, divorce and living in stepfamilies

Families are complex, dynamic systems, with members entering and leaving through birth, adoption, death, marriage and cohabitation. Adaptation and adjustment are central to how family groups maintain a balance in the midst of many internal and external demands for change. In this section, we focus on the processes of separation, divorce and remarriage for both adults and children. While these experiences may come as a relief and safety, as a source of happiness, as an opportunity for economic betterment and so on, we wish to help articulate the experiences of loss embedded in these processes, as the loss may be hidden, masked or denied. For example, in attachment terms, the end of a marriage may signal loss of connection and/or loss of earlier hopes and the wished-for future. For children, they may still be grieving the loss of the non-residential parent, while their residential parent may be happy to have found a new partner. There is potential here for family members to hold different experiences of loss at different times, and if the loss cannot be straightforwardly acknowledged, the risk is that loss will show itself in disguised ways, that are open to frank misinterpretation, such as behavioural problems in children.

The six stations of divorce

Bohannan (1970) writes of the six stations of divorce, indicating multi-layered processes involved in separation and divorce, for different members of the family system, over an extended period of time. His schema helps to unpick the complexities of loss, decision making, and the relational consequences of actions, in ways that mitigate against the 'taken for granted' and that keep us working in culturally attuned ways:

1   *The emotional divorce.* This is the process whereby the marriage/partnership loses its meaning, for one or both partners. This may have been happening for some years, at different rates for each partner, or it may come as a surprise to one of the partners, and if there are children, they will have observed this. It is no surprise to us that many children, following their parents' divorce, for years afterwards harbour the desire that their parents will reunite (Visher and Visher, 1985). It also highlights for children the complexity of one of their birth parent's decision to re-partner, whereby the parent may be joyful about the decision, but the child still grieves the lost 'family'. If the divorce has been acrimonious, and the child finds that they are not permitted to speak well of one parent, or about their affection for one parent in the hearing of the other, their sense of divided loyalties, and inability to please either parent under these circumstances, can lead to emotional withdrawal, or behavioural acting out.

2   *The community divorce.* This is the process whereby friends and relations might take sides and one partner loses contact with a group of people who may have provided social support, or where the partner who moves out of the family home, often the father, may need to change neighbourhoods to find affordable housing, and thus loses contact immediately with a neighbourhood. Sometimes, other couples may be emotionally threatened by the divorcing couple as it forces them to think about rifts in their own relationship, so some friends simply seem to 'disappear'.

Relatives may disapprove of divorce and emotional distance obtains as a result. All of these possibilities can combine to leave divorced and separated couples somewhat exposed and lonely at a time when social support and confiding relationships are even more crucial.

3 *The psychic divorce.* This refers to the process of adjusting and accommodating to the role and status of a 'single' person, when a sense of personal identity may have become invested in being a couple.

4 *The economic divorce.* During separation and divorce, many financial decisions have to be made about allocating resources and supporting the children. For example, the sale of the family home to provide two separate living units can mean a move out of the neighbourhood, with multiple transitions for children, of moving school and leaving friends and activities, at a time of adjusting to the major loss of one parent living elsewhere.

5 *The legal divorce.* These are the grounds on which the divorce is granted, or the separation is enacted. In these times of 'no fault' divorce laws in the West, there may be less public humiliation in identifying whose behaviour led to the 'breakdown' of the marriage, but privately we see the same dynamics of loss, anger, hurt, humiliation and disappointed dreams, alongside the possibility of relief and safety if the marriage was unsafe. For children, who may be caught up in continuing parental disputes, as the 'battle' is fought over contact and custody, the dilemma of divided loyalty poses a major developmental crisis, for which they often do not have the personal resources to understand and manage the impact of the conflicts (Blow and Daniel, 2002).

6 *The co-parental divorce.* This relates to the decision making about the care of the children, such as where they live, who looks after them, how they have contact with both parents and so on.

Each stage of divorce and separation requires tasks of grief and mourning, for all members of the household, and kin system. Bohannan's schema reminds us that different family members may be living through different experiences of loss and grieving at different times and in different ways, and difficulties might occur when one family member expects others to be responding similarly to them.

Divorce and separation

For many families, nearly a third of families in the UK, one or other parent has experienced separation or divorce. This also means that for many children they will experience divorce or separation in their family. Divorce can represent one of the greatest attachment disturbances for children and families. Frequently, prior to a divorce there will have been argument, conflict and in some cases violence, which will be experienced as extremely frightening for children and often for the parents. For the child it represents fear and anxiety as they see their parents upset, distressed and distracted. At the same time, the children will be fearful that they may lose one or other parents, be anxious about where they will live, how they will cope and so on. In some cases, children frame this in positive terms since they hope it will be an end to the tension and fighting that they have witnessed.

> They were supposed to break up this time last year, they had all the divorce papers and I was so sad, and then they decided to change their minds, and it's just like . . . messing me about.
>
> (Kathy)

Children, as in Kathy's case above, may also feel some relief that they may no longer have to occupy the position as go-between for their parents and can lead their own lives. However, frequently in the process of divorce, children often feel compelled to take sides:

> They used to really hurt me because they used to play each other off . . . and they'd be like – 'go on tell me all the bad stuff about the other one'. And I used to sit there and think I'm made up of half of each of these people and they hate each other and do they hate me? That used to play on my mind for ages.
>
> (Kathy)

As with all of these life-cycle stages there can be positive reorganisations as well. For example, some children develop a sense of independence, learn to make use of friendships more openly and in some cases develop closer relationships with each parent. Typically through this period, parents are emotionally distracted and less able to be attachment figures for their children. In some cases, children develop a more parentified role in looking after their parents (Byng-Hall, 1995).

A less-documented possibility is that children also learn to rely on other siblings and these relationships can become strong – in effect they may become substitute attachment figures for each other (Dowling and Gorell Barnes, 1999). In a research study on how siblings coped with divorce (Abbey and Dallos, 2004) we found that often they described changes in their relationship with each other, such that they became closer. In some cases the children were also drawn to take different sides, such that one sibling looked after one parent and the other sibling the other parent. Although not necessarily becoming closer, the children appeared to agree on this division, recognising that both parents needed 'looking after'. How this occurs varies with the age of the children and may also change following the divorce. For example, there is also a tendency for children to make a choice (Dowling and Gorell Barnes, 1999) to cut off relationships with one of the parents following a divorce as it becomes too emotionally difficult to continue to manage the tensions between their two parents.

Remarriage and partnership

Transition through divorce can involve moving from a two-parent household, to living with a lone parent, and staying with a non-residential parent, to living with a remarried parent – with any number of potential combinations of these transitions, with the incumbent demands for role and task reorganisation, and the profound implications for the development of secure attachments within the family groupings. Frequently following divorce, one or other parent remarries, or starts a permanent relationship. There may be some shorter relationships before this occurs, which children may find problematic because they may be fearful that difficulties may arise again, they want to keep a peaceful family life and also want to keep the emotional closeness to the parents. For many parents these explorations and the eventual settling down may mean that they are relatively distracted emotionally from their children. For example, in falling in love with a new partner the parents may be happy and excited but may not be so aware that they are becoming more focused on themselves than their children. This can be particularly difficult for the children since they have already experienced a period of disruption and the possible emotional unavailability of their parents leading up to the divorce. For teenagers there can also be some uncomfortable tensions as they are entering into sexuality and they see their parents likewise 'on the market' and looking for partners and being more overtly sexual than they would be as parents in the original family. A parent distracted with their own romances may even turn to their child to help regulate their own feelings, ups and downs, doubts, jealousies and so on, rather than being emotionally available and focused for their child.

When the new partner enters into the family there is again a further intense period of emotional change and adjustment. There may be preparation for this or the change may happen relatively suddenly. Children find that they have to share their home and their parent with a new partner, who may also have children from a previous relationship. Their parent may hope that the children can become close to the new partner but there may be a range of mixed feelings. For example, the children may resent the intrusion into their lives, blame the new partner for the demise of their family, resent the new partner for taking their parent's attention, feel unloved by the new partner and so on. Alternatively, there are also safeguards required, for example a sense of some appropriate emotional distance between a stepfather and his adolescent stepdaughter for instance.

Families may struggle in learning how to renegotiate the complex attachment roles involved. For example, should the step-parents be substitute parental attachment figures or hold a more distant role, like an uncle or friend. If the incoming step-parent is a woman there may be a host of gendered expectations that she will 'mother' her partner's children. Often the parent feels guilty that the children are missing out on a parent when the other birth parent has disappeared off the scene or there is minimal contact. There is a variety of emotional dilemmas for the new parent: they may feel that the children resent them because they are not as 'good', nice, loving, fair, caring or clever as their birth parents. On the other hand, they may also experience resentment because they are in some sense better than the non-residential parent, leaving the children sad about their birth parent's failings. The new parent may also find it difficult to cope with the fact that the children continue to be attached to a seemingly irresponsible, non-caring parent when they in contrast try a lot harder to be there for the children.

The complexity of living in stepfamilies and the careful negotiation of these developmental pathways for children and parents is not to be underestimated. We can summarise some of the attachment implications for stepfamilies in the following ways:

- The children and one of the parents have had a longer relationship than the new couple, which is the newest relationship in the family system, with implications for loyalty and the strength of the attachment bonds – in attachment terms, the incoming step-parent has to learn about the intimacy, rhythm and history of the parent–child relationships.
- For many family members the new family was forged and formed through loss – through separation or death, with the potential for loss of hope, loss of dreams, perhaps loss of community if a move was involved, and for the children, the very real loss of day-to-day contact with their non-residential parent. Thus, while the new couple may rejoice in their new-found relationship, the children may be in mourning – almost as if they are missing someone most of the time.
- There may have been a period of lone parenting predating the new couple relationship, whereby one or more of the children assumed greater responsibility and/or became a confidante to the parent – these arrangements are likely to be disrupted by the arrival of a new partner, and the children may or may not wish to relinquish these new roles and responsibilities.
- When any new couple get together, they bring traditions from their previous experiences in families that necessitate some accommodation and adaptation, for example in how family and cultural rituals are celebrated, or in how food is best cooked. Thus, with a stepfamily the number of traditions that are brought together increases.
- Children are often members of two households, and need help with understanding and negotiating different rules and ways of being in different households.

- Little if any legal relationship exists between the step-parent and the stepchildren, unless the children are adopted by the new step-parent.
- The life-cycle stages in the stepfamily for the adults may not be congruent. For example, an older man with children from a previous relationship may marry a younger woman with no experience of looking after children, such that the new stepmother and her stepchildren may find that there is not a generational gap in their ages; and she may want children of her own, so to speak, and he may not.

Thus, in working with families in transition, we need to pay attention to how people are helped to accommodate to processes of loss and mourning, how they develop resilience and ways of coping, how they make sense of their own and others' experiences and how they negotiate conflict and difference in the best interests of all family members at times when emotions can run high. As we have suggested throughout this chapter, the transitional stages offer both challenges and opportunities for change. It seems to us to make considerable sense to consider these times of change as times when emotional changes are also primary as are shifts in the nature of the attachment connections between family members and also in terms of shifts in each family member's internal worlds. In this chapter we have not offered an ANT framework for how to deal with these changes; rather, we offer this quite extended discussion as a potentially helpful framework for considering the shift that families are needing to make. We think that an explicit discussion with families of these changes in their emotional connections can helpfully inform the work that we describe in the chapters in this book and this may also apply to a wide variety of family circumstances, tasks and problems.

Chapter 4

Emotion regulation

Aggression, ADHD and violence in families

In this chapter we want to look at how people manage their strong negative feelings and anxieties. Many serious problems are seen to be associated with difficulties relating to the regulation of emotions, for example, various forms of anxiety and fear including specific forms of phobia, depression and problems in managing anger and aggression – the so-called 'conduct disorders' – and problems of family violence. It is also possible that one of the most widely diagnosed problems of childhood – attention deficit hyperactive disorder (ADHD) – may also predominantly be a problem that is related to the regulation of emotions. Since attachment theory is primarily concerned with how children learn, with the assistance of their parents, to manage their feelings and calm themselves down when unhelpfully aroused, it is helpful to consider in more detail how it may illuminate our understanding of the above problems. In fact, from an attachment theory perspective, many forms of interpersonal problems can be seen in terms of issues of emotion regulation. We will, however, restrict our focus in this chapter to work with problems where the emotional regulatory process seems to be clearly central to the problems, namely aggression and violence, mood disorders and hyperactive conditions.

The chapter will take a look at emotional regulation in general terms with some detailed exploration of attachment theory as offering a model of how children develop strategies to manage their feelings. The focus will then be on an exploration of problems of attention/hyperactivity and aggression. Finally, we shall consider the problems of violence in adult intimate relationships and the intergenerational effects on children.

Attachment patterns

Attachment theory can be regarded as predominantly a theory of emotional regulation: When an infant is frightened, distressed or anxious they turn to their parents for protection and reassurance. The comfort that is offered provides safety and as such has a survival value but also serves to help the child to learn to manage their feelings. How parents respond to the signals of distress and anxiety from the infant is seen to shape their patterns of emotional regulation. For the young infant their initial responses are behaviours or primary attachment strategies wherein they directly attempt to seek reassurance and protection from carers. As the child develops they become capable of not just responding to but internally representing the attachment figures and their relationships with them. Through the development of this 'working model' of attachment they are able to employ 'secondary attachment strategies'. Essentially, two main types of patterns are seen to emerge: secure and insecure. Insecure patterns have been described as avoidant/dismissing, and anxious/ambivalent:

Avoidant/dismissing patterns

If the child's cumulative experience is that the parents or carers will be unresponsive and possibly even punitive towards signals of distress or demands for comfort, the consequence may be that the child develops a *deactivation* strategy in that attempts are made to shut down the emotional system. This pattern occurs when seeking support from others is seen as a non-viable option and attempts are made to reduce the risk of frustration or further distress by the attachment figure being unavailable. It is suggested that this strategy broadens to distancing oneself from any form of distress whether it is attachment related or not. It involves active inattention to threatening events and personal vulnerabilities as well as suppression of thoughts and memories that might evoke distress. If this feature of the strategy does not work, for example if a painful memory is unexpectedly aroused by association, then the thoughts are actively suppressed or repressed. Broadly, the strategy also involves withdrawing from close relationships, suppression of painful negative memories, repression of negative memories, failure to acknowledge negative feelings and denial of basic fears. There is a development of a belief in the need for self-reliance, which may encourage a denial of one's own vulnerabilities. In contrast to the hyperactivating strategies the person's internal world may be tidy and ordered but an emotional desert that is devoid of the clutter of feelings, needs, distress and other significant people.

Anxious–ambivalent patterns

Here the parents are likely to have been inconsistent and unpredictable in terms of their responses to the child's signals of distress and demands for comfort. The child may therefore maintain excessive displays of distress and emotion, as they learn that they are attended to eventually. Sometimes we hear children say they prefer negative attention to being ignored. This can also mean that other features of the environment may become associated with anxieties and fear as the child remains in a distressed state for extensive periods of time. This pattern also prompts the child to become *hypervigilant* so as to maximise the possibility of any attention and care as soon as it appears to be available. In a context of uncertainty the only reliable prediction may become the child's own display of affect: If I am crying, demanding and angry, eventually I will have my needs met. However, the crying and demands may in turn be met by angry responses from the parent, 'shut up' which provoke further distress and anger in the child.

There is a self-amplifying process whereby the person is chronically pre-occupied with possible signs of disapproval, waning interest or fear of possible abandonment. With the advent of language, the internal dialogues are likely to be saturated with a pessimistic view of the world, others, and possible negative outcomes. There may also be a negative view of self alternating with anger at others' imagined betrayals. Activation of attachment-related worries may be activated even when there is no actual external threat:

> Hyperactivating strategies produce a self-amplifying cycle of distress in which chronic attachment-system activation interferes with engagement in non attachment-related activities and makes it likely that new sources of distress will mingle with old ones, thereby creating a chaotic and undifferentiated mental architecture.
>
> (Mikulincer *et al.*, 2003, p. 85)

Importantly both of these insecure strategies imply that attachment needs continue to occupy a large part of the child's thinking and experience (Kobak and Cole, 1994). In effect, both types of strategies leave the child distracted by attachments and less available to engage in other activities. In particular, they are more likely to lead to the child being stuck inside a loop of continually striving to avoid or gain care.

In *secure* patterns the child experiences a consistent response from the parents to provide comfort and reassurance as required. The child is therefore able to predict the parents' behaviour cognitively and is also able to express their feelings. This allows the possibility that the child progressively becomes more able to use cognitive information to predict events and also to employ a wider repertoire of emotions, including positive ones. It may also mean that they are able to regard situations as safe and be less distressed by new contexts. Their experience is likely to have been that any anxieties that may have been triggered by their exploration in new situations were consistently followed by receiving comfort from their parent or carer.

Attachment strategies as filtering our experiences

Attachment strategies influence how people react cognitively to both negative and positive emotional experiences. Attempts have been made in various studies to manipulate participants' emotions to see how this interacted with their attachment styles. For example, in an experimental study (Pereg, 2001) people were asked to read either a distressing account of a car accident or a neutral account of assembling a hobby kit. Following this induction of negative or neutral, they were asked to list the causes of a negative relationship event, such as 'your partner revealing something that you wanted them to keep secret'. Participants who displayed hyperactivating strategies (anxious–ambivalent patterns) remembered more negative headlines and saw the relationship problem in terms of more enduring and general causes. Participants with deactivating strategies were not influenced by the induced negative event. However, those with secure strategies remembered more positive headlines and saw the relationship problem in less enduring and general ways. Mikulincer *et al.* (2003, p. 88) suggest some important aspects of studies such as these:

> Importantly, the findings indicated that hyperactivating strategies ended up negatively biasing attributions about a relationship partner even when the partner was not the source of the negative affect. That is, negative cognitions about a partner can be triggered not only when a partner behaves in a relationship – threatening manner but also when negative affect is elicited by other relationship – irrelevant sources.

Such findings fit with much research and clinical evidence for example in relation to domestic violence where a preoccupied and fearful partner appears to entertain negative and threatened thoughts with no apparent triggering action from their partner (Dutton, 2003). Equally interesting are findings relating to differences regarding the influence of positive emotional experiences. Mikulincer and Sheffi (2000) found that the induction of positive feelings could enhance creative problem solving for people classified as secure and had no effect on those classified as avoidant. Interestingly, though, positive mood induction could reduce problem solving for those classified as anxious–ambivalent. People who show an avoidant, or deactivating, style appear to disregard both negative and positive feelings and seem to shut down the opportunity for developing an awareness of feelings. In contrast, for people showing the anxious, hyperactivating strategies, either negative or positive feelings may activate negative feelings. Possibly, positive feelings may trigger a reminder that in the past many positive feelings ended painfully or with deeply held resentments about parents' faults. This is also consistent with clinical experience where, for example, memories of more positive times can produce a release of distressing emotions. Partly, this may also be about negative predictions about the future – a person's belief or story that their life will continue on its unhappy course. For example, Kathy, the young woman diagnosed with an eating disorder introduced in Chapter 2 described how 'there was a picture of me and her [mother] when we were little, cuddling, and I was only young and I was looking at this picture and I was crying so much because I thought because they're older than most parents that she was going to die really soon'.

From self to joint regulation of feelings

Attachment-seeking behaviours are evident not only during childhood but during the whole of our lives. Attachment theory suggests that there are patterns for how children learn to expect to be looked after when they feel anxious or distressed. More broadly, we can see this as the need we all have to rely on others for support and comfort in times not just of physical danger but also of emotional distress. As children develop, these attachment figures may become people outside of the immediate family, such as friends and, later, romantic and sexual partners and, increasingly perhaps for some people, counsellors and therapists.

The ability to use other people to manage our feelings of threat is synonymous with the attachment styles. Mikulincer *et al.* (2003) add that the child's developing working model comes to contain two aspects: declarative knowledge, which is a set of beliefs or expectations that embody their ability to trust others – the extent to which they have faith in others' goodwill and about their own ability to manage distress; and procedural knowledge – what the child is learning to do. The latter is seen to include the willingness to show fear and distress to others, seek support from others and engage in problem solving to reduce the distress. Relatively secure people have learnt that acknowledging and displaying distress elicits support from others. They have also learnt that they can often cope themselves but turning to others can assist coping when necessary. Arguably there is a positive cycle inherent in this since these beliefs allow greater exploration, fun with others and in turn looking after others as well as being looked after. These help to build a sense of competence and trust and further develop self-regulation capacities and a sense of autonomy. These people are able to choose when to be autonomous and when to seek help. Unlike, for example, those with an avoidant attachment style they do not feel compelled to always try to resolve their distress alone. Kathy puts this poignantly:

> Nobody. I wouldn't go to anybody. . . . I went down to Dad and he was like 'Don't be stupid and go back to bed', and I had to go back to bed. And. And after that I didn't bother going to him. I would just bottle it all up and just not bother.

In Kathy's account there is also a broader sense that she has decided that the best strategy is to keep things to herself and not expect to turn to anybody.

Dependency and independence

Attachment strategies can be seen as on a continuum from an extreme independence where a child gradually learns that they must never depend on anyone else – a form of compulsive self-reliance – to an extreme anxious enmeshment with others. The balanced or secure attachment styles can be seen where the person can both find ways of managing their feelings by themselves and also turn to others for emotional support and to help process their feelings. From needing initially to largely rely on parents and carers to help manage their feelings to comfort and soothe themselves, children become able to do this for themselves and to decide when and how to involve other people to help them when necessary. As we have seen earlier, a child develops secondary strategies when the actual attachment figure is not phys-ically available and a part of this involves developing and turning to *internal representations* of our attachment figures:

> As a person gains experience and develops cognitively, more and more of the role of a security enhancing attachment figure can be 'internalised' and become part of a personal strength and resilience. In adulthood, the question about literal attachment figures becomes transformed into a question about the adequacy of internal as well as external attachment-related resources for coping with stress. In many cases, internal resources are likely to be sufficient, but when they are not, the person with a secure attachment history is willing and able to depend on actual attachment figures for support.
>
> (Mikulincer *et al.*, 2003, pp. 82–83)

Mikulincer *et al.* (2003) suggest that situations which are emotionally threatening, which can include, for example, even the experience of reading threatening words, arouse attachment-related thoughts. In effect, we seem to start to think about our attachment figures when we experience threat even of a mild level. They go on to suggest that the roles of our attachment figures become internalised and we come to apply to our self what we remember the attachment figure having done in the past. This may mean that we can imagine what they would do in a situation themselves and what they do or say to make us feel better.

Shaver and Mikulincer (2002) suggest that children proceed from co-regulation of their feelings to being able to manage some of this them-selves by three related processes: The first is through exploration. As the child learns that it is safe to venture out into the world they are exposed to new experiences and may learn that they can manage on their own and even that they are able to assist others with their feelings. The second process is described as an expansion of the self. When an adult comforts the child their responses are synchronised with the child's needs. This can foster a feeling of contact, of being joined and experiencing the adult as part of oneself. The strengths and competencies of the adult are in this way incorporated into a sense of the self. This might include how the parent is emotionally, how they set about solving problems and what they say. Finally, it is suggested that the child is also able to internalise or mirror the actions of the adult, for example how they compliment, approve, celebrate the child's actions and successes. The child can come to imagine or replay in their minds what a parent or other adult figure would say to them. When these three processes occur positively the child may be able to develop in confidence and in their ability to regulate their own feelings (Figure 4.1).

But what happens when these three processes do not occur in a constructive manner? Mikulincer *et al.* (2003) put forward a possible phenomenological account, suggesting that a child may experience two different kinds of mental pain. One results from a frustration of the child's attachment needs and their failure to remain close to the attachment figure. The second is a sense that the child is unable to work together with the attachment figure in the face of dealing with distress and anxiety. In the first state of mind, closeness to the attachment figure is experienced as non-rewarding or even punishing so the child becomes afraid of punishment in the future should they seek attention. The parent may engage in various behaviours that foster this feeling, such as consistent inattention, threats of punishment for showing negative feelings, traumatic abusive experiences when the child seeks closeness, or explicit or implicit messages that encourage self-reliance and prohibit

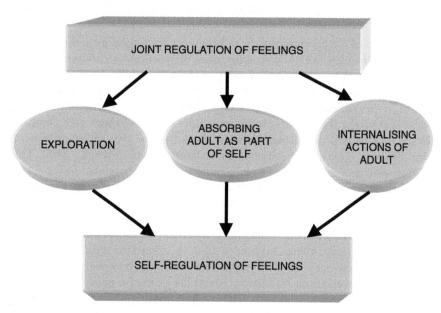

Figure 4.1 Processes in developing self-regulation of feelings.

the expression of neediness or vulnerability. Rather than a source of comfort, the attachment figure, and proximity to them, may become the main sources of threat. Here the child comes to feel that they can only regulate their feelings and cannot rely on others.

In contrast, Mikulincer *et al.* (2003) argue that a different state of mind develops when the child experiences that inconsistency and intrusiveness leaves them helpless and vulnerable and that they must try harder to gain the protection and comfort they need from the attachment figure. In this case, distance from them is experienced as distressing. The behaviours of the caregiver here may include inconsistency, intrusiveness and blocking of autonomy, explicit or implicit messages emphasising the child's incompetence, vulnerability and helplessness, and traumatic or abusive experiences when the child is separated from the attachment figure. The prospect of managing their feelings on their own is therefore experienced as frightening and they feel helpless and alone. In this case the child is likely to feel that they cannot possibly manage on their own, that they are helpless, but also angry, if the parent is unavailable to help sort their feelings out for them.

Problems of attention/hyperactivity and aggression

One of the most widespread clinical conditions seen to be affecting children, and now also becoming diagnosed for adults, relates to problems associated with hyperactivity and an inability to remain attentive and concentrate on tasks and activities and conduct disorders. Furthermore, although there are distinct diagnoses of these conditions there is also a tendency to see them as related.

A cluster of such symptoms have been conceptualised as a distinct syndrome or disorder: ADHD. A substantial proportion of children, between 3 and 9 per cent of school-age children in the UK (NICE, 2006), are said to have this disorder (1 per cent having severe symptoms) and they can take up about 15 per cent of the work of Child and Adolescent Mental Health Services (CAMHS). There are substantial gender differences such that clinically based diagnosis is nine times higher in boys than in girls although general prevalence is found to be only two to four times higher (NICE, 2006). This difference is seen to be linked to referral biases, possibly related to the possibility that the features of ADHD are seen to be more clearly aspects of expected male as opposed to female identities.

The condition is classified as having two components:

- *Inattentivity*: for these children or adults it is hard for them to pay attention to their activity, to organise their work, to complete a task or to follow conversations and instructions. They are also easily distracted or forget details of routines, are likely to lose things and do not seem to like tasks requiring mental effort.

- *Hyperactive–impulsive*: these children or adults are generally extremely active and find it hard to keep still, to cease talking, and they fidget and talk a lot. Younger children are likely to run, jump, climb and make noises and tend to interrupt others and grab things from them. They also find it hard to take their turn in conversations or activities or to listen to directions. There are also likely to have more accidents and injuries.

Some children have both groups of features and the criteria for the diagnosis include that the symptoms must have been present for over six months, and in more than one social setting, for example at both home and school.

There are various assessments employed to diagnose the condition, the most widely used being the Connor's Parent and School Rating Scales (Conners *et al.*, 1998). This test indicates that these children are likely to show rapid and drastic mood changes and 'temper outbursts, explosive and unpredictable behaviour'. In particular, it is possible that the last of these has led many parents to consider that angry, rude, disruptive, risky or violent behaviours may be indicative of the condition. One core problem, as with many other diagnostic conditions, is that there may be other complicating features. In particular, many children seen in the CAMHS setting also show indications of traumatic conditions. For example, children who have experienced or witnessed domestic violence may also demonstrate symptoms of inattentiveness, inability to concentrate and sudden and unexpected intrusions of anger (Vetere and Cooper, 2005).

There are powerful contemporary debates about whether and to what extent ADHD is a form of illness that has some biological or dispositional basis (Schore, 1994; Roy *et al.*, 2004; NICE, 2006). There is also considerable controversy regarding one of the central aspects of contemporary treatment, which is the use of the medication methylphenidate (Ritalin or Concerta), which had been seen as providing a rapid and effective form of treatment. Its usage has accelerated, for example in 1998 there were 220,000 prescriptions made for methylphenadite and dexamfetamine and this had nearly doubled by 2004 (NICE, 2006). However, there has been accumulating evidence that these drugs are not effective for all children diagnosed with the condition, that the long-term effects may be insignificant and also that, for Ritalin, there is a danger of producing a substantial decrease in growth rate (Jensen, 2007; Swanson *et al.*, 2007). It is also recognised that, as with most conditions, there are secondary consequences in that children may develop low self-esteem and depression, in part stemming from negative feedback regarding their symptoms from peers and teachers.

The clinical picture is quite complex and confusing. Not only is there an increasing tendency to see problems of aggression as within this diagnosis but there may be an overlap with post-traumatic stress disorders and the effects on children of witnessing continuous domestic violence (Schore, 1994; Spatz-Wisdom, 2007; Vetere and Cooper, 2006). Children who have been physically or sexually abused, emotionally neglected, exposed to frightening family contexts, have witnessed domestic or other forms of violence or have experienced repeated disruptions in family life due to separations of parents or periods in institutions also show many features of the behaviours included in the ADHD diagnosis. Hence, in the following clinical discussion we are in effect treating these as a broad spectrum of problems of emotional regulation. We are focusing on the term ADHD since many families are influenced by this diagnosis and seek it as a way of making sense of and hoping to gain some support for and respite from their problems.

Implications for therapy: an attachment formulation

We do not wish to enter into unhelpful debates about the extent to which the problems associated with ADHD have an organic as opposed to a social basis. It may well be the case that there are biological components or even a predisposition, such as a high level of arousal and activity which promotes a greater degree of restlessness and need for activity by some children. However, it may be helpful to take a broader perspective and contemplate an alternative perspective that some behaviours labelled as 'ADHD' may be a learnt behaviour pattern (Wiener, 2007), which is also influenced by the nature of attachment patterns in the child's family or social context (Lewis et al., 2007). Arguably, it was similar patterns of behaviour that Bowlby (1979) first recognised in children who had been institutionalised. He described that they were frequently failing educationally, disruptive, sometimes engaging in criminal activities, lacked self-control and the ability to inhibit their actions based on contemplating possible negative consequences. A recent study (Lewis et al., 2007) has supported these initial findings specifically in that adopted children who had experienced instability in their placements were more likely to have difficulty on a task measuring inhibition and also displayed more oppositional behaviours.

From an attachment theory perspective we can see two related conceptualisations of the behaviours described under the diagnosis of ADHD. First, they can be seen as exemplifying features of the anxious–ambivalent attachment strategies. Second, they can be seen as exemplifying features of the extreme or 'disorganised' attachment strategies where the child has experienced the attachment figure/s as confusing, contradictory and frightening (see Chapter 2, p. 28 for a further description).

Anxious–ambivalent patterns

As we described earlier in this chapter, in these types of family interactions the child's experience is likely to have been that the parents are unpredictable, sometimes unavailable and at other times intrusive and disrupting the child's attempts to engage in autonomous activity. It may be significant here that the rates for ADHD are found to be higher in boys and we can speculate that this may relate to the two types of anxious–ambivalent patterns. In one the child adopts a passive, helpless pattern where they appear to abandon attempts to be autonomous in the face of parental intrusions and interference. So, insistent crying, hurting themselves, failing at tasks and thereby eliciting the support of parents may be a way of gaining emotional attention. This may still be, in many cultures, a more acceptable pattern for girls. In contrast to this anxious pole of the ambivalent attachment patterns, there is the aggressive coercive pattern, which appears to be more common in boys. This is likely to involve coercive activities: shouting, breaking things, hitting people and generally running riot (Patterson *et al.*, 1989). An important part of the interactional cycles in families may be that parents over time habituate to these activities such that there is a gradual escalation of behaviours. Parents typically describe a powerful sense of confusion and even helplessness as they become entangled in these patterns with their children. Descriptions of such futile and never-ending struggles are common from parents who have a child with a diagnosis or suspected diagnosis of ADHD. In fact, many parents in CAMHS appear to wish for a diagnosis of ADHD to help them to make sense of their child's behaviours.

In systemic therapy such patterns have also been described as enmeshed – where the separation between the parent and child is amorphous and their actions, emotions and thoughts appear to be entangled (Minuchin, 1974). Arguably, the children in these patterns have found it difficult to proceed to increased self-regulation of their affect. In contrast, children in the avoidant patterns have learnt that they can only rely on themselves to manage their feelings. For children showing anxious–ambivalent patterns the prospects of managing their own anxieties and fears may be extremely anxiety provoking. This may seem strange since some children show angry attacks and apparent rejection of their parents. However, these may in turn produce at first an angry response from their parents and in many cases a failure by the parents to maintain a clear stance with eventual capitulations to the child's demands. In effect, the child and parent/s can be seen to be mutually caught up in an emotional vortex where it becomes very difficult to develop and employ information about the causes and sequences of events. Instead, both come to rely on emotional information, anger, helplessness, anxiety and distress to manage their relationship.

This in turn involves a high state of arousal, as is common in the hyperactive attachment patterns and a vigilant monitoring of the parents' and other's emotional states. The language use of these children may be less developed since their experience has been that language is less useful in predicting events since parents often do not consistently fulfil what they say verbally. Also as the children become caught up in cycles of emotionally laden interactions with their parents their ability to cognitively process events becomes increasingly more difficult. Hence, to employ language to help understand and integrate the various aspects of their experiences becomes difficult. Importantly, children need to develop through conversations with their parents an ability to self-sooth through internal conversations. As Vygotsky (1962) has described, a central aspect of development is the ability to employ inner speech to regulate our actions and our feelings. In the anxious–avoidant attachment patterns this inner speech does not appear to develop effectively. Instead, the child remains entangled with their parents, often engaging in emotionally laden and escalating conversations. These may be either bouts of angry accusations or counter-accusations, or a clingy, anxious dependency on the parent to help them manage their feelings. Either way, the child develops a sense that managing their feelings is not predominantly their own but their parents', or other people's responsibility – 'It is your fault I feel this way'. Figure 4.2 displays a basic example of this overlapping of the selves in families according to the different patterns. In the complex,

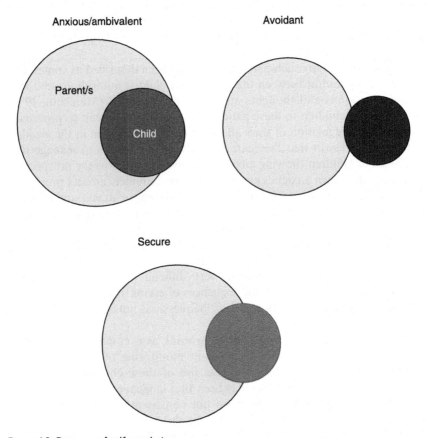

Figure 4.2 Patterns of self-regulation.

'disorganised' patterns there may be an alternating between the anxious–ambivalent and avoidant pattern such that the child alternates between feeling neglected and rejected and also intruded upon and emotionally entangled with the parents.

Creating a secure base

In our clinical experience many families have in a sense established a relationship with the diagnosis as a part solution to constructing some sense of safety in the face of the turmoil that the symptoms described as ADHD can generate. They often describe a sense of chaos, of failure and desperation and even of danger. Frequently the child is described as extremely demanding, aggressive, out of control and also failing in situations outside of the home – at school and in friendships. Parents also describe that whatever they have tried to do seems if anything to make things worse. Often the parents are in a state of oscillation between explanations of their child's behaviours as either wilful, destructive and a personal attack on them or, alternatively, as signs of a form of illness. A commonly attempted solution in many families has also been to attempt to utilise some form of behavioural strategies. There are a variety of self-help books on these topics and also television programmes, such as *Super Nanny*, which utilise a mixture of behavioural, developmental, psychological and occasionally systemic ideas. However, one of the core techniques that captures the imagination of many families is that of a form of extinction described as the 'naughty step'. This contains the idea that 'bad' behaviours are not to be tolerated or rewarded in any way and are clearly indicated by the removal of the child to a quiet and isolated space in the home. Unfortunately, such behavioural techniques, unless combined within a wider therapeutic framework, are frequently counterproductive, producing more rather than less anger in the child. The wider framework, such as a need for consistency in the parents, a calm response to the child, clear setting of goals and parameters, consistent and clear use of language to help the child predict events and so on, may become lost in a reactive and emotional use of such time-out techniques. Furthermore, the parents stay at the level of descriptions of behaviours rather than making an attempt to connect with the child's inner world – their intentions, needs, anxieties and wishes (Hughes, 2007).

Given this context of protracted experience of chaos, distress, anger and frustration along with a sense that psychological approaches such as those above have been tried and failed, families are understandably drawn to the possibility of viewing the problems in terms of an illness. It has also been found that such diagnoses can have, at least in the short term, a beneficial effect for family members. For example, they allow the parents not to feel blamed and likewise the young person is absolved of responsibility for their actions, since they are deemed to be 'ill'. However, parents have described

(Lloyd and Dallos, 2006) that the perceived benefits may erode as the parents come to see some of the more negative aspects of the child gaining a psychiatric label. For example, in a piece of (unpublished) research we conducted, mothers described that their children started to feel singled out at school as odd, Ritalin 'nutters', and that they came to realise the prospect that their child might need to be on medication for their lifetime and so on.

The experience for many families can be of a sense of loss: They feel that they have lost a well, healthy child and have to come to terms with the fact their child has a substantial and potentially lifelong problem. Likewise, children may experience a sense of loss of their childhood and normality. Many appear to resent taking medication and want to be 'normal' like their friends. Some children also describe that the medication can make them feel removed from their real self – in a sort of chemical straightjacket.

For some families it may be some time following a diagnosis but the medication is no longer proving to be effective. How families react to this may vary. For example, some families feel that the medication should therefore be increased or some other stronger substances used. Others may blame the child for not having taken the medication properly and hence having disrupted its effects. Others may now be more angry with the child on the basis that the problem was not medical but due to their 'naughtiness'.

Given that parents and children have had considerable difficulty talking and managing their feelings together, processing these further anxieties may be unlikely. We may also be curious about the attachment patterns of the parents. One possibility is that they too have had a history of ADHD-type symptoms. As a poignant example, one father described to us that he had been so out of control himself as a boy that his parents at one stage resorted to lashing him with rope to a boulder in the garden. The transgenerational patterns, however, are complex and we are not suggesting one simple form of cross-generational transmission. Instead, we can just point to a few patterns that we have observed:

- As in the case above, the parents themselves describe a childhood where they have experienced similar problems. Not infrequently parents may describe each other as lacking emotional control and ability to self-regulate and self-sooth.
- Parents may feel that as children they were over-controlled and not allowed to express their feelings. Hence, they may adopt a 'corrective script' whereby they vow to allow their children more space to express their feelings to the point where this becomes problematic since they may confuse the child by, on the one hand, encouraging such expression but, on the other, becoming angry and reactive when it happens or alternatively passive and unable to set any clear boundaries. The latter can be combined with an incongruity between what parents say explicitly – it's

okay to show negative feeling – and implicitly – non-verbally that they are actually upset and hurt but denying that they are feeling this.

- Another possibility is that parents have experienced traumas in their own childhoods and become highly anxious, angry and fearful at the child's displays of anger. As we shall see in Chapters 6 and 7 this can produce a deep sense of anxiety and confusion in children. It can also produce a tendency for the child to try to monitor, become hypervigilant towards, their parents in order to be able to predict and adjust to their mood changes.

The therapist may at this stage hold some of these potential family dynamics in mind as an alternative to or complementary to medical diagnoses. However, it is likely that a key component of building a secure base with families will be to find a way of being able to work alongside the labelling processes. In some cases families have not received a diagnosis of ADHD and feel as a consequence that the mental health services have let them down. Family therapy can therefore be seen as a bit of an insult or as a way to convince people that the problem is not medical but to do with family relationships. However, the processing of labelling is generally a particularly strong feature of work with ADHD in that the diagnostic process can start so early for so many children. As therapists we may feel some sadness, or even anger that children so young start to be labelled and medicated. A related consequence of this is that the therapist may experience the parents in an antagonistic way. For example, we can start to sympathise with the child and resent the parents' insistence that the problem has some medical basis. An attachment framework reminds us that there is inevitably a flip side of vulnerability and distress to the parents' impatience and anger. A helpful question can be to consider how desperate, at their wit's end and anxious parents must feel that they seek the solution and/or the relief of a medical label with their offspring.

Open communication – discussing the therapeutic relationship

It can be helpful to discuss the issues outlined above with family at the start, for example to inquire about what they think and feel about a referral for family therapy. In this context it may be useful to explain that we (professionals) do not have definitive knowledge about whether the condition is somehow organic, learnt, due to events that have occurred in the family and elsewhere and so on. This can allow the family to voice some anger, for example about the failure to receive a diagnosis without them worrying that they are insulting or attacking us. Hopefully this will promote a sense of working alongside as opposed to against them. Such communication about their feelings can also start a process whereby difficult feelings are expressed but do not escalate out of control and instead can lead to some integration and cognitive processing. A helpful overall narrative at this stage may be that although we do not definitively know the cause of the symptoms we do know that whether it is a medical condition or not there may be some ways in which the family can work together to manage the problems on a daily basis.

This stage of the therapy is extremely delicate and needs particular care. Some families despite anything we say or do may be convinced that the problem is completely medical and it is a waste of time attending for family therapy. However, they do not want to say this since it is all that is on offer, or they are fearful of alienating the professional system.

Working with subsystems

It can be very helpful to follow the above by an indication that we realise that the family has tried to solve the difficulties previously and have struggled with a sense of failure. A way of signalling that we are aware of this can be to offer to do some work with the child alongside work with the parents. In our experience, parents often feel a wave of relief that someone is going to try and help their child and not just expect them to do it all, or accuse them indirectly that they have done it wrong so far. This way of working can also offer a compromise position between seeing the problem as totally in the child or as predominantly a family problem. In our experience it can also offer an opportunity for the softening of the feelings in the family and allows both the child and the parents to receive some support and comfort – caring from the therapy team.

It can also be easier for the child and the parents to acknowledge their vulnerabilities, sense of hurt, loss and sadness about what has happened in and to the family. Often in sessions with the parents and the child there can be a danger of an extended cataloguing of the child's actions. These descriptions can be tinged with anger and bewilderment from the parents and by an angry, sullen silence from the child. What is harder to open up at this stage is how both may feel very sad about this situation, afraid of rejection, and their wish to change it.

On their own, parents and the child often speak very differently from how they do when they are together. For example, the parents are often much more able to talk about what they value in the child and how sad they feel about the child's inability to fulfil their potential. Ironically, parents often appear to feel that sharing these softer sentiments with their child will upset the child. Working with the subsystems also allows us to act as translators for the family members. For example, we typically reconvene as a whole family to end the session and can help the child and parents feed back to each other what they have discussed. This enables an opportunity to emphasise some of these vulnerabilities and start to contemplate whether there might be ways of building on these points of connection.

Exploring the problems

It is important to keep checking the nature of the family's conceptualisations about the causes of the problems. Crittenden (2005) describes one of the narrative styles associated with the anxious–ambivalent patterns as a form of reductionist thinking. People experience the emotional complexity of events and relationships but have developed relatively polarised ways of seeing the problems. As we discussed earlier, this typically is in terms of an essentially medical 'illness' view versus a view of the child as 'naughty' or malevolent towards them. This contrast may reflect the parents' own childhood attachment experiences, such that their own attachment patterns embody a form of narrative that seeks to reduce cognitive complexity, lacks integration and reflection and focuses on emotional responses. However, in addition, this may reflect the wider tensions and polarisations in the professional discourses.

An over-riding strategy is to help families develop a more cognitive and reflective as opposed to emotionally reactive style of communication and dynamics. The focus may therefore be on techniques or orientations that help to 'cool' feelings and promote cognitive processes, for example consideration of the causal and temporal connections in behaviour. This can be fostered by use of various visual techniques, such as use of genograms, time lines – depicting when events happened – or mapping circularities or patterns of interactions in the family drawing out what are seen as acceptable rules of behaviour. Importantly this also needs to address family members' abilities to empathise or understand each other's perspectives. Use of empathetic questioning may be useful to help to move to an awareness of each other's beliefs and intentions as opposed to emotionally driven and reactive processes. Use of paper or whiteboards to map family members' beliefs and positions on the family dimensions can facilitate this (Figure 4.3). For example, we can draw out various dimensions to consider how aspects of the problems may be shared by family members. This can introduce a little humour, such as including the therapist or members of the team in order to help communicate a non-blaming approach.

One approach we find helpful in the initial explorations is to map the professional context in which the family is immersed. This often reveals the preponderance of medical professionals, for example the general practitioner

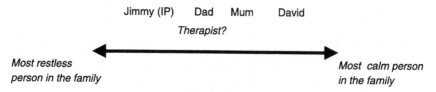

Figure 4.3 Scaling the problems among family members.

Note: IP = identified patient.

(GP), paediatrician, psychiatrist and nursing staff. However, in our experience some of the most forceful advocacy of a medical model may come from extended family and friends who have found or have heard that the diagnosis and medication can be helpful. This consideration of professional and social systems surrounding the family (Figure 4.4) can lead to discussions of different explanations although at this stage we need to be careful not to make the family feel that their beliefs are being unhelpfully challenged.

By drawing up a map of the professional systems with which the family is involved we can also open up a discussion about how the family wish the family therapy team to communicate and liaise with the various professional groups. We have found that many families are very confused about the roles of the different professional groups and agencies and may feel that they are receiving conflicting types of advice. Clarification of how we will engage in communication with these different professions and agencies can help to prevent families from rattling between different systems and can more broadly foster a process of planned rather than reactive responding in the family. In effect, we help them navigate their way through the professional network and its workings, hopefully fostering a more cooperative set of working relationships.

Combined with such mapping and exploration we can draw the family genogram to explore other family members, the lives of people in the family and whether similar problems have been experienced by others in the family. A useful approach can be to enquire who the child takes after in the family. Often this reveals that one or other parent or a more distant relative,

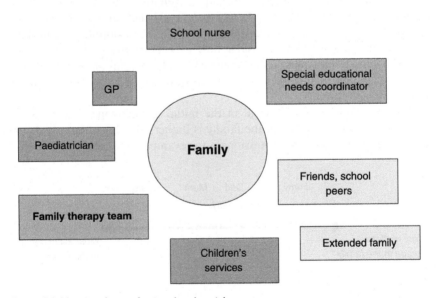

Figure 4.4 Mapping the professional and social systems.

'uncle Jim', was just like the child when they were at that age'. This can help develop and promote a narrative about how such problems may alter and ameliorate as the child matures. It is also possible to start to introduce some less medical terminology, such as who in the family is particularly active, energetic, alert, noisy, boisterous, curious and so on.

Such discussions also connect with an exploration of the delineation between being active as a problem (ADHD) and what might constitute normal boisterous, active behaviour in a child that age and the associated gendered expectations of children's behaviour (Figure 4.5). Again, care has to be taken in order not to appear to confront the family but to start to loosen the polarised narratives that the child is either 'ill' or 'bad'. In such discussions there is sometimes a spontaneous recounting of how a family member identified as having similar problems was seen as problematic but looking back on it, some of what they were doing was seen as normal. Sometimes this leads to a revelation by one or other parent that they had become anxious that the child was following in their footsteps, for example in not completing school successfully, being distracted by other activities, failing to gain a good education or apply themselves to an occupation. Such corrective scripts can be confusing for the child especially if they get an incongruent message, for example that their father is a highly active man who has little time for quiet contemplation but is urging their child in this direction. Alternatively, the parents may reveal different and contradictory beliefs about the value of education, focusing one's attention and persevering with tasks. Often the parents acknowledge that they struggle to pull together as a team and the child has learned to play them off, or a single parent might report exhaustion, with no other adult to help and 'pick up the slack' for them.

It is possible through this discussion to enlarge the shared area such that ADHD has a lesser grip on their lives as there is a move towards somewhat less medical and problem-saturated narratives. This also fits with the idea of externalising the problems and looking at what problems ADHD has created for all of them.

It may also be useful to explore the family environment, how family members do things together, whether they engage in shared and pleasurable activities, and how people focus their attention. For example, some families are extremely noisy and there is a struggle for anyone to find any personal space

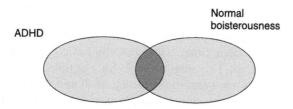

Figure 4.5 Mapping the overlap of 'problem' and 'normal' behaviours.

to engage in quiet contemplation. Some children describe a constant battle with their siblings to protect their property, toys, clothes, books, DVDs etc. and there is a sense that they need to be vigilant to each others' intrusions, leading to a constant bickering and noisiness in the family. There may also be a pattern where in order to be heard or get any attention, a child needs to be the one who shouts loudest or finds some other way of getting attention, hurting themselves or others, getting upset and so on. This type of behaviour may thus be a family pattern rather than simply or predominantly an individual child's problems, that is, it is reinforced behaviour because the child learns to get what they want and need by persisting. It is also important to explore what activities the family engage in that have a focus and require freedom from distraction and consistent attention. Examples may be where family members have an allocated household task, engage in structured play, or reading at bedtime. Not infrequently this reveals, for example, that children spend a lot of time on aggressive videogames, which tend to lead to arousal and frustration and this often occurs before bedtime, leading to problems with sleep. This can of course construct a cycle of tiredness, irritability, further bickering, fights, punishments from the parents and so on.

Throughout these explorations it is essential to be wary of promoting a feeling of failure by the parents or of unhelpfully challenging their belief that this is an illness. Instead, these discussions can focus on ways in which some of these issues may be relevant to managing the problem and building on what if anything seems to work – and when all is said and done, however this is caused, it still has to be lived with!

Considering alternatives

Throughout this work it is important to check with families that the work is meeting their needs. Given the widespread belief that these symptoms are signs of an illness, we find that families may in a sense 'relapse' into a medical framework and move away from any consideration of how the family environment, their relationships and other factors may play a part. It can be helpful to check especially at this stage whether they are willing to continue and to explore ways in which they may be able to change the situation at least to some extent. Along with this we can check whether they might value some advice or suggestions from us. Families sometimes comment that we just ask a lot of questions but never actually suggest anything useful, until we move into working with enactments and work with behavioural experiments!

The exploration of the problems can move on at this stage to look at whether there have been times when the child was relatively free of the problems – exceptions. This might reveal, for example, that the difficulties escalated following some event in the family, such as a divorce, an incidence of violence, a loss or bereavement. This discussion can move onto a discussion of the family's feelings and needs and to a consideration of how the symptoms might be ways of distracting from the underlying feelings. More broadly this can involve a discussion of how people deal with difficulties issues, vulnerabilities. There may be underlying family patterns, such that some people deal with difficult issues by becoming over-excited, distractible and continually changing their focus. Importantly, there can be a discussion of times where the symptoms were not so overwhelming or where the family managed to find pockets of relief from them. For example, they might report times when they engaged in some structured activity, family games or were able to have a discussion that helped resolve the problems. Families often describe that the child showed examples of being calm and focused when they had individual time with one of their parents. This is often portrayed as a problem of the child – needing excessive attention and not being able to tolerate the distraction of peers at school or other siblings at home.

In looking for these 'unique outcomes' it is again important to connect with the possibility that the parents have become disheartened and feel they have failed. Hence, this activity of seeking exceptions can be framed as an opportunity to gather together some ideas that may help the 'illness'. This can then be incorporated with research findings that breaking up tasks into smaller manageable chunks, giving frequent rewards and praise, offering frequent breaks and modifying the environment to be less distracting are all helpful – and of course the parents need praise and support from us! Along with this it is important that the parents try to identify activities that will be interesting to the child rather than activities that will be considered by the child to be aversive and likely to lead to boredom and failure. Spending some individual time with the child can also be framed as helping to identify what the child needs and facilitating communication between the parent and the child.

It is also important to focus on stories that are more hopeful and which also allow a softening of blame and feeling blamed, and of the parents' views of their child and vice versa. It is helpful for parents to recognise that many children with a diagnosis of ADHD have developed an extremely low self-esteem. A reaction to this sense of failure can be that the child becomes angry with themselves and others but is likely to externalise this anger as attacks on their parents. Parents may be helped to connect with the child's vulnerabilities but a danger can be if the swing then is from anger to excessive sadness, tears and displays of distress, which may not assist the move to a less emotionally aroused process in the family. However, the display of warmer feelings can be fostered by developing narratives regarding the child's strengths and competencies. Some different ways of seeing the behaviours can be considered, for example as energetic and spirited as opposed to hyperactive, or alert as opposed to distractible, or enthusiastic as opposed to uninhibited.

There can also be a discussion of the parents' own childhoods and their experiences of parenting. This can include a discussion of what, if any, aspects of their child's behaviour they shared and how they came to overcome or manage these. An important focus of this discussion can be how their own parents spent time with them, what activities they enjoyed with them and how the parents helped them to be able to attend to and focus on tasks. In some cases, parents can recount examples that can be discussed in relation to attempts to replicate these with their own child. In many cases, parents do not have memories of such activity and it can be helpful to consider hypothetical scenarios of what difference it might have made to them had their parents been able to do such activities with them. Such discussion can also reveal that the parents themselves were emotionally deprived, neglected, left to entertain themselves and so on. Rather than replicating these patterns, many parents are actively trying to compensate and to do a better job for their children. However, not having had the experience of their parents supporting them emotionally and experiencing what such shared activity is like it is difficult for them to undertake it with their own children despite their best intentions.

Maintaining change and integration

Many of the families we have worked with have shown a pattern of dropping out of therapeutic contact or becoming somewhat unreliable in terms of attending for sessions. This of course is not unique to this type of problem but is consistent with an attachment formulation that the families may be organised around an anxious–ambivalent pattern. One aspect of this pattern may be that there is a tendency to be emotionally reactive such that their attendance is crisis driven, for example they may be more likely to attend when problems are severe. With some families it can be useful to discuss how they wish to continue to use us or to end their therapeutic contact with us. A useful strategy can be to offer to continue to be a resource for them should problems arise. This may have a fit with their general emotional strategy and by accepting and validating this we can also gain some potential to suggest that, even if problems have subsided, meetings might be helpful in order to consolidate changes.

We also recognise that the wider social contexts, extended family, friends, the media and professional systems may draw families back into a more medically oriented view. Part of our discussions with them can include a reflection on the continuing conflicts they may feel between a medical and a more psychological perspective on the problems. It can be helpful to return to our diagram of the professional systems in order to consider what contact and support they wish to receive from these various professional systems. Along with this we can ask what they would find helpful for us to communicate to these various groups about our work with them. We sometimes discover that families have some very practical concerns, for example a wish not to lose the ADHD diagnosis so that they are able to claim disability benefits, or so that the child can continue to receive special educational support as a consequence of an educational Statement.

By reflecting with them on their continuing practical needs we can also more easily find some emotional space with them to be able to reflect on the relational and emotional processes in the family and what they have gained from their work with us. Some explicit statement of what these gains may have been can be very important since many families may not have integrated our discussions into a more explicit reflective framework that they can draw on to deal with future problems. Specifically, we can discuss what they think may be future challenges and what they can helpfully apply from the sessions to address these more effectively. We also think that it can be very important to offer a continuity of contact so that we can be a resource for them to discuss problems that arise either in further sessions or more informally through a telephone call or e-mail.

The intergenerational effects of family violence

Interpersonal violence, especially violence experienced by children, is the largest single preventable cause of mental illness. What cigarette smoking is to the rest of medicine, early childhood violence is to psychiatry.

(Scharfstein, 2006, p. 2)

Thus far we have been writing from the perspective of the child who may be labelled and diagnosed within a psychiatric system, and suggesting that an attachment perspective both illuminates our understanding of the child's difficulties and gives us a road map for helping families change their usual responses around one another. In this section we wish to elaborate further on the impact of continuous trauma on family systems and to consider in particular the developmental dilemma for children when one or both parents/ carers are frightened and/or frightening, and may even hold mal intent towards the child. When children or adults are afraid, in the face of real or imagined loss, abandonment, threat and harm, their ability to process negatively laden material slows down. They become preoccupied with regulating their own anxiety and fear and become less adept at reading others' emotional and relationship cues. In more extreme circumstances when children are chronically worried and afraid, perhaps they cannot sit still and cannot bear to contemplate their worry or even worse that their carer wishes them harm. Perhaps one way to resolve that dilemma is to dissociate from feeling, or to identify with the abuser to foster an illusion of control.

Family violence can be defined as any act or omission committed within the context of family life that threatens or abuses others, such as psychological, physical, sexual, financial or emotional harm (Council of Europe, 1985). Such a definition with its emphasis on both action and omission, draws our attention to safety, and how we learn to keep ourselves and others safe, and the development of a sense of entitlement to be safe and to be kept safe, and what happens when safety is not part of our lived experience. The Department of Health (1995) estimated that over 750,000 children a year witness domestic violence in England. The British Crime Survey (Home Office, 1996, 2000) estimated that at least one third of all violent crime was domestic assault, with women much more likely to be assaulted and harmed by their male partners. Moffit and Caspi (1998) estimated that over two-thirds of domestic assaults are witnessed by children, and children are four to nine times at greater risk of being assaulted themselves when they live in households where domestic violence takes place, than in households where the adults do not assault each other. They summarise the risks to children of developing both internalising and externalising problems and showing trauma symptoms. Browne and Herbert (1997), writing from a social learning perspective, summarise the impact thus:

- Children learn aggressive styles of conduct.
- Children learn reduced restraint and increased arousal to aggressive situations.
- Children learn to be desensitised to violence.
- Children's views about conflict resolution are distorted.

We find it helpful to think of children's developmental dilemmas in terms of exposure to continuous trauma and the associated problems of affect regulation – and to think of the adults we work with therapeutically as children once themselves – so we always work with intergenerational emotional legacies. These can be summarised as affecting the child's:

- ability to trust;
- ability to concentrate and engage with learning;
- ability to manage anger;
- ability to regulate emotion and learn self-control;
- ability to play, explore and be curious;
- ability to develop a sense of self-worth; and
- social and emotional development more broadly.

The Dunedin Study in South Island, New Zealand, identified a group of at-risk 3-year-olds in their sample and compared them at age 21 with other young people in the sample. At age 3, these children were restless, negative and distractible. At age 21, half of the young men had abused their partner compared to one-fifth of the others and were 2.5 times more likely to have a criminal conviction; and of the young women, nearly half were in a violent relationship and nearly one-third had a teenage birth, compared to the rest of the sample (Silva and Stanton, 1996).

Trauma can be defined as an exceptional experience of powerful and dangerous stimuli that overwhelm the child's capacity to regulate their own emotions (van der Kolk *et al.*, 1996). Children show the same signs of distress when they are exposed to violence as when they are physically abused. It was this well-replicated research finding that led the UK government to extend the legal definition of harm to children to include the impairment suffered from seeing or hearing the ill-treatment of another, particularly in the home. The National Service Framework for Children, Young People and Maternity Services (DH and DfES, 2004) reports that violence starts or escalates during pregnancy, and is associated with a greater incidence of miscarriage, foetal injury and prematurity.

Vetere and Cooper (2001, 2003, 2005) have written extensively of their therapeutic work with domestic violence. Here we shall emphasise the importance of creating a safe context for practice, and the necessity of a safety methodology that both families and the professional network can use as a platform for shared planning, goal setting and collaborative working. When family violence is known or suspected, we work with a 'stable third', to form a triangle as our minimum sufficient network for safe practice. The stable third can be the referrer, especially if it is a social worker, or a trusted adult in the community, such as a health visitor, faith leader, grandparent, community worker and so on. The stable third meets initially with us and the parents to agree a safety plan, and helps us monitor the safety plan with the family. They are not present at all meetings, just those meetings where we review safety with a view to taking another step towards rehabilitation or therapeutic work. The stable third is someone who knows the children, and has access to the family home, and who can corroborate what we are being told about violent behaviour. They also help us to manage the anxiety around risk of future violence held by the family and professional systems.

We do not meet the children in the company of the parents/carers until we know it is safe enough to do so. We hold the parents responsible and accountable for their safety, the safety of others, and for behaviour that harms, threatens and intimidates others, while at the same time using explanation to illuminate, expand and reprocess frightening and dangerous experiences. We start by developing a safety plan, and usually work with a no-violence contract (see Cooper and Vetere, 2005, for a detailed explanation). When the no-violence contract appears to be working, we gradually move to working therapeutically around emotional vulnerability and with the legacies of shame, humiliation, disappointment, sadness and fear so often associated with intergenerational violence. These emotions are seen as primary in attachment terms, and often buried, covered up and denied – whereas, anger, as the secondary emotion, is what everyone notices and responds to!

Our work with adults in families is with those whose violence comes out of a 'hot' place, so to speak – with anger, frustration, resentment and their associated entitlements and expectations. We do not work therapeutically with adults who use violence coolly, calmly and instrumentally to control others. Our attachment-informed couples and family therapies are developed to work with people who show some capacity for empathy. Our responsibility as therapists lies in helping people develop further their capacity for empathy and for emotionally attuned responding in their intimate relationships. In assessing for empathy we recognise that anyone can tell us they know their child might be frightened if they loom over them, for example. Rather, we are interested in the capacity to stand in the emotional shoes of the other, to partly suppress our own emotional needs to appreciate and experience the other's needs, as much as is possible, and to do this involves recognising that the other is *like* you. Empathy is thought to be the single greatest inhibitor of the development of the propensity to violence (Wave Trust, 2005). Empathy emerges from early experiences of emotional attunement, whereby the person looking after the child responds emotionally to the child's needs in a way that the child feels understood, supported and valued (Stern, 1985; Schore, 1994).

As therapists, we pay attention to how people talk about their experience of anger and violence towards others. Phrases like 'I lost it'; 'The red mist came down'; or 'I go from 0–100 in ten seconds' are common – suggesting the speed with which some people feel anger and the associated unexpectedness and loss of control. We notice these descriptions, pause, and slow down our work to encourage people to walk around in these phrases with us. We also notice that alongside these descriptions of speed of response, other family members will say they felt tension building all day! In our work with men who have behaved violently towards others we often find they are not very prac-tised at monitoring their own arousal. Part of the safety planning work we do, is to help them learn to monitor and regulate their own arousal, and to begin to learn to calm themselves down in more constructive ways. We use some of the cognitive behavioural ideas around anger management work:

- to help people experience and predict the build-up of tension in their bodies, such as muscle tension, changes in breathing and heart rate, and so on;
- to help them learn to monitor their self-talk, which can contribute to an escalation of conflict through entitlement talk, defensive protection against shame, such as 'how dare she look at me like that', and so on; and
- to help them identify triggers for anger by carefully tracking the last or worst episode of violent behaviour (Novaco, 1993).

These early warning signs can contribute to safety planning and the devel-opment of safety strategies, such as the use of time out. It is important to recruit the partner's agreement to the safety plan, as we have noticed that women often fear that men will use time out to avoid difficult or important discussions, or they fear that men might not return. Thus, we pay attention to how they make up and reconcile following a conflict or emotionally difficult interaction – in the early stages of our safety work, they may take the issue to their stable third, leave it to discuss with us, or take it to another trusted adult, such as a friend, relative or faith leader.

In our experience, rehearsal of these safety strategies is key, as under future conditions of arousal people are more likely to remember them and put them into action. We plan what the man will do while taking time out – how will he take action to calm himself down. We carefully follow the man's feedback following his successful implementation of a safety strategy when he noticed his arousal levels rising unhelpfully in interaction with his partner – we want to know what he noticed about himself as he calmed down!

We support the parents in listening to their children – no mean feat when the parents themselves may be traumatised. Hearing their children talk about their fears and distress, learning to listen in a way that is non-defensive and learning to bear to hear what they have to say often needs considerable and extended therapeutic containment and support. Importantly, this demands that the therapist too can bear to hear what the children and adults have to say, and does not move too quickly to distract and comfort, thus shutting down the opportunity to illuminate, expand and process traumatic material.

The effects of exposure to family violence can be dependent on a number of interrelated factors, such as the nature of the violence, the age of the child, their familiarity with and dependence on the victim or perpetrator, and responses from within the extended family and local community. If schools, neighbourhoods and extended family do not keep violence a secret, if they are committed to supporting non-violence, and to providing children with safety, reassurance, normal routines and opportunities to process their experiences, then children fare better in the long run.

Family violence thrives in secrecy. So when you see in children a picture of somatic symptoms, repetitive play, numbing and a marked inability to comfort self, a lack of interest in activities, a high activity level (constantly moving and distractible), new fears, sleep problems and/or behaviour changes, consider whether fear and violence might be the cause.

Chapter 5

Love and sexuality

Systemic therapy and attachment narratives: applications with couples

> Many of the most intense emotions arise during the formation, the main-
> tenance, the disruption and the renewal of attachment relationships. The
> formation of a bond is described as falling in love, maintaining a bond as
> loving someone, and losing a partner as grieving over someone. Similarly,
> threat of loss arouses anxiety, and actual loss gives rise to sorrow; whilst
> each of these situations is likely to arouse anger. The unchallenged main-
> tenance of a bond is experienced as a source of security and the renewal
> of a bond as a source of joy.
>
> (Bowlby, 1979, p. 74)

This chapter will explore the relationship between systemic theory and
attachment theory in therapeutic work with distressed couples. Working systemically with distressed couples has been a later development in the field of
systemic psychotherapy, compared to work with family groups and kin systems, and the application of systemic thinking to organisational dilemmas.
Systemic theory has been less concerned with theorising emotion and emotional experience, rather it has emphasised context, power, circularity, feedback, connection, process and narrative. In many respects, emotion, and
emotional experiences in relationships, have been implicit in our work, for
example understanding the effects of anxiety or anger in family systems, or
the impact of loss and trauma, but perhaps less explicit in being a primary
focus of our writing (Vetere and Dallos, 2003; Vetere and Dowling, 2005).
Throughout the wider therapeutic literature there has been less emphasis on
understanding joy, happiness and creativity compared to the more negative
emotional experiences such as sadness and shame. Perhaps this is not surprising, as therapists are asked to help alleviate distress, and need to understand
its source, maintaining factors and relational effects. But as systemic therapists, we need a road map to help us find a way for people to achieve calm and
soothing for themselves and others they love, to de-escalate distressing and
destructive interactions and to create more satisfying and more bonding
interactions. Attachment theory offers systemic practitioners a way of understanding and promoting experiences of felt security, and emotional bonding

(Bowlby, 1988). Thus, including emotional experience, and how it is constructed and processed in intimate relationships, is essential to a systemic understanding of distressed relationships, and how to help promote more positive bonding. Sue Johnson (1998) argues that we need to attend to affect, and how it impacts on an individual's interactional position and on their relationships. If we are not clear how to use emotion in the change process, we are at risk of avoiding it. Such avoidance of affect, she points out, can block avenues of therapeutic change.

Adult attachment theory views adult intimate relationships both as representational, that is, shaped by the ways in which earlier attachment experiences have been represented as expectations of caregiving, affection and sexuality, and as embodied experiences of affection, caregiving and sexual intimacy (Hazan and Shaver, 1987). The focus on sexuality both as an experience and as an expression of love in an intimate adult romantic relationship is welcome in the field of systemic work with couples, which curiously has neglected this aspect of love in the wider systemic literature. This chapter establishes the link between attachment theory and systemic understandings of couple relationships and explores the potential of integrative, collaborative formulation for practice, using the attachment narrative therapy (ANT) framework. We suggest that collaborative formulation offers both us and the couples we work with, a map to guide our work towards helping to de-escalate distressing interactions and to promoting more rewarding and secure intimate connections.

The couple relationship can be an enormous and rich resource for each partner, promoting economic security, and providing an emotional safe haven and secure base within a confiding relationship (Byng-Hall, 1995). The relationship itself can be seen to either foster or undermine the sense of security of each partner, and family systems thinking would suggest that felt security in the couple relationship contributes to the psychological development and well-being of children in the family (Steele and Fonagy, 1995). Access to a confiding relationship has long been understood to help buffer against the experience of depression for adults (Brown and Harris, 1978).

Attachment theory has been criticised for its apparent essentialism in assuming that attachment experiences are transcultural. In this chapter, we shall assume that people living in intimate relationships attach meaning to their felt experiences, and that these meanings are influenced both by wider societal and ethnic discourses, and by psychosocial development in families, and that they are subject to change. On the other hand, attachment theory can helpfully encourage us to think about what is common about our emotional experiences across different cultures and what may connect people in their experience of passion, loyalty, love and loss. It is important to re-emphasise what we noted at the start of this book: that the very roots of attachment theory were based in cross-cultural observations, for example Mary Ainsworth's pioneering observations of children in Uganda. We try to practise in a culturally attuned way, by remaining as open as we can to others' understandings and ways of appreciating the relational world, and by asking for information and help when we do not understand. We also acknowledge the possibility of commonalities, such as the importance of safety and protection, and that within or across cultures we may share common features of the need to be attached and connected to others. The ANT framework emphasises the importance of exploring narratives and attachments within a systemic framework. Equally, we do not assume we understand relational experiences just because we share a cultural background with couples, and again we try to stay open and curious in our work.

Our attachment strategies are based on our observations of how others respond to us when we need them – when we are upset, distressed, unhappy or frightened. We are all from birth participant observers of our own lives. An important issue in extending attachment theory to work with couples is that, unlike children, adults possess sophisticated language and the capacity to place their observation of themselves and their relationships into abstract and generalisable forms. A young infant is predominantly responding to their parents but for adults in a relationship they each respond to and also prompt each other's actions. These in turn are based on their understandings. It is a central question though how much each partner is acting towards the other in terms of previously learnt attachment patterns and how much these are shaped or altered by their observations of their relationship; likewise, how much their observation is shaped and coloured by their prior experiences – or transferences. More broadly, adults are also influenced by a variety of wider ideas and influences. Language therefore offers the potential for adults to elaborate and reflect on their relationships. However, it is also apparent from an attachment perspective that it also permits increasingly sophisticated distortion to their experience with each other, for example by the use of sophisticated cognitive and semantic wording to hide and conceal their feelings, or alternatively by the use of reductionism and blaming language to oversimplify and promote negative emotions. Cultural contexts in turn shape adults' expectations and ideas but at the same time their attachment strategies may function to selectively direct attention to certain features of the cultural context, for example to make reference to what is 'normal' or expected of a 'decent' mother, a 'good' partner or a 'responsible' father.

As systemic practitioners we are mindful of the wider family and social context for each couple we see, and the mutual influences between the couple and the other family and kin subsystems. We also see a two-way process of how culture shapes couples' lives and also how couples actively and strategically draw on culturally shared discourses. Life cycle theory and intergenerational approaches to family therapy provide a framework within which we can explore transition points as a particular challenge to the couple system, as partners seek either to re-establish familiar interaction patterns or to develop new patterns (Carter and McGoldrick, 1988). For example, we find that when a couple's union is not recognised by one or both extended families, it can place an additional burden on the couple's attempts to develop their sense of trust and intimacy in their relationship, to manage conflict and to heal and befriend following a rift. However, whether the union is recognised or not there is likely to be a prevalent discourse in Western cultures that the relationship should be based, at least in part, on a mutual emotional attraction. However, in other cultures this is not so clearly the case.

In our work with a Pakistani couple, in an arranged marriage, it seemed they had decided to separate, at the point when their families were pressing them to have children, but they did not know how to discuss this with their families, and feared shame and opprobrium. Interestingly, we can see in attachment terms that this is the point where a strategy, such as avoidance or a dismissive minimisation of the importance of attachment, may be pushed into a crisis. Not only are the couple required here to be sexually intimate but also for the union to produce a new life – a person they need to love and nurture. If they are unable to resolve the potential lack of interest or disdain in each other, how do they come to be able to love their child, which embodies each of them? The couple became drawn towards an avoidant, distancing solution, which was to separate, and wanted our help with managing the process of separation. Both partners had been born in Pakistan and came to the UK as children to live with their parents. Their families lived in the same village in Pakistan and had feuded for years, for reasons the couple thought had been long forgotten. They described the feud itself as coming to be important, stretching across continents and defining relationships between the two families. The elders in the families decided to try to stop the feud and bring the two families together through an arranged marriage. The expectation was that an attachment would form between the couple as part of an arranged marriage, rather than marrying on the basis of an existing attachment. It seemed to us that this couple had never been able to form an emotional attachment to each other, and their position remained a more semantic one driven on by beliefs in the values of duty and responsibility. Although the couple had been living in the UK with their parents, and the feud had originated elsewhere, they approached their marriage with a mix of hope and trepidation. As time went by, they found that the demand that they heal the rift, albeit symbolically, too pressing, especially as the feud continued unabated, and they found themselves asked to arbitrate and take sides and, of course, they could never please both families at the same time. They did not wish to bring children into this context of feuding and divided loyalties.

The stress and distress they experienced in this context of frozen loyalties had become internalised as a problem of their relationship, wherein they regularly fell out with each other over the actions and perceived intentions of the family of the other one. Arguably, this in turn prevented the possibility that they might be able to build connections and emotional intimacy between them. We offered them a series of consultation meetings initially, where they

explored their separate and shared understanding of their family circumstances. Using a modified genogram, our questioning focused around:

- the couple's attachments to their respective parents and grandparents;
- their parents' and grandparents' relationships with each other;
- the influence of these relationships on them as children growing up, and
  as a young couple;
- the intergenerational legacy of feuding and the felt experience of living
  with complex, rigid and divided loyalties.

This exploration of the tangled emotional loyalties and emotional cut-offs
within a small village community, which had been transported to another
time and place, provided the basis on which the couple reassessed their original decision to separate. They decided to engage in systemic couple's work.
As a result of this work they decided to stay together, and began discussions
about whether they wanted children. They worked hard to contextualise the
family feud and track its effects within their relationship. They strived to hold
a respectful relationship with their parents and kin and slowly initiated a
discussion with their own parents about how the feud had been affecting
them. The success of this tentative approach for them lay in the explicit
acknowledgement received from their parents about the importance of their
future together and an expressed wish to offer them more support. On this
basis they committed to more couples work and ended the therapy at the
point when they felt more confident in their own and each other's ability to
speak and to listen, to offer and take support, and to trust in each other's
ability to respond to separate and shared concerns.

Any attempt to integrate systemic theory with attachment theory needs to
take account of the social and political context within which we work, and
the wider postmodern critiques of theory and practice. The overarching integrative framework for the book and this chapter takes a social constructionist
position, within which systems theory helps us understand relationship
processes, and feedback loops and so on, while attachment theory helps us
theorise the emotional experience felt and constructed within relationships –
working within and between, so to speak.

Sexuality and gender

We work with couples in a Western cultural context, many of whom are white
British and in opposite-sex relationships. We do, however, also work with
same-sex couples and with couples where their ethnic heritages are mixed. We
hold the view that in many ways we all inhabit cultural borderlands, to use
Falicov's (1998) term, and have experience of different roles and expectations
within and across various cultural groupings, and in the present authors' case,
groups of women and men, older people, people who migrate in childhood,

working-class and professional people and so on. Our ability to move in and out of these different groupings, adopting different roles and responsibilities, is the basis on which we stay curious about others' cultural competence. Regular supervision with a systemically trained supervisor helps us maintain a collaborative stance. We all have competence in these various groupings, and we sometimes find ourselves being defined, or we define ourselves in relation to 'others'. When it comes to considerations of expressed sexual orientation, we do not assume that these are categorical descriptions, given that we work with couples who have had experiences in both same-sex and opposite-sex relationships, at different times in their life cycle, have chosen celibacy, and may have had sexual relationships outside their couple relationship.

We are also interested in the notion of 'cultural embeddedness', so we also take the view that higher context markers for intimate relationships can have an influence at the level of cultural discourses about the nature of and expectations around couple relationships. The significance of this interplay between subcultural competencies and cultural influences for attachment thinking in our work finds expression in the work of some of the feminist thinkers. For example, Wendy Hollway's (1989) work with white British opposite-sex couples explored significant cultural discourses in the development and maintenance of their relationships. The discourses of influence were found to be of: fidelity – 'to have and to hold'; permissiveness; and the male sexual drive discourse. So whatever the cultural groupings and multiplicity of influences of the couples we see, we wonder how discourses in the wider host culture permeate and influence expectations and behaviour across generations. From a life cycle perspective we are always working with couples embedded in three- or four-generational systems, sometimes with marked cohort difference in attitudes and beliefs, for example around the meaning of love, or the acceptability of divorce, or duties and responsibilities around sexual behaviour.

Foucault (1967, 1975), in writing about the history of sexuality in Europe, has suggested that 'sex' has developed as a concept that has somehow rendered it separate from intimacy, sensuality and relating to become a 'technology' and a 'science'. It has become a commodity that is used to sell products and is framed as an activity, a sport, a bit of release, fun, pleasure, a competition – something we are good or bad at – 'no good in bed' and so on. This can separate and also 'tame' sex so that the attachment anxieties of losing our connections and dependency on the love of another person are avoided. It fits with observations that promiscuity seems to be associated with avoidant/dismissive attachment patterns: Moving from or between one sexual partner to another may seem to help avoid the risk that any one of them will reject us. Or a 'casual' sexual contact may be our only way to obtain affection and warmth, albeit from relative strangers. From an attachment perspective, we as therapists may find ourselves working with some men, and sometimes women, where the 'acceptable' way for them to express their desire for close-ness and affection is through sex – the context where they may allow them-selves to hold and to be held and stroked, and to engage in mutual eye gaze. However, to gaze into a sexual partner's eyes lovingly may be harder for some people who can only approach intimacy at a distance through sex – perhaps by noisy, frantic, energetic sex, which helpfully avoids the need to be tender and to feel tender and be vulnerable as a result. Attachment and intimacy are expressed through various modalities: sensory, visual, smell and touch, actions, words and stories. Such sex can therefore be a way of meeting some needs to touch and be touched.

It is no accident in our view that sometimes couples need the help of a psychoactive substance like alcohol to give freer expression for their desire for closeness. We hear how drinking alcohol makes it much more likely that the couple will have sex when they find emotional connection challenging and/or intimidating. Under these circumstances we explore in therapy the meaning of intimacy, the origins of shyness and self-consciousness, the potential impact of past hurts in the relationship, current threats to trust and the impact of drinking on the couple's relating (see Chapter 8 for an extended discussion).

When a couple complains or worries about the lesser sexual desire of one of the partners, or the demands of the other, we often start by exploring with the couple what we might call 'ordinary intimacy'. Thinking about affection, closeness, sex and touch as an extraordinarily rich continuum from sensuality to frank sexuality may come as a surprise to some couples. We ask about ordinary touch, such as holding hands, or hugs, small rituals and routines, such as giving each other small treats, or how they say hello and bid farewell, who sits next to whom, whether they share a bed or bedroom, how they comfort when one is ill or unhappy, whether they share activities, hobbies, artistic appreciation and so on. Most couples seem to have developed a shared language and a shorthand way of communicating, which can put a momentary boundary of intimacy around their relationship when in the company of others, for example. It could be a humorous exchange such as a shared joke, or a meaningful look or a way of describing something. Constructing their everyday shared activities, rituals and routines and shared language as an expression of sensuality is often the start of a process of deconstructing unfulfilled hopes, desires and unhelpful expectations around their behaviour and their partner's behaviour. Such a framework can help-fully de-escalate a pattern of demand and withdraw, or withdraw–withdraw in moments of sexual tension as 'low desire' can be seen to be a richer sensual experience than had been imagined, and demand is seen to be contextualised and fulfilled in a wider context of everyday intimacy. Each person's contribu-tion to the relationship is validated. Such conversations help to further deconstruct taken-for-granted gender expectations that both partners hold for themselves and each other and the implicit contract partners hold for each other. Implicit contracts may reflect explicit contracts for our intimate relationships, or they may be awkwardly at variance. Our more deeply held wishes for our relationships that may not be so easily discussed, particularly in the context of emotional and sexual responding, may be expressed indirectly, such that their intent is not understood by the other. As therapists we may help intuit the unsaid or the unsayable.

We fall ill in the face of complex obstacles to love. . . .

(Juan Linares, 2007)

Research in the social sciences and in the field of health psychology lends some support to the implications of attachment theory for therapy practice, as outlined above. Couple distress can be seen in parallel with recent research. For example, AV is involved in a series of research studies that explore the link between repressive coping style and adult avoidant attachment style (Vetere and Myers, 2006). It has been found that people who reported themselves to be avoidantly attached also met the criteria for a repressive coping style. A repressive coping style is thought to be a conscious attempt to deactivate emotional arousal, almost to the point where a person is more interested in convincing themselves than others, that they are not anxious, despite physiological data that would indicate that they are emotionally aroused. This is operationalised as a low score on trait measures of anxiety and a high score on a measure of psychological defensiveness. Some longitudinal research suggests that a repressive coping style has implications for elevated health risk in a number of serious illness conditions, such as some forms of cancer, heart disease, immune system illnesses and so on (Vetere and Myers, 2006). Kiekolt Glaser and Newton (2001) have researched the positive relationship between reported marital satisfaction and enhanced immune system functioning in recovery from cancer. Brown and Harris (1978), in their landmark study on the social origins of depression, reported the presence of a confiding relationship to act as a buffer against depression for young women, raising children under the age of five, who were not in paid employment. The London Depression Intervention Trial (Leff *et al.*, 2000) found that women with regular partners who were diagnosed with moderate to severe depression significantly improved with systemic couples therapy relative to treatment with prescription medication and cognitive behaviour therapy. In a final example, a magnetic resonance imaging (MRI) study showed that women with chronic pain who were in supportive marriages, self-reported less pain when their hand was held by their partner than when it was held by a nurse (Johnson, 2004). The self-report data were supported by the MRI data. The opposite effect was found for the group where the women were living in unsatisfactory marriages. Sue Johnson (2004) summarises research that shows a strong positive relationship between felt security in a relationship and:

- affect regulation, that is, less emotional reactivity, hyperarousal and underarousal;
- more support seeking;
- information processing, that is, more curiosity, more open to new ideas, more tolerant of uncertainty;
- communication, that is, more disclosing of personal information, empathic and assertive, and able to meta-communicate;
- a more robust sense of 'self', that is, a more positive view of the self, a more elaborated and articulated view of the self.

Adult attachment relationships and internal working models

The academic field of adult attachment research offers some useful insights to us as couples therapists, for example the concept of 'internal working models' and their developmental origins (Shaver and Brennan, 1992; Clulow, 2001). Internal working models of relationships are our beliefs and expectations about (a) our own and other people's behaviour in intimate relationships; (b) our views of the self, for example how loveable, worthy, acceptable and deserving of others' care we are; and (c) how available, responsive and interested others are in caring for and looking after us. This conceptualisation of how we perceive, construct and co-construct a view of ourselves, and others, and of ourselves in relation to others, sits well with current systemic thinking and narrative practice, but what attachment theory offers is a *developmental* perspective. For example, if people's thinking and responses can be characterised in this way, how does it come to pass? What experiences do we have along the way that teach us that we are deserving of others' care, or in some cases, that we are worthless and are not deserving of comfort and care? If as a child, one of our parents turns to us for comfort and solace and confides in us in such a way that we cannot ask for comfort and care in return, we may learn to be very good at looking after others, but not so good at looking after ourselves. Byng-Hall (1995) has written about the development of the parental child, and Crittenden (1997) has written about the development of compulsive caring. Both roles are thought to develop over time, as a result of our childhood needs for comfort and security being met with injunctions to suppress our feelings. So, not only do we learn to suppress our own feelings and needs, and to pretend that we are alright, we also learn that by anticipating and meeting others' needs we gain approval and some comfort in return, such as feeling good about ourselves. If these beliefs and response styles are not challenged and changed by subsequent life experience, we may enter into our adulthood romantic relationships looking for people we can care for, and who want to be looked after. Such a relationship is described in systemic terms as complementary, wherein the mutual roles are more fixed, with less flexibility and capacity for adaptation. These roles tend to carry a lot of responsibility and are actually very emotionally demanding, in the absence of mutual reciprocity. In our view, such positions are not sustainable in the longer term, and we see in couple relationships awkward attempts at having needs acknowledged and met, or even where one or both partners slip into depression. This is sometimes what brings couples into therapy.

Similarly, when working therapeutically with a couple, if one of them believes they do not deserve comfort or care, then in moments of peak distress, they may be less likely to turn to their partner for comfort and support, and may even rebuff offers of help. If this response tendency becomes patterned, and the couple seek to avoid these painful moments, it can lead to communication misunderstandings, relationship dissatisfaction and loneliness. This partner may feel increasingly lonely and believe they cannot turn to anyone for support, while their partner increasingly sees them as distant, cold and stand-offish, and comes to believe that their partner does not need them. Seeking to understand the system of beliefs and expectations held separately and together by the couple, helps the couples therapist work to develop a deep understanding and appreciation within the couple, that their partner's behaviour is not designed to hurt them deliberately, nor is it thoughtless and so on, but rather it is triggered by the perception of relationship threat – a fear that they are really unloveable and unworthy, and that their partner will love them less, or may abandon them if they find out the 'truth' about them. Achieving an understanding and appreciation of these complex intentions fosters the capacity in one partner to tolerate strong negative emotion in their partner, so that as a couple, they can continue to communicate and iron out misunderstandings without reverting to earlier and less helpful interactions.

In order to do this, the therapist also needs to tolerate working with strong emotion in the moment, and not seek to avoid emotion or soothe too soon. If a therapist's tendency is to find strong emotion alarming because their own family of origin experiences have taught them to look after others, say, and not to express their own strong feelings and wishes, they may need careful supervision to help them monitor a reflexive desire to avoid or prevent the expression and illumination of strong emotion. Working in this way means that the therapist needs to be able to slow the interaction down, so that the couple can walk around in their emotions and process their responses. Constantly maintaining a semantic therapeutic position does not foster emotional reprocessing, thought to be so important in trauma work (Foa and Kozak, 1986). Clearly, we are not talking about abusive interactions, which demand a safety response from the therapist. In this chapter we shall not be writing about working with abusive and violent behaviour – for a full discussion of how to create safety for couples and family work in the aftermath of violence, see Cooper and Vetere (2005).

Although the research on attachment theory for children and parents/ carers and for adult intimate relationships has been developed and conducted in separate fields of inquiry, there is some useful overlap from the lifespan developmental literature for couples therapists in the area of response styles under conditions of perceived relationship threat. We do not wish to suggest that adult intimate relationships are the same as parent–child relationships in attachment terms, but we do want to emphasise the lifespan developmental approach of Bowlby (1988), when he formulated his ideas on the human wish for connection, and the need for a safe haven and a secure base in our intimate relationships. We acknowledge that couple relationships are social systems in the wider sense and subject to forces and processes outwith adult attachment theory's explanatory scope, as we saw earlier in the example of our work with the Pakistani couple (Blom and van Dijk, 2007). But for us, the explanatory and predictive power of the synthesis between attachment theory and systemic psychotherapy lies in the road map it gives us for change towards more positive bonding interactions (Johnson, 2004). And this synthesis puts emotion at the leading edge of our thinking and practice: emotion, as it is both individually constructed and experienced, and constructed in relationships over time. So, in those moments of perceived or real attachment threat, when couples think that their partner does not care for them or loves them less, is about to abandon or reject them, or will not be interested or emotionally available at a time of felt need, it can be said that certain response tendencies might prevail, such as avoidance of emotion, or feeling overwhelmed by emotion.

We can see the relevance of some of these ideas in the typical scenarios we encounter in our therapeutic work with families and couples. For example, perhaps (and somewhat rarely for us as therapists?) we may meet with adults who use both their feelings and cognitions to make sense of emotionally significant events. Such people can be described as having a more *secure* response style, because although they might struggle to connect thoughts and feelings, they are capable of integrating and processing emotion as part of their relationship experiences. In our past experience we have sometimes wrongly assumed that one partner is secure in contrast to the other partner when they display a lack of emotions, and downplay the significance of their feelings, or even deny their feelings. We have learned through our experience of working with couples, that a partner so described can be said to distrust feelings – and to exhibit a more *avoidant* response style in these difficult attachment-related moments.

Similarly, those who might respond with hyperarousal in moments of attachment threat, who anxiously pursue a partner to secure attention and caring, can be said to distrust words, that is, what we might say in response to their distress. Finally, those whose experiences of care have been frightening or confusing may find if difficult to develop and predict a consistent pattern of caring, which may lead to a distrust of both words and feelings. In our experience of working in NHS-based adult and adolescent mental health settings, such a response pattern may be described with terms such as 'borderline personality disorder'. Attachment thinking, in our view, goes a long way in helping to illuminate confused and confusing responses in emotionally significant moments, and helps us as practitioners to ground our therapeutic responses, as we hope to show in this chapter.

Attachment strategies

The behavioural attachment strategies that can be said to flow from these anxiety responses tend to be at times when we are afraid and need comfort and support from a partner and further, can be said to be governed by how we make predictions for ourselves and others at these moments (using our internal working models!).

Our internal working models then are seen to be a set of beliefs, predictions and expectations about the accessibility, responsiveness and worthiness of ourselves and others in our intimate relationships. From these beliefs flow our emotions, behaviours and actions in recursive feedback loops, which can further reinforce or challenge our beliefs. For example, if we predict that our partner is emotionally unavailable or insensitive to us, then we might develop alternate strategies for coping, such as a deactivating strategy whereby we do not seek contact or support, or a hyperactivating strategy, whereby we closely monitor our partner, increasing our demands and insisting on contact. This evolution in responding within our current significant relationships will be influenced by many factors, past and present, such as earlier experiences of receiving and giving care, which will vary in importance from couple to couple. Hence, for us, this demonstrates the need to have a set of theoretical ideas that can be brought together in discussion with the couple to help formulate our shared understandings and plan how we might help them build more satisfying interactions.

To conclude, then, insecure attachment patterns in couple relationships involve both emotional and physiological arousal, with avoidant responding putting cognitive and emotional effort into distraction strategies, and anxious responding putting cognitive and emotional effort into continually monitoring the partner; whereas those with a more securely felt connection have spare mental capacity for reflection, integration and play – and this is what we are trying to help couples achieve.

Thus, an experiential/structural orientation is helpful when working with couples when one or both is likely to respond with avoidance and dismissal of the significance of emotional responding in the face of perceived attachment threat. An experiential orientation fosters the slow and careful illumination of feelings and the importance of relationships in narratives about ourselves and others. The emphasis is more on being inside the narrative, by focusing on experience in the here and now, validating those experiences and using episodic memories to link past events to current experience. Feelings can be discussed in relation to the therapist and the therapeutic process, which helps to emphasise a growing awareness of the self as relational. Thus, the

ANT approach to considering alternatives, here makes central the need to promote more secure bonding interactions, using 'family experiments' in and outside the therapy room. Therapists can comment on their observed process in the room, and can help to model openness, a commitment to straight talking and safety in expressing a range of feelings, both negative and positive.

Similarly, we find that a more cognitive style (often associated with the Milan/post-Milan therapies, and adaptations of cognitive behaviour therapy to work with couples) is helpful when one or both partners tend to respond with ambivalence and preoccupation in the face of perceived attachment threat. This can be fostered by emphasising thoughts and meanings held in relationship narratives. Using the ANT approach of considering alternatives, the therapist can model an approach that encourages thoughtful reflection, leading to thinking through actions and their consequences and helping to reduce impulsive responding based on unprocessed anxiety. A focus on semantic memories helps to link past events to current feelings, and leads the way to experimentation with being outside the narrative, rather than within the narrative and feeling overwhelmed. The therapist helps to focus on current events, by mapping patterns and enabling prediction. The ANT framework promotes thinking about narratives and attachments within a systemic framework. Current attachments are explored, perhaps using an attachment-based genogram to focus on traditions of transgenerational attachments. The emphasis is on understanding, helped by the structure, goals and aims of the therapeutic process.

When working with a partner whose life experience has taught them not to trust people, and not to trust their own feelings or their thoughts in relationships, aspects of both the above approaches in combination are helpful. A strong emphasis on emotional safety in all relationships needs to be held throughout the work. This emphasis helps to build and encourage some predictability within and outside the therapy sessions (Dallos, 2006b). The ANT approach to creating a secure base for therapy relies on the pioneering work of Byng-Hall (1995) in its emphasis on warm and open communication and mapping the context for therapy with clarity about what might be expected from the work.

The field of systemic psychotherapy has developed a range of techniques to encourage both the expression of feelings and the expression of cognitions. Action techniques, rooted in structural and gestalt work, encourage the expression of feelings, such as use of enactment, role play, empathic questioning, internalised other interviewing techniques, promoting conflict management, and promoting caring and comforting in relationships. Reflective techniques encourage the expression of cognitions, such as the use of genograms, life lines, tracking circularities, mapping relationships, scaling questions, circular questions and questions that focus on shared beliefs (Vetere and Dallos, 2003). Reflecting teams and reflecting processes can be shaped to support both the expression of feelings and the expression of cognitions (Cooper and Vetere, 2005). The ANT approach is an attempt to reconcile and integrate the contributions from these major traditions of systemic psychotherapy using attachment theory and the focus on emotion as the cement.

Couples therapy and attachment theory

Systemic theory describes a mutual influence between the couple and other subsystems within the family and kin group. The couple unit can be said to be nested within overlapping groups and relationships, which provide support, resources and sometimes constraints for the couple. Resilience in family groups is likely to be constructed with intimacy, shared humour, a balance of control, shared positive emotions, low levels of conflict and hostility and a sense of connectedness. We recognise that it is unlikely to be reducible to a single process involving attachment security (Rutter, 1999). Thus, our focus in this chapter is specific: we focus on emotional engagement within the couple relationship as a source of distress, and with the potential for healing.

When working therapeutically with couples, attachment theory focuses our attention on their attachment needs and the ways in which they emotionally engage with one another, and on those moments when they feel emotionally disengaged. Emotion and emotional experience is at the forefront of our thinking – it is seen as 'the music of the attachment dance' (Johnson, 1998). Times of transition can provide particular challenges for the couple, as the partners seek either to re-establish familiar patterns of reaction, or to develop new responses. In order to develop an emotion focus in our work, we need to establish a secure base first. We can work towards building therapeutic trust in how we explore the couple's complaints and dilemmas – identifying unhelpful arousal and distressing interactions. Systemic theory assumes that some of these interactions will have become patterned and habitual. If so, the task is to identify these distressing interactions with a view to helping the couple de-escalate them, either by preventing them or by reducing their frequency and intensity. This can be described as a form of externalising, whereby the *pattern* is seen as the problem, not the partner. Therapy is collaborative in so far as the couple identify their sources of distress, and agree the descriptions of how they find their interactions unsatisfying. In any couple relationship there will be many potential sources of stress and distress, some of which are outside the couple/family, but impact directly and indirectly. Emotion-focused work is more organised around those interactions that feel unsatisfactory, because in those moments, partners feel that the other is not emotionally available to them, or they themselves are unworthy of care and comfort. These experiences can arise directly within the relationship, and in response to external sources of stress. The issue for the couples therapist is not to ignore the partners' felt experience. It is of interest to us that couples will often turn to more pragmatic issues and problem-solving tasks when they report that they feel more secure in their relationship. This seems to be the context within which their creativity and problem-solving skills are liberated. So it is not that we teach couples to communicate or problem solve, rather we help them to explore and establish what a secure base looks and feels like, so that they can develop and promote more positive and satisfying interactions. Therapy continues into a stage of consolidation, whereby the therapist continues to support the couple's attempts to restructure their emotional responses towards each other, in ways that promote secure bonding.

Implications of attachment theory for systemic couples therapy

The implications of attachment theory for systemic therapeutic work with couples are clear (Vetere and Dallos, 2007):

1 *Naming and exploring emotions*: helping couples access, illuminate, expand and reprocess their emotional experiences. For example, we can work alongside a couple to help them to explore what it means to be angry: anger may be a response to fear of loss, or of rejection. Anger can be hopeful – 'what do I have to do to get you to pay attention to me!'; or it can be despairing – 'you are a waste of space!'. But in each of its forms it can be seen to reflect the continuing wish for connection.

2 *Standing in the emotional shoes of the other*: helping couples listen to each other, and learn to tolerate and bear each other's emotional arousal when they themselves might be unhelpfully aroused. Importantly, this involves helping them to feel how it feels for the other person.

3 *Comforting and self-soothing*: helping couples de-escalate unhelpful interaction patterns, to manage their emotional arousal at times of conflict, to seek and give comfort and to find ways to reconnect following a disagreement. Importantly, this giving of comfort is something that we come to be able to 'carry with us' to draw on when we need. For example, on a train journey away from our partner in some new and lonely place we may remember their affection, reassurance and jokes and, as we do, we feel comforted and reassured. We might even, when we call them later to talk to them, speak to them as if they had actually said the things we had thought rather than remembering that it was our internal conversation with them!

4 *Information processing*. At times of attachment threat, we may be afraid of abandonment or rejection. Trauma theory teaches us that the processing of negative emotionally laden material is slower under conditions of fear (Herman, 1992). Couples become preoccupied with monitoring and regulating their own fear and arousal and find it hard to listen to what the

other is saying and to 'read' relationship cues. Feeling heard is soothing and calming and hence why the creation of a safe therapeutic space is so helpful in these moments.

John Byng-Hall (1995) describes therapy as a secure base, as a safe and secure position from which to explore and experiment with change in relationships. Safety in the therapeutic space facilitates exploration of both the internal and external world – beliefs, expectations, emotion, reflection, empathy and relationships. When working with couples, if a partner tends towards dismissing or denying feelings, we help them illuminate and expand their emotional experience by making contact with defended, cut-off feelings, encouraging emotional expression and reprocessing, and making connections with others. In some instances, we can think of the therapist acting as a stable third, bridging couples' relationships – by learning to trust the therapist, people can learn to reconnect to intimate others. It may well be that the therapeutic relationship represents the first trusting emotional connection for one or both partners for some time. Similarly, a partner who is preoccupied with anxious responding can be helped to think and reflect and to lessen their unhelpful emotional arousal, sometimes rooted in earlier experiences of unpredictable or unavailable caregiving. If the preoccupation is articulated as angry and blaming, it is necessary to help soften their position so that they can be more responsive when their more withdrawn partner takes the risk of speaking about their feelings. The ANT approach to creating and to maintaining a secure therapeutic base emphasises the importance of trust, soothing and calming as a context for de-escalating unhelpful patterns of interaction.

Case example: Working with Claire and Jim

The cycle of 'pursuer–distancer' is especially important to an understanding of couples' attachment relationships. We find an example in our work with Claire and Jim. If Claire thought Jim had hurt her feelings in some way, she would demand an apology. Jim would feel criticised and attacked, and unhappy that he had yet again disappointed Claire (and perhaps think about having a drink of vodka for comfort). Jim would consider it unsafe to engage with Claire at these moments. Claire would see Jim's hesitation to speak and his emotional withdrawal as a sign that he did not love her enough to attend to her emotional distress. She would then increase her demand for an apology and accuse him of not caring about her. This hurt Jim's feelings, and by now he would be sure it was not safe to talk to Claire, so he would withdraw further. By now Claire would feel his withdrawal as punishment – that he was doing it deliberately to hurt her. Claire would cry and be very demanding of a particular response from Jim.

However, if we wind the clock back to the 'start' of the interaction, Claire was seeking reassurance that Jim still loved her – her initial demand for an apology was based on the wish for reassurance and wanting to have a cuddle. Jim's withdrawal response was largely determined by feeling very criticised and that he was a disappointment to her. Therapy helped the couple identify these sequences, and to explore the unspoken emotional experience and the unspoken wish for comfort and reassurance. Arguably, in any couple relationship, there will be difficult moments, and therapy also explores how the couple reconnects and 'makes up'. Do they carry on with their lives, sweeping the previous distress aside, as if it did not matter; do they not speak for a few days; and/or do they return to the incident when calm, sort out misunderstandings and try to repair their relationship? However they manage the process of reconnection, if they have children, their children will be exposed to forms of conflict resolution and comforting between adult partners that may influence their later preferred styles for relating.

Case example: Working with Peter and Mary

In another example, Peter suggests going out as a couple in the evening. Mary makes excuses, saying she feels too tired. Peter feels rejected and hurt, and in seeking reassurance, makes more demands on Mary. Mary feels imposed upon and suffocated, and resists Peter's demands. Both of them end up feeling unhappy and dissatisfied, and when they come into therapy, they struggle to understand why they feel so disappointed in their marriage. We can show the systemic nature of these feedback loops diagrammatically, as shown in Figure 5.1.

If we were to try to be helpful to Peter and Mary using the ANT framework, and thus incorporating adult attachment theory, we would use an emotion focus as a road map to change (Johnson, 2004). In the first phase of the couples work we would try to identify with them the patterns that contribute to their sense of emotional distance and dissatisfaction in their marriage. Thus, a pattern as illustrated in Figure 5.1 might emerge from the discussion, which both partners agreed was unhelpful, and represented a familiar cycle

Suggests going out
Feels rejected

BOTH *FEEL* UNHAPPY

Peter

Mary

Makes excuses, too tired
Feels imposed upon

Figure 5.1 Systemic feedback loops fuelled by emotion.

of interaction to them, and they both wanted to change. This form of externalisation leaves the couple in agreement that they both want to change a (this) pattern, and thus this makes it less likely that they will blame themselves, or each other, and more likely that they will take responsibility for what they can do, and most importantly in this work, begin to take emotional risks, with the support of the therapy process. In our experience it is helpful to draw these patterns as they are described and agreed. This is not just because some people think better with the aid of diagrams, but the diagram is visual and immediate, can be referred to many times and concentrates on the 'here and now' aspect of their relationship. In this phase we are helping them to identify unhelpful patterns and to develop strategies for avoiding these patterns or reducing their negative emotional intensity.

Observation and reflection

This process of de-escalation is helped by the capacity to observe oneself, so that one or both partners, under conditions of negative and anxiety-provoking emotional arousal, can spot the process and meta-comment on it, both to themselves and to each other. All of this acts to help people stay reflective when sad, distressed, irritated and anxious with themselves or with their partner. In the second phase of the work, examples are used to help build and reinforce more secure bonding interactions. All the systemic couples techniques are helpful here, such as reframing, a solution focus (i.e. doing more of what is satisfying etc.), enhancing accessibility and responsiveness, practical problem solving and so on. The final phase of the work consolidates achievements and helps the couple grow in confidence in their ability to give and receive emotional trust, given the daily rigours of their lives. We are grateful to Sue Johnson for her pioneering work in bringing an emotion focus to systemic couples work (Johnson, 2004) and showing through her work and research how it can facilitate the change process.

So, in returning to the example above, both Peter and Mary withdraw emotionally, feeling rejected and hurt, and feel let down, and that they have let the other down in some way. We would talk to the partner who appears to use blame more in these moments (let us say it is Peter for the purpose of this example) and help them soften their position by talking with them about what happens to them in these moments: their thoughts, feelings and actions. We would support the other partner (Mary) in listening. Then we would turn to Mary and similarly talk through with her what happens for her in these moments. We would encourage Peter to listen. Feeling properly listened to, validated and soothed during this process, encourages people to walk around in their feelings and to develop a good understanding of what is happening for them, and helps them develop a more relational and empathic perspective. This sets the scene for partners to take risks, and literally come out from their more withdrawn state, and begin to trust that their partner can be accessible and responsive to them. This is a mutual process, and becomes a positive and mutually reinforcing cycle, which helps to reduce and replace the hurt, angry, disappointed and withdrawn cycle they first described. The therapist and the couple need to be patient and persistent. Time is needed for slow and careful illumination of warded-off feelings, or for soothing and calming of unhelpful arousal, to encourage reflection in the face of attachment threat. If past experience has taught people that it is safer not to trust their feelings to anyone, then it takes a while for people to reconnect emotionally in a different, and hopefully more satisfying way.

Attachment injuries

The couple relationship can either promote or undermine the sense of security of the partners. As couples therapists we pay attention to key emotional responses that maintain distress, within the safety of the therapy alliance. Johnson writes of the importance of addressing emotional impasses and 'attachment injuries' (Johnson *et al.*, 2001). An attachment injury, so called, may have occurred some time previously, when one of the partners had a high need for connection and reassurance, and the other partner did not realise, and thus did not respond in the way that was sought. This can occur in an otherwise satisfactory relationship. But the emotional legacy from that moment of untended need can linger on, and create a sense of doubt that has the potential to undermine trust at moments of future emotional need. It is important to explore such doubts and if possible to help the couple heal the 'injury', which may emerge as a surprise to the other partner, but then helps them explain their sense that their partner sometimes holds back from them emotionally.

We find an example of an 'attachment injury' in our work with Bill and Mavis, a couple in their mid-forties raising their young son. Both Bill and Mavis recovered from years of alcohol abuse earlier in their relationship. Mavis has children from her former marriage who are still living with their father. During a therapy conversation Bill mentioned in passing that his recent birthday had been 'rubbish'. We noted that and asked Bill what he meant. He gave his account of his birthday with bitterness and disappointment. We listened for the source of his disappointment – he thought Mavis had not cared about his birthday (and therefore, about him). He softened in the telling and expressed his sadness. We asked Mavis what she thought happened, and she told something different, and with a sense of shame (at having disappointed Bill). As a couple they do not have much money, so Mavis had planned Bill's party and his present very carefully for many months beforehand. She had bought him a personal item as a present, which she had specially engraved with his initials, but she was so convinced it was not good enough, and that he would not like it, that when she gave it to him she offered it with her face turned away and almost slung it at him, she was so anxious. He only saw her body language and responded by tearing off the paper and tossing the present to one side – and that set the tone for the rest of the party. Mavis was very sad as she gave her account. Bill saw her sadness and responded with kindness and warmth. They went on to discuss fully what happened, and began to sort our their mixed feelings and misunderstandings in such a way that they both contributed to healing their own and each other's sense of hurt.

Johnson (2004) writes that the attachment significance of the 'injury' is important, rather than the content of the interaction *per se*. The therapist encourages the partner to talk about the injury and its continuing impact in the relationship. The other partner is encouraged to listen and to acknowledge the hurt partner's distress, and then to talk about their experience of the event. The hurt partner is helped to connect the narrative with the emotions, so that they can access their attachment fears and longings. The other partner acknowledges their responsibility and expresses regret for what happened, while staying therapeutically engaged. The hurt partner is helped to ask for comfort and reassurance, and the other responds. This exchange can work both ways, as it were, as in the example with Bill and Mavis above. This re-enactment helps to heal the injury and overcome the legacy of insecurity, thus helping both partners redefine their relationship as a safe haven, and construct a healing narrative.

Softening feelings

Running throughout the work is a recognition that when couples come to us for help they are often displaying angry feelings, engaging in mutual and sometimes escalating accusations, making threats, feeling blamed, wanting revenge and so on. An attachment perspective helps us to recognise that within or underneath these protests there lies hurt, vulnerability, fear, disappointment and the wish and need for love, comfort and connection. Attachment experiences always have this dialectic: the child is both angry at the unavailability of his mother/carer and also desperately vulnerable and needy for her. Likewise, in couples when we see the explicit anger we help couples to find the other side – the softer emotions of hurt and the need for care, love and connection. Initially we work to understand and validate each partner's position. If we find one partner more critical and blaming in their responses, or both partners engaged in mutual blaming, we work hard to help them soften their position first, as in our experience, the more withdrawn partner will not take emotional risks and come forward with an expression of vulnerability until it can feel safe enough to do so. We have to help them in these early moments, as the partner who tends to blame when hurt, may well blame again when vulnerability is shown, almost as though they show their hurt with anger at their imagined or real rejection.

We find an example in our work with Claire and Jim, described earlier. Jim wanted Claire to look after him and meet his emotional needs after years, as he put it, of supporting her, and helping her overcome her drink problems. He asked for this from her directly. She in that moment turned her head away, looked out the window and her eyes filled with tears. Jim saw her head turn away, and when she turned to face him and to tell him she did want to care for him and look after him, he retorted angrily, 'There you go again, turning on the waterworks . . .!' Claire dropped her head in her lap. It is important for the therapist to validate both partners, while 'holding' the other, always checking back and helping them stay attuned, listening and available. This early work can cover a few sessions, slowly and carefully validating and illuminating experience, helping the partner to listen and working to de-escalate dangerous and unhelpful interactions. We are often asked if this work can be done with couples where violence has taken place between them. Our experience is to work for safety first and then assess whether couples work can follow (see Cooper and Vetere, 2005, for a full description of a safety methodology that includes attachment thinking). In any event, we always meet a couple both separately and together at the start of our work, for example if one partner is having an affair and refuses to disclose and/or give up the affair, we may not proceed with couples work.

Of course, a recognition at some level that the other is hurt and needy is what keeps many couples together through the periods when they are angry with each other. They can remember, just about, how they were once soft and vulnerable with each other and want that to return. Arguably, in the early systemic therapies, techniques such as reframing and positive connotation also covered this terrain although they talked about it differently. In fact, the classic reframe of a couple's anger with each other as an expression of their passion for each other fits well with an attachment perspective that emphasises the strength of hope and a wish for connection. However, in early systemic and strategic therapies there was less of a recognition that a good reframe also had a quality of softening the feelings, as it was less targeting and blaming and focused on these important attachment ideas.

Attachment narrative therapy with couples

Systemic therapy with couples can be organised into four phases, broadly speaking, of creating a secure base, exploring attachments and narratives within a systemic framework, considering alternatives, and maintaining the therapeutic base. These phases reflect the interweave of attachment thinking and narrative practices. They now will be discussed in turn, using the developmental idea of scaffolding to inform practice.

Therapy as scaffolding: emotional and cognitive

According to Vygotsky (1962), the development of social competence occurs by learning what we can do with the assistance of another person. Social development is encouraged by a process of challenge and risk taking, which occurs within the zone of the not too familiar and the not too different. Learning can be said to be a process of gentle scaffolding where existing competencies are developed and new competencies learned. Conversations about the development of social competence are internalised, and help us predict action and interaction in the moment and for the future. More recently, narrative practice in psychotherapy has adapted Vygotsky's ideas, exploring how therapeutic questioning and encouragement can assist people in challenging unhelpful views of their social competence and social resources and developing their options for effective action (White and Epston, 1990). Within an attachment narrative frame, the implications of scaffolding for couples work are many, and include:

- using trust in the therapeutic process as the base to develop mutual feelings of safety and security, and to reduce negative patterns of arousal;
- assisting in identifying and regulating strong negative feelings, such as fear and anger;
- encouraging the capacity for reflexivity, such as 'standing in the emotional shoes of the other';
- exploring processes of comforting and self-soothing under different circumstances;
- exploring expectations of intimacy;
- assisting with the integration of feelings and events; and
- assisting coherence, for example helping couples develop a narrative of how they healed their relationship.

Creating a secure base

Creating a secure base in therapeutic work with couples is the main task in this approach, it is the main focus in the early part of the work, and continues to strongly underpin later work. It is the vehicle through which therapeutic change is wrought. We carry out a four-session assessment at the start of our work, meeting the couple twice and each partner on their own once. This allows us to ask questions about risk and safety. We try to engage warmly with each partner, using ourselves to reflect on our own experience as appropriate. We reflect on the relationship process in the room, both between the couple and between the couple and ourselves, in an attempt to model safe and open communication. We try to work collaboratively, in a non-blaming manner. When partners are defensive and used to patterns of blame and counter-blame in their relationship, we help them identify these patterns and thus to identify the pattern as the enemy, rather than each other! This is done through a slow, gentle, careful and detailed process of identifying the patterns and focusing on each partner's felt emotional experiences within the pattern, while the other partner is supported in listening. We gently bring emotion to the forefront, while encouraging exploration of beliefs and explanations. We do not push for change as such, rather we encourage the softening of a blaming position through validating that person's experiences. When a blaming position has softened, we consider it safer then to encourage a more withdrawn and emotionally distant partner to access, expand and reprocess their emotional experience. We should note here that in order for this softening to occur it is necessary for couples to be able to express their anger and frustration. We do not seek to avoid or detour such expression, perhaps as solution-focused approaches are more likely to do. But neither do we want to become problem-saturated or trapped in the quicksands of blame and anger.

Validating emotional experience is done with the other partner listening, and being supported in their listening. When it feels safer, we encourage the partners to seek comfort and reassurance from each other. Anger softens and fear is made more evident: fear of loss, of rejection and of abandonment. This process of detailed, slow and careful exploration helps to de-escalate unhelpful patterns of interaction. In our experience, therapists and trainee systemic therapists sometimes rush this part of the work. We encourage people to work slowly and carefully. Partners then become better able to predict and avoid such patterns, at best, and to experiment with alternative responses (Johnson, 2004).

Exploring narratives and attachments within a systemic framework

Current and past attachments are explored, often with the help of a family genogram (Lieberman, 1979), for example, trans-generational patterns of attachment, of closeness and distance in relationships, of seeking and giving comfort, of emotional cut-off and re-connection; corrective and replicative scripts; and corrective relational experiences. If partners respond with a more emotionally dismissive style, we begin with circular questions and move towards more direct questioning that allows for the illumination of inner experience in relation to others. If partners tend to respond with anxiety we rely more on circular questions to encourage them to stay focused on thinking, in an effort to help them calm and de-escalate their arousal. We have found that exploration of attachment narratives encourages the expression of curiosity, sociality and empathy. As systemic practitioners we try not to lose sight of the impact of the couple's problem on wider family relationships, and vice versa. Such exploration encourages awareness of self and other in intimate partnerships, and allows us to work therapeutically 'within and between'.

Considering alternatives

Alternative narrative explanations and ways of ascribing meaning to couples' experiences (both as couples and as individuals within those couples), the couple relationship and wider family relationships are generated and developed within the therapeutic conversation, and rehearsed outside therapy. Systemic psychotherapists draw on a range of techniques and ways of questioning to help couples illuminate and reprocess experience, and rehearse more positive relational connections. Much of this work is mediated through language informed by attachment theory and narrative practice, for example searching for unique outcomes as building blocks of relationship security, and moving the conversation between intrapersonal and interpersonal narratives of affection, intimacy, caregiving and bonding. Supporting the wish for connection, and slowly and carefully helping couples take emotional risks in terms of asking for and giving support, affirmation and comfort, in the face of reduced defensiveness and blaming, helps to promote a sense of secure bonding.

Exploring alternatives can move backwards and forwards in time. For example, many couples have an image of a 'golden age' when things were wonderful between them and they yearn to return to this period. We can explore this but also how things change and may be different, perhaps even better than those heady but often insecure early days of lust, drugs, drinking, and flirting for some . . .

The future and maintaining the therapeutic base

This phase of the work aims to help couples consolidate therapeutic change, by contemplating desired futures, rehearsing achievements and planning to deal with future disappointments. Systemic future questions are helpful, such as: how do you see your relationship in one year's time; what will help you achieve/maintain that?; what are your hopes for yourself and each other?; and so on. Ending therapy can evoke feelings of loss and separation. Endings can be negotiated to involve follow-up and review meetings, or to phase out meetings more slowly, according to preference. Anticipating the ending of the work early on can help couples manage endings with confidence. Couples work by its very nature engenders an intimate connection between the therapist and the couple. Therapists are allowed a glimpse of couples' most deeply felt hopes and fears and trusted to help the couple navigate a safer route home. Clearly, not all couples work achieves secure bonding. Some couples seek therapy to help with safe separation, and the promotion of more cooperative parenting if children are involved. Sometimes one partner has decided to leave and enters therapy in the hope that the therapist will look after the other partner. Whatever the wishes and intentions, the therapeutic connection has the potential to promote intimacy and fosters felt security for the future, albeit in another relationship.

In closing this chapter, we shall summarise the benefits of attachment theory and the idea of attachment styles for systemic psychotherapists in their formulation and interventions with distressed couples. We try to hold both partners in mind, where their styles might be both similar and different, and work with both styles, constructively and simultaneously. The core features include:

- fostering a secure therapeutic base;
- helping to identify and de-escalate negative patterns of interaction, softening emotional responses, using and modelling affirmative practices, close and careful listening, and using positive connotation, reframing and externalisation;
- helping to promote and develop more secure bonding interactions;
- consolidating secure bonding experiences and developing a shared narrative of what helped and why, as a means to prevent a retreat into insecure patterns of responding and to reduce the likelihood of the perception of attachment threat, when none perhaps is intended.

Chapter 6

Trauma and dissociation

The idea of trauma and being traumatised has become increasingly employed in everyday language and also in clinical practice. Many people describe that they feel that they have been 'traumatised' by an event, or that certain events are traumatic. This is often equivalent to a statement that the experience was frightening and upsetting and that it continues to play on their mind – that they cannot stop thinking about it or alternatively that thoughts about the events break through or interrupt their thinking processes in unpleasant and uncontrollable ways. An aspect of such statements is that although the event may not be consciously in our awareness, painful memories of it can be unexpectedly and uncontrollably triggered by some chance reminders, such as the smell of the floor polish in a hospital or the sound of a car door closing reminding us of an illness or an attack. Embedded in such statements can be an idea that there are some qualities of events that in themselves are inherently traumatic, that they will invariably produce a traumatic state. It is important to draw out of this a distinction that events in themselves may not in fact be trauma inducing, rather there is some process whereby they come to be so. This is in contrast to explanations that feature individual vulnerability, for example that some people are prone to be traumatised, that they are somehow vulnerable or in some way 'weak'. Arguably, it was such thinking that suggested that only some soldiers were prone to shellshock in conditions of battle in wars.

Throughout this book we are adopting the perspective that experiences and the nature of a variety of problems can be seen as connected with how individuals have learnt to process events, which might in turn be greatly influenced by their attachment strategies. At the same time we are suggesting that we make sense of events, and importantly are helped to cope with danger and fear, through the emotional support of people close to us, particularly our family members and partners. Furthermore, we can think of not just individuals but also of family groups as traumatised or disrupted by dangerous, threatening and painful experiences. In this context, perhaps counterintuitively, we can start to see that statements such as 'I feel traumatised' can be seen to indicate that the person, although still upset by the events, is engaging in two related processes, which may be helping to contribute to overcoming the negative impacts of a difficult experience. First, they may be showing some awareness of the impact of this experience on their functioning, in statements such as 'I just cannot stop thinking about it'. This may indicate that the person is engaged in a process of integration of the experience. Although still painful, the early process of making sense of the experience appears to be taking place. Particularly important in this is that this storying of the experience is assisting the person to develop strategies for anticipating and dealing with future events. Second, in articulating their experiences they may be able to draw support and assistance from people close to them to help them in this process. In particular, help from others to regulate or control difficult and painful feelings may give the person an opportunity to continue to engage in the integrative processes required to help overcome the impact of the distressing experience. Related to this, the person may find it useful to connect with others who have had similar experiences in that attempts to assist them can also assist their own reflective and integrative processes and help their coping strategies to develop.

What is trauma?

There is a wide variety of events that many of us will experience that have the potential to lead us to become traumatised. The events include extreme forms of danger to oneself, such as physical attacks, accidents and injuries. They also include these events occurring to others – vicarious traumas – and arguably one of the most difficult is attacks or injuries to those close to us – our children, partners, parents, siblings or friends. Trauma can also result from the kinds of natural and inevitable losses that we all experience, such as the death of family members, friends and lovers. However, this list starts to point to some apparent paradoxes regarding trauma. On the one hand, the above list of dangerous events does not inevitably lead to trauma. On the other hand, inevitable life events sometimes can lead to trauma. What is more, in some cases what most of us might consider relatively minor events, such as a separation or ending of a relationship, or loss of a loved pet, do seem to lead to traumatic responses or states. An event, then, is not in itself inherently traumatic: many people experience violence, serious injuries, sexual abuse or rape without developing a traumatic condition. Furthermore, it is possible that we need not even directly experience an event to become traumatised. For example, we may respond vicariously to what has happened to someone who is close to us or even imagine or anticipate some dangerous event.

Clinical definitions of trauma have emphasised that it can be *triggered* by a specific life-threatening event. However, revisions to this definition have taken into account that traumatic states can also develop as a consequence of the accumulation of everyday events, such as bereavement, bullying, interpersonal conflict, marital disharmony, failures at work or working for emergency services (see *Diagnostic and Statistical Manual of Mental Disorders* (DSM); American Psychiatric Association, 2007). The *reactions* to the triggering events are seen as falling within two groups:

- preoccupying – the person may experience recurring memories of the event, dreams and nightmares, flashbacks, intense reactions to a wide variety of cues associated with the event;
- dismissing – the person may make continued efforts to avoid thinking about the event, avoid activities associated with the event, be unable to remember important aspects of the event, withdraw and generally diminish activity levels, and shut down their feelings.

With the patterns of either a preoccupying or a dismissive reaction there may be embodied states of increased arousal, shown by difficulty in sleeping, difficulty in concentrating, hypervigilance and outbursts or intrusions of anger. These symptoms are seen to have lasted for some period of time (over a month) and are causing significant impairment in social, occupational and relational functioning with accompanying levels of distress.

Traumatic states include the important feature that psychological processing, and importantly the ability to protect oneself and one's loved ones in the future, may be incapacitated. As the DSM definition above suggests, it appears that the nature of the reactions and related psychological processes appear to take two major forms:

- The memories and emotions associated with an event continue to preoccupy us and fill our minds such that we are unable to think coherently about other aspects of our lives. We may even become unable to take care of our own basic needs, to feed for and care for ourselves. Moreover, this can mean that we become similarly unable to take care of others but may become preoccupied with anxiety about our own safety. Although continually preoccupied with thinking about the painful event, we do not develop any coherent ideas of how we can protect ourselves in the future. Instead, we may become obsessed with every detail of the event or situation and become generally very fearful of a wide range of irrelevant details. In case of a violent attack, such as a physical assault or rape, we may become generally very distrustful of people and hence unable to draw on appropriate assistance to help ensure our safety in the future.
- Alternatively, our response may be to push the experience out of conscious thought. What may then result is that fragments of memories from the experience, such as visual images, sensations and negative emotions may intrude into consciousness. During a conversation or various activities we may become distracted or absent from the interaction as our attention is taken up by the intruding fragmented memories. In turn,

these states of distraction may be triggered inadvertently by images, smells, sounds and tones of voice, for example.

Functions of trauma

The diagnostic definitions above have running through them the idea that trauma can be seen as the extreme poles of two types of reactions. On the one hand, we become primed to defend ourselves either by being prepared to fight and retaliate or to flee and avoid the danger. This is to stay in a vigilant and hyperaroused state. Arguably in conditions of continued danger, such as war, this state may have a protective role in that we avoid immediate danger and are ready to act quickly if necessary. On the other hand, we may develop a state whereby we deny or minimise the danger in an attempt to try to maintain some form of life. Again in war situations we avoid thinking about the danger or try to minimise it so that we are able to take some actions (risks) necessary to stay alive. Were we to correctly evaluate the dangers we might, for example, never cross the road for the (real) fear of being shot. So both responses can be seen in certain situations to be functional and adaptive. However, both appear to involve a considerable emotional cost and in the longer term may lead to conditions that become fixed and non-adaptive. A powerful example is where troops returning home to relative safety from wars (e.g. Vietnam or Iraq) continue with one or both of these strategies and they disrupt their ability to function under safe conditions where more considered and less extreme responses are required. In effect, what has been learnt as a form of survival in one context may not be functional or appropriate in another.

Trauma, dissociation and attachment theory

From its inception the issues of trauma and dissociation have been central to attachment theory. Danger and threat are the bases of attachment theory in that the function of parents is to provide protection and comfort for the infant when they are threatened. Rather than regarding danger as unusual or an exception to life, attachment theory regards it as inevitable and central. In turn, humans, and animals, are seen as having evolved to be able to effectively deal with danger and threat. In order to be able to survive, a species has to develop adequate strategies for dealing effectively with high levels of danger and threat, first and foremost of which is the instinct to attach to others to ensure protection. These characteristically involve basic flight and fight reactions (and, in some circumstances, freeze) but as a child becomes increasingly psychologically sophisticated, abilities develop to be able to predict and anticipate dangers and to work out solutions or strategies for dealing with these. Essentially this means that the child needs to be able to learn from situations of danger to be able to carry forward information about the event, the circumstances, setting, people involved, how they came to be there and so on in order to be able to anticipate and avoid the danger in the future. The child needs to learn what information from the dangerous situation is relevant, and generalisable for future safety and what is not relevant for future events but was unique or specific to that particular setting. To take an example, the patterns on the wallpaper in the room where a young woman was sexually abused may serve as triggers of the abuse but carry no particular self-protective function in the future. In contrast, paying attention to details of the neighbourhood, the expressions on people's faces, the types of drugs being used, the fact that some were carrying weapons may help us to avoid being attacked again at a 'party'.

Trauma responses can in this way be defined as the ability to make use of information from events in our lives. To build on the example above where a woman was abused, if we become preoccupied with every single detail of the situation we may develop a preoccupying trauma whereby we become fearful and ruminate about every single detail of the above situation including the colour of the wallpaper. However, this may ultimately be dysfunctional since we may attend to the wrong cues or attempt to completely cut ourselves off from any social contact. Alternatively, a dismissing form of trauma reaction may be where we attempt to block just about all aspects of the experience from consciousness. This then leaves us vulnerable since we may enter into a similar situation since we still do not attend to the cues that signal a danger-ous context. We act as if nothing had happened and in effect have not learnt from the experience. In cases of domestic violence a woman may become attached to yet another violent and abusive partner.

Bowlby (1980, 1988) described how attachments are represented in differ-ent modalities as behavioural, sensory, visual and semantic information. For a young infant without language, attachment experiences are held as conditioned responses, for example they learn that their mother's footsteps are a precursor to their hunger being satisfied. They might also learn to associate her smell and touch with relief from hunger and anxiety. As the child grows older she becomes capable of representing these experiences in more sophisticated images and then verbally as internalised speech or semantic thought. In turn, these cognitions, images and sensory impressions start to be built into short stories or episodes that later may become more complex narratives about our experiences. Alongside this, the child gradually learns to be able to integrate and reflect on their mental processes. So, for example, they might come to recognise that they do not have an image of an event and wonder why, or even that having said that they enjoyed an experience with a parent the image that arises contradicts this.

Bowlby (1988) described this process as 'Not knowing what you know and knowing what you don't know'. By this he meant that children may be instructed by parents to deny their own experiences and memories: To tow the family story or party line and accept a version of events, such as that the parents were kind and not abusive in the face of the child's embodied memory of hurt and pain having been inflicted on them. When we try to recall early childhood experiences many of us will find some points where we are not sure if we are actually remembering the event ourself or we are recalling a story that has been told to us by our parents. This is a normal and inevitable process since as young children our language abilities are limited and we require our parents to help us place events into language. We even require our parents to help us make sense of our internal bodily states and find ways of communicating these (Stern, 1998). Bowlby (1980) made the important point that this is a process of negotiation and co-construction between child and parent and where the parents distort events to their purposes then the child is left in a particularly confused and vulnerable position. In order to belie the adult's version of events they may need to distort their own experience or to hold on to their own experience they need to reject their attachment figure's version of reality. It is possible that extreme and continuous experience of these processes can promote a sense of loss of reality or even psychotic states in a child. Attachment theorists have argued that a secure attachment consists of our ability to weave together these different memory systems into a coherent whole in order to make sense of our experiences. This involves open communication with our parents so that gaps, discrepancies and inconsistencies can be resolved.

Family patterns and trauma

People are engaged in two twin processes in response to potentially traumatic events: first, there is a survival response of trying to ensure their safety and, second, connected with this, there is an attempt to understand the experience and hopefully to learn from it in order to be able to avoid or deal with such dangers in the future. There appear to be three main ways in which people organise their narratives regarding threat and danger. The first is to develop narratives that help them to dismiss or minimise danger. The second is to become increasingly preoccupied and fearful about danger. The third is to develop a balance whereby they can realistically evaluate the danger but also decide how to prioritise the possible sources of danger and make plans that allow them to organise to make themselves safe in future but also enable them to continue with their lives. Families, friends and others who are close or connected to them are involved in a process of helping them to make sense of painful and dangerous events (Harvey et al., 1992). A critical step in this resolution is that others are willing to acknowledge and accept their experiences and also to offer support to help them to continue their lives. Crittenden (1997) has described where she suffered a 'minor mugging' on the metro in Paris and then spent the following days alternating between dismissing the experience in order to cope with immediate events, and being preoccupied by it, in order to learn what she needed to learn from it.

Likewise, the conversations with friends that initially can appear to be a form of rumination can help to identify what features of the experience people need to learn from in the future. This process may need to be repeated and exhaustive so that they do not miss vital clues. On the other hand, friends and family members can also help them to put this thinking aside in order to get on with other activities and regain a sense of confidence and competence.

The way in which families' members have learnt to deal with painful and dangerous events – their attachment strategies – shapes the ways in which they are able to make sense of these experiences. Central to this is the way in which they are able to develop their narratives of these experiences. These narratives are multi-layered representations of the events and the narratives serve a variety of psychological functions to help protect family members. However, families can be seen as connected with traumatic events in two ways. On the one hand, we can see families as responding to outside threats and attacks – where dangerous events are imposed on them from the 'outside'. On the other hand, they can be seen as inflicting traumatic events, danger and attack on each other from the 'inside' – where the source of danger appears to be clearly inside the family. This distinction is not quite so straightforward since family members may themselves be carrying past experiences of abuse, neglect and attack from their own earlier experiences, for example in childhood, into the heart of their own family.

The family as a source of protection and the development of meaning

Trauma and loss are in a sense the extreme ends of the general process whereby children in families require comforting and soothing. Learning to comfort and soothe requires support from parents and how they respond not only assists the child to return to a calmer state but also becomes internalised (Mikulincer *et al.*, 2003; Mikulincer and Shaver, 2007). How the parents help the child to calm down, by calm talk, reassurance, touching, stroking, distraction into a pleasurable activity, allowing the child to express their fears, forming plans for ways of dealing with the event in the future and so on, becomes internalised and eventually part of the child's repertoire. In effect, the child learns to do to themself what they have seen, felt and heard their parents do to them. Further to this, they also learn vicariously by seeing how their parents sooth their siblings and each other. An important part of this process can be described as 'containment' (Winnicott, 1965; Fonagy *et al.*, 1991b) where the parents are able to show empathy and awareness of how the child is feeling but at the same time the parents do not indicate that they are overwhelmed or incapacitated by feelings themselves. For example, if parents becomes extremely distressed in response to the child's experience this may serve to increase the child's distress rather than help to soothe the child. Younger children may feel frightened that their parent are so vulnerable, older ones may feel guilty that they have caused their parents to be distressed and perhaps also angry and disappointed that they end up having to protect their parents when they needed help. In contrast, parents may respond with too much apparent calm and distance such that the child does not feel connected or understood and feels little empathy from the parents. Many adolescents we have seen appear to fall into these patterns. For example, one young woman had been repeatedly sexually attacked at school by an older boy. However, she felt that revealing this to her parents was not viable since her mother would become so upset and also that her father might blame her for being provocative or make things worse for her by taking on the school. Her attempts to manage her feelings herself appeared to lead to increasing distress and a sense of being alone with her problems to the point that she took a dangerous overdose of medication.

In more extreme circumstances of severe danger and threat, children require their parents to help cope with potentially traumatic events by helping to attach meaning and help process the experience, and also together to develop strategies that will ensure safety. How and whether the attachment figures are able to comfort, reassure and empower children or their partners who have experienced potentially traumatic events is vital to the successful management of the problems that may have occurred outside of the family such as attacks or accidents. Harvey *et al.* (1992) indicate that the positive responses of family members, such as acknowledgement of the pain, sympathy, offer of emotional support and being willing to talk over the events, are critical in shaping whether the experience deteriorates into an unresolved traumatic state. In particular, parents who refused to believe that an event, such as sexual abuse by a grandparent, had occurred had the effect of making the person feel alone, uncared for and trapped in their distress.

The family as a source of danger

We want to say at the outset in this section that we recognise that parents who may be dangerous to their children have very often been traumatised themselves. This is crucial. Hence, we attempt in our conceptualisation and clinical work to support the parents as well as listen to their children's experiences.

In some situations the attachment figure may themselves become the source of danger rather than comfort or safety for the child: These are the situations of intra-family physical and sexual abuse (Bentovim, 1992). Here the parents and other family figures who the child needs to provide protection, safety and comfort instead become the sources of danger, fear and distress. Bowlby (1980) has argued that not only does the child in these circumstances experience danger but that being in this unsafe situation with their parents impedes the child's ability to process and make sense of dangerous events in various ways. He refers here to the child developing 'multiple models', for example that at an embodied and sensory level the child remembers abusive, frightening acts but these may be disordered and disconfirmed by the parents so that at a semantic level the child is required to believe that they were responsible for these events because of their 'naughty' behaviour, or even more extremely, that the events did not happen and that they are a warm, harmonious family. Bentovim (1992) emphasises that such family abuse is often an ongoing, continuing process rather than a one-off traumatic event. Over time the child learns that they have no possibility of escape or even relief from these events. There are various ways in which a child may respond, but arguably the range of possibilities may appear limited to many children, and in some cases they are trapped by fear and threat. Here it is possible that some forms of behaviour, such as self-harming behaviours, may offer a form of distraction or even emotional relief. A related possibility is that the child comes to engage in a form of self-hypnosis – dissociative states – a sort of daydream state where they cease to be in the present. An extended version of this may be forms of multiple personalities where the dissociative state becomes more complex and extended. For example, a child might develop one self-state in which they are a victim and abused and another where they are a naughty girl who enjoys the sexual abuse and is somehow responsible for it. The processes can also be seen to resemble Seligman's (1975) accounts of learnt helplessness where over time in response to uncontrollable and unbearable events the person becomes passive, helpless and depressed.

Liotti (2004) likewise describes how the child in the situation of experiencing abuse from their parents can experience an acute and irresolvable dilemma: The child both turns to the attachment figure for security and comfort in the face of danger but is placed in a very difficult situation when this same figure is the cause of danger, for example a physically or sexually abusive parent (Figure 6.1).

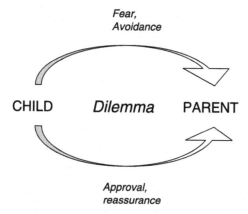

Fear,
Avoidance

CHILD   *Dilemma*   PARENT

Approval,
reassurance

Figure 6.1 Dilemma for a child in an abusive attachment pattern.

Liotti (2004) emphasises that the child is placed in an inescapable dilemma in such situations of abuse because the need to be attached to, to seek comfort and security, to be loved by a parent or attachment figure is fundamental. A child in this situation cannot trust the reassurance when it is given by a parent who is frightening and/or frightened. The child cannot eliminate the need to be attached and hence the child in the above situation of abuse is placed in a dilemma or a no–win situation wherein whatever they do will most likely gain further abuse and pain: If they approach the parent they may be further hurt and not comforted, and if they do not then they may feel abandoned and rejected. Even more likely they may be punished further for being rude, for not being available for their parents needs or even for causing their parents' anger. In a couple's relationship it may be possible for a partner to at least partially resolve this dilemma by becoming aware of it and seeking help, turning to others for support and so on. A young child, however, has fewer options. As described earlier the responses may be dissociative states, depression and self-harm. Liotti (2004) summarises the situation for the child as one in which they strive to push away the memories of the abuse suffered at the hands of their parents, for example by dissociation or memory loss. This helps them to maintain, or at least attempt to maintain, the needed attachment to their parents. At the same time, in order to protect themselves from further abuse, they also try to deny or disavow their need for attachment (Figure 6.2).

We can see in this process that the child is constructing an internal working model that may become increasingly problematic for them. In adult relationships, for example, this tendency to avoid memories of abuse may mean that they do not develop strategies for anticipating and removing themselves from potential or actual scenarios of abuse. Further to this, in attempting to deny their needs, they may not be aware of what is driving them to engage in potentially difficult and dangerous relationships.

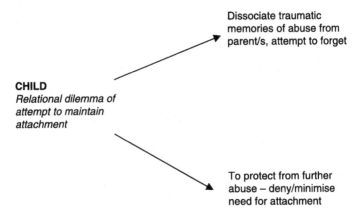

Figure 6.2 Relational dilemma for the child of attempting to maintain attachments.

A further important layer is that the abusive parents may themselves have been exposed to abuse and suffering in their own childhood. This may mean that the parents are also suffering with traumatic states. A consequence for the child may be that the relationship with their parents is even more complex and confusing, for example that the parents is not only frightening but at times themselves very frightened and vulnerable (Cooper and Vetere, 2005) (Figure 6.3).

A child, for example in relation to a parent who has been physically abused, may experience the parent as frightened and vulnerable and respond to this by attempting to comfort and reassure them. In fact, the child may even experience their own actions of demanding attention or of showing some anger towards the parent as themselves being abusive. The parent may in turn react with tears or panic as a victim of the child's apparent 'attack' on them. This vulnerability can turn to anger in the parent, resulting in an attack on the child for 'making' the parent have these bad feelings. This may be without realisation that the child had not caused these feeling but may have inadvertently triggered the parent's unresolved experiences – trauma. At other times, the parent may act in a loving and caring way so that the child can, at least temporarily, experience themselves as cared for and loved. This mixture of contradictory experiences may be very difficult for a young child to understand and resolve. Furthermore, it is likely that the child will develop a sense that they cannot make sense of events and alternate between extremes of self-loathing, intrusions of anger and depressed withdrawal. Such a mixture has been described as a 'disorganised' attachment process (Main *et al.*, 1985; Fonagy *et al.*, 1996). Interestingly, it can also be seen as connecting with Bateson's early formulation of the double-bind. In the description of this, Bateson had similarly described a process where the mother shows rejection of the child and also demonstrates anxiety that the child might reject her. In turn, the

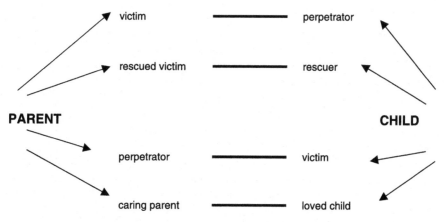

Figure 6.3 Multiple and contradictory roles for the child in a traumatic system.

child responds by disguising their need and affection for the parent such that a mutual cycle becomes constructed whereby neither is able to clearly and unambiguously express their needs and feelings for and about each other.

A child's attempts to make sense of these experiences may be impeded by the parent's response. For example, the parent may falsify or repress the child's experience, for example when a child is told that what was experienced emotionally as a frightening event was in fact an example of affection or even that they were mistaken and, for example, domestic violence did not happen. Also, a child may be instructed not to mention certain events with the consequence that they are unable to emotionally have their experiences validated, and attach meaning to them. Likewise, the parent may themselves be over-anxious about an event such that the child is kept continually vigilant and anxious in relation to it.

Implications for therapy

Central to our approach is the creation of a secure base for families for re-experiencing, reprocessing and renegotiating interpersonal responses and difficulties. In the discussion so far of trauma and loss we have seen that trauma is not simply or predominantly an internal and individual state but is woven into the emotional dynamics of a family. As we described earlier we can see this in one of two main ways. First, an external event/s has produced a traumatic process in the family such that family members are no longer able to care for and comfort each other. Second, the family itself is the source of danger and trauma for its members. These two sets of circumstances are not simply separate, however, since parents may, for example, have themselves experienced trauma as children themselves, which is making it difficult for them to respond to the needs of their children or partner.

Creating a secure base

From our discussion so far it is clear that families where trauma is a central feature are struggling to be able to provide a secure base for each other. In some cases it may appear that in fact they are operating in such a way that what is happening is quite the opposite of creating safety and what is being created is increasing levels of fear and danger. In speaking of 'families' here we also need to be cautious to clarify that in many instances it will be the case that one member of the family is particularly dangerous to the others. Systemic perspectives have debated issues of power but Haley (1987) and Minuchin (1974) were two of the early pioneers who argued that power was central to family life and that any and all family communications conveyed a message about whose view of reality was dominant and would prevail. There may also be cases where danger is imagined or anticipated as there has not been a physical attack or other direct indication of actual danger. For example:

They [parents] used to hate each other so much I always used to be so scared that one of them would do something stupid and I would come home and, I used to hate coming home just in case something happened. And they've both got the worst tempers, even Dad . . . Dad's is I've rarely seen but it is really bad. . . .

(Kate – young woman with anorexia – age 17)

Kate described her anxiety about her parents but had never seen the parents being physically violent to each other.

Case example

James, aged 12, was experienced by his stepmother Claire as an extremely aggressive and potentially very dangerous boy. James had been living with his mother who started a relationship with a man who had a conviction for sexual abuse. Social Services became extremely concerned and asked his father to accommodate James with his new family. James said little about his mother and had little contact with her, acting now as if he did not want to know and was trying to forget all about her.

We were puzzled about the descriptions of his anger and violence since James was a slight, quiet diminutive boy who was extremely compliant, somewhat sad and eager to please in our family sessions and in the individual sessions with him. In the sessions with his stepmother he looked over to her continually as if to check out that what he was saying was acceptable. In sessions she would talk with a frosty determination that her ideas of behavioural management of his tantrums, including time out, rewards and punishment schedules and use of strict boundaries, were necessary. At the same time, she would at times display extreme sadness, despair and vulnerability regarding her experiences and frustrations at her attempts to cope. We felt a breakthrough in our work with Claire and James when, talking on her own, Claire revealed that she had been physically and emotionally abused by her stepfather and at times James reminded her of these experiences. She did not want to see another man in her own life bullying, frightening and making her and her other children (girls) feel unsafe. Our hypothesis shifted and we also began to see Claire in a different way, as not a rather harsh, unforgiving stepmother but as a vulnerable, traumatised woman trying her best to help her husband bring up his son despite the fact that he was triggering extremely distressing traumatic memories. We were able to share her discussion with James and it helped him to see why his actions produced such strong reactions in his stepmother. Subsequently, Claire's reactions to his naughtiness decreased in intensity as did the level of James's aggression and the continuation of his behaviours.

Although creating a secure base is a central feature of our approach for all kinds of problems and distress, it is arguably all the more important for families where trauma is evident. For these families not only feel unsafe, but they also distrust attempts to offer comfort, reassurance and warmth. As we have seen, the difficulties may in turn have their roots in experiences across generations. Although each family is in a sense unique, we suggest that where trauma is a leading element in the family's experience the above is a core dilemma for the family. In fact, given this dilemma, we need to consider very carefully how it is that a family or parts of a family have come for any therapeutic input.

The therapeutic invitation

A key question that frames our work with such families is how will they see the therapy and what will they feel about attending therapy sessions? Our general formulation is that they will experience the core dilemma above as their experiences have taught them that people who should offer them comfort actually hurt them, and it is best to try to deny any emotional needs and vulnerabilities. Within this framework, the more we might strive to offer them reassurance and comfort, the more it may arouse suspicion that this is essentially a trap or a set-up so that they will be punished and abused. Why should we (therapists) expect that they will immediately see us as any different to what the sum of their life experiences has been to date? In contrast, we know that some families where trauma is not prevalent are able relatively quickly to trust the therapy setting and to utilise the help available from the therapy team. A helpful approach may be for the therapist, if they have the benefit of a team, to emphasise that the team will be able to support both them and the family. It may be especially important to emphasise this since the family may feel that the team is there to judge, evaluate, conspire against them and so on, rather than being a source of emotional support for both the family and the therapist. This may also mean that silent teams behind a mirror may not be so appropriate for these families or that we find ways of helping this arrangement to be less threatening, for example warm introductions to the team, inviting the family to observe us from behind the screen when we discuss their concerns, or using a reflecting process with a lead therapist and in-room consultant (Cooper and Vetere, 2005).

We have called this initial process with families *talk about talk*, which connects with systemic family therapy's emphasis on the importance of discussing with a family what has led them to come for therapy and what they think and feel about attending. Included in this conversation with a family is also the possibility that they may not want to talk about problems straight away, and alternatively that they may want to launch in fairly quickly. In this conversation we can discuss clarifying how we will know if people are not feeling safe to communicate about some areas and what is the best course of action – to take a break, change the topic and so on. Above all the conversation needs to convey to the family that the therapist respects that communication can be difficult and painful and that they will not be tricked, persuaded or pushed into revealing anything that may be dangerous and have negative consequences outside the therapy room. It also important to emphasise that we as therapists might get things wrong and can apologise if we do so.

Central to the approach is also to adopt a non-blaming stance, a focus on competencies and on our willingness to understand things from their perspectives. If the family process is organised around blame and guilt, both for the victims of abuse and also the perpetrators, then they will be extremely susceptible to feeling accused and judged. This will leave the family feeling extremely insecure and unsafe emotionally and this is a state in which it will be very hard for them to start to think and integrate, revise, re-story and transcend their negative experiences. An approach of externalising the problems, that is, conversations about how, for example, anger has been allowed into family life and damaged their relationships, can offer a safer place to start. It can also help to start to create a therapeutic relationship where the therapy team are seen to be working alongside rather than against the family. This stance can also help to make the problems seem more emotionally manageable and allow us to think.

Importantly, an approach that reduces blame, emphasises responsibility and as a start externalises the problems can create a safer space for families to start to make sense of events. Once a safety plan has been agreed, we can work with the family to maintain physical safety and to develop their sense of emotional safety:

Conversation focuses on how, for example, a pattern of violence may have become a part of the family's life, both currently and intergenerationally.

⇩

This externalising reduces the potential blame felt by family members, but care must be taken not to dilute responsibility.

⇩

There may be a reduced emotional stance of anxiety and an attempt to defend self – leading to an enhanced sense of responsibility for choices and actions.

⇩

Family members can see the therapist as not blaming but being sympathetic about the topic, while holding onto ideas of responsibility and accountability.

⇩

This can offer family members a *vicarious experience of safety* – they can see the therapist as non-blaming and sympathetic.

⇩

This may facilitate a sense of emotional safety and containment. This work may be done with individuals, different family members and with family groups separately and concurrently depending on the assessment of risk.

⇩

This allows the family to start to engage in attachment seeking and comfort seeking from the therapist.

Where the trauma has resulted from actions within the family, for example from abuse by one or both parents, there is of course the danger that an externalising stance may appear to be colluding with the abuse. For example, a victim of the abuse may feel very strongly that it was her father's fault and he must accept responsibility for this. Therefore it is important at this stage for the therapist to be able to reflect back that they understand how people feel in terms of the distress, the anger and fear that people may be experiencing, and show how they keep the legal context and the professional network in mind. In some cases it may be helpful to discuss how the parent who perpetrated the abuse may feel trapped by it, wants to stop but does not always know how to do this. All this needs to be done carefully, and initially with perpetrators of abuse on their own, and perhaps leading in to a family meeting, and without suggesting that explanation reduces or eliminates responsibility for actions that hurt, frighten and intimidate others. There is also a need to recognise with the family that they may have a sense that they do not want to raise false hopes of things being better only to see it all fall apart as it has in the past.

Exploring the problems: communication and representational systems

A cornerstone of attachment theory is that insecure attachments involve various forms of difficulties with interpersonal communication. This occurs both in terms of what people are able to communicate to themselves and in turn to each other. With trauma there is a schism between different representational systems such that embodied and sensory experiences are disconnected from semantic and episodic ones. For example, people may experience flashbacks, outburst of anger and fear and be unaware of what the causes of these experiences are. This disconnection can be extremely problematic for communication in families since both the person emitting the behaviour and the person responding to it may be distorting its underlying core meaning and causes through their own traumas. Hence, in the first few sessions a focus on communication and a careful analysis of how people react and a consideration of what attributions people make about each other's actions is central. In the case described above, James's anger was apparently construed by his stepmother as abusive anger – like her stepfather's. In turn his stepmother's actions possibly reminded him of the painful rejection by his mother and the risk she had exposed him to with her paedophile partner.

Inherent in this process is a consideration with the family about what is being communicated in different representational systems. Again in relation to James it was too threatening for his stepmother to discuss initially that James's actions, especially his anger, might have been a form of protest for his own sense of loss. However, through the use of his visual representations, such as drawing, it was possible to communicate with his stepmother's vulnerable and softer side. Use of visual material in families can be helpful not only for children like James to express his feelings and to help him make connections but also as a way for parents to connect both with their children and their own childhood experiences. For example, parents in seeing their children's drawings can connect with their visual representations of childhood, of being little, vulnerable and afraid. Visual material contains, and is a often a vehicle for, emotions that are denied at a semantic, language level and can help a parent like Claire to connect with a child's vulnerability instead of holding a fixed view of them as bad, evil, dangerous and so on. The therapist may also be helpful in this process by both encouraging the use of multiple representations for the family, for example asking questions about what things looked and felt like, inviting examples of episodes or stories to describe their experiences. This can be done in a reflective way in the session so that the therapist talks about images that come into their minds, comments on what images they may have noticed from the family and helps to make connections between feelings, images, words, stories and the family's theories and explanations (integration).

Through this exploration we also start to be able to consider how family members perceive the problems. As with Claire and James it can be important to try and track with them transgenerational patterns of relating in the family. The most common tool to facilitate this is the family genogram, which can reveal important themes across the generations. Within an attachment perspective a part of this exploration can be to consider danger, fear and comfort in the families. Again for these families this will be an especially delicate task since they may quickly come to feel blamed and there is the potential that very painful feelings from, for example, the parents' childhood may be activated. It may in fact be helpful for the therapist to reflect with the family that they agree to tread carefully and that 'landmines' may appear – although hopefully we will not stand on too many!

Exploring alternatives and change

Again, for families with trauma, moving to a consideration of alternatives and, for example, a discussion of unique outcomes, may be difficult. For example, a consideration of how things might have been different for the parents as children or examples of times that were good may provoke power-ful defended feelings. Likewise, a consideration of times when things are well in the current family may simply provoke the position that this is when the child who is abused is totally compliant and capitulating, being no problem. Again for James this could be times when he was particularly depressed but at least quiet and not making trouble for his stepmother and father. The explor-ation of unique outcomes therefore needs to go towards an exploration of when people felt really safe and comforted, or if this is not possible to remember what this might hypothetically have felt like. It may also be helpful to bring this process into the therapy room so that there is a consideration of what has gone on and at what times there has been a feeling of safety and how this happened and what could help to make it happen again in the session and, possibly, eventually outside. In our experience it is crucial to validate people's experiences and their attempts to do things differently, and to give people credit for trying.

We also utilise the idea of different representational systems to prompt experiences of relating in the family in different sensory systems, for example, through the use of visual materials such as drawings, by facilitating different types of emotional responding in the session and through suggesting struc-tural changes. With James and his stepmother Claire, one aspect of this was when we suggested that for part of the session we split into two groups: James was to talk to one half of the team and his stepmother to the other. Working with the two parts of the family system separately allowed us to have a softer and calmer conversation with each. It then allowed us to share positive information from these two sessions when we came back together as a large group. This then facilitated a warmer, softer and more positive interaction between James and Claire at the end of the session.

It is possible that Claire essentially framed (semantically) this as something that was being done to, and for, James to make him better but it was apparent that she also appreciated the support that she was able to receive for herself. The sense of each of them being given some attention and comfort appeared to create a unique outcome – a safe space for them to try being closer and more trusting of each other. The experience of a warmer way of being together may have a created a warmer experience for both of them at an embodied and emotional level. Such structural interventions can create opportunities for experiences at different sensory levels and may create some potential for change, for example Claire and James's new experience of seeing his stepmother smile and touch him when we told Claire about how James had told us how much he appreciated all she was trying to do for him. These interactions can help to promote positive bonding and mutually rewarding interactions. As Watzlawick *et al.* (1974) used to say, 'nothing convinces like success'.

Corrective and replicative scripts

An important aspect of the work at this stage is the exploration of corrective and replicative scripts. Again there is an important additional layer where there is significant trauma. In particular it may be that the corrective or replicative processes operate in a particularly powerful and sometimes inflexible way. The emotional pain from the parents' early childhood experiences may mean that they are extremely mobilised to do things very differently from the experiences that they had. However, in some cases they may not be aware of what is driving them to do things differently, having blocked out the abuse from conscious awareness or blocked out the idea that it is informing their lives now. Also, the process may be that, although semantically they are determined to do things differently, the memories at an embodied level, visually and in terms of awareness and ability to recall episodes of what they experienced and felt, may be blocked. Another consequence may be that when attempts to do things differently do not appear to be working, the parents may experience some of the full force of the anxieties and pain they had as children – a similar sense of powerlessness. Again for Claire this seemed to be relevant in that her attempts to be a good, considerate, organised, predictable mother to James seemed to lead to the same kind of violence that she had experienced. In effect she was trying to be a 'good girl' again and getting violence and attack as a result, as she had throughout her childhood. This retraumatisation as a consequence of the attempt of a corrective script may feel like a crushing blow to parents. It is unlikely that they possess the emotional resources, the experience of being held and supported themselves or of how to deal with a child's difficult emotions without anger and abusing them. Their corrective scripts are therefore based on a semantic attempt without the supporting emotional experience to draw on.

In one family, the father who was now an actor who had spent his childhood in various children's homes described how he had tried to learn how to be a parent like a part in play. He had read books, watched films and plays, talked to friends and so on – learnt his script – but the practice of doing it for real with his own daughter and wife had proved very hard since he lacked the emotional experiences to draw on as a resource.

Integration and maintaining contact

Integration of experiences, and from our attachment perspective an ability to integrate the experiences from the different representational systems, is central to therapy. Again, difficulties with this process lie at the heart of problems related to trauma. Perhaps this is a central feature in that such integration, sometimes also termed 'reflective functioning' (Fonagy *et al.*, 1991b) is particularly problematic. In order for family members to be able to defend themselves from the pain of traumatic events these memories may be suppressed or dissociations frequently occur. Fonagy (1991) warns of possible iatrogenic effects such that too rapid attempts to integrate experiences and to engage in full reflective appraisal of one's experiences and relationships can be overwhelming for some people, especially those with 'personality disorders' associated with severe abuse.

Integration is a process that occurs throughout therapy, but as it progresses the family needs to make attempts to be able to reflect on their experiences in increasingly less distorted ways and as fully as possible, employing more material from each of their representational systems. A relatively gentle way of encouraging this is for the therapist to reflect on their relationship with the family, to offer reflections about their own family and circumstances and connections with the family's experiences. This can both offer families an example or model of how to develop integrative stories but also communicate that it is safe to do so. However, with these families there may be a choice not to communicate about or to integrate certain very negative and painful experiences. It may be helpful to discuss this openly with a family, perhaps that through recognising the impact of some traumatic events they are choosing to close the book on these for now but may possibly attend to them later. This in effect helps move the family to a different position whereby they are less at the mercy of the traumatic events and more choosing to employ some forms of defensive measures. Arguably, secure attachments constitute just such a choice or flexibility so that we may choose, for example, to adopt a dismissive, avoidant strategy at times. However, we are deliberately using this as a strategy and are not therefore so trapped or compelled to stick with it if it becomes ineffective or inappropriate at a later stage.

Finally, another central issue for these families is that their experiences of attachment and trust have been very shaky. The 'ending' of therapy can critically reactivate a sense that as soon as they form an attachment, come to trust someone, this is destroyed, they are abandoned and even at worst that it was all just a con. The therapist/s were just being paid to fix them and did not really give a damn. This position is made worse by a dominant discourse in the mental health professions that warns against 'dependency' and the risks of clients becoming dependent. This is particularly inappropriate as a guiding concept when we consider that many families with trauma have been through the care system and have experienced a string of broken attachments to carers. If the therapy reproduces this experience of a sense of trust developing and then being broken it may add up to having been totally useless, and at worse making the family worse in terms of being even less trusting. A discussion of issues of separation by the therapist is therefore important. In addition, it can be extremely helpful to offer ways of maintaining contact – of showing the family that we are holding them in mind. It is interesting to speculate here about our own needs as therapists, and it may be that some of us avoid further contact with our clients for fear that they relapse and show that our work was not very helpful! Our own experience is that it can be delightful to hear from a family that they are doing well and that we were of some help in this. On the other side, it is important to acknowledge that we want and need to feel this and may feel disappointed and worry about our own competence if we hear the reverse.

Chapter 7

Loss, grief and attachment

Many of the most intense emotions arise during the formation, the maintenance, the disruption and the renewal of attachment relationships. The formation of a bond is described as falling in love, maintaining a bond as loving someone, and losing a partner as grieving over someone. Similarly, threat of loss arouses anxiety, and actual loss gives rise to sorrow; whilst each of these situations is likely to arouse anger. The unchallenged maintenance of a bond is experienced as a source of security and the renewal of a bond as a source of joy.

(Bowlby, 1980, p. 3)

Beautiful words. Bowlby's description evokes the dynamic relationship between joy and sorrow, mediated by our experiences of love. In the words of C. S. Lewis' beloved wife, Helen, 'it's part of the deal. . . .'. In C. S. Lewis' words, following her death, 'No one ever told me that grief felt so like fear' (Lewis, 1961, p. 2). This is what we have found, both in our clinical practice and in our own life experience, that there still exists a profound misunderstanding of the nature of grief, a wish for denial of the impact and length of the grieving process and a tendency to pathologise what is, after all, an everyday emotional process. We resist the description of grief as sickness or illness, or that people are seeking a cure. We find that people seek us out because they are experiencing distress or emotional pain as it is more popularly called, and they recognise that they are living and functioning below their own optimal capacity. They wish to function better in how they face current life dilemmas and challenges, and they hope to improve the felt quality of their interpersonal relationships. But they do not ask us to help them find resolution or acceptance. Instead, they ask us to help them pick up the threads of their lives, to help one another, and to learn to live alongside their sorrow.

In this chapter, we shall focus more on sorrow, arising in relationships, and how it finds its embodied expression in grief, and the cultural practices around mourning. We shall explore the contribution of attachment thinking to systemic practice when working with people who are bereaved, and people who have endured losses of many kinds, including the losses experienced by family members during the processes of separation, divorce and the formation of stepfamilies. The chapter will focus on bereavement and mourning, while Chapter 3 outlines the relational impact of loss for children and adults through separation and divorce. Grief and loss are, and always will be, experienced by all of us as an inevitable part of life. Grief and loss take many forms. The most obvious is when someone close to us dies. However, there are many variations: the loss of a partner's love, a divorce, the moving away of a close friend or colleague, a severe illness or accident that so changes someone who is close to us that in a sense we have lost them as the person we knew. We can also experience loss when a friend succumbs to alcohol or appears to change or reject the values that once connected us. Conversely, for some people, the passing away of a relative who was severely disabled by illness, pain and suffering can be experienced more as a relief than as a loss – as an end to suffering. In effect what constitutes loss is both a personal and a social construction – it differs for different people – and we have much in common in how we experience sorrow and sorrowing.

Thus, we do not want to suggest that there might be a right or a wrong way of dealing with grief. We are not proposing grief therapy or a therapy for grief. Instead, we want to consider how we might respond therapeutically when family members describe their grief responses as complicated, stuck, preoccupied or traumatised (Murray Parkes, 2006). Using our attachment lens, we shall explore ways of working with loss and with the bereaved that both honour the grieving process and help to make it more explicable and endurable, and in using examples from our practice, show how to reformulate depression and anxiety as sadness, grief and mourning, when appropriate. It was Bion who wrote that it was our ability to suffer our emotional pain, and the resultant anxiety about our emotional 'truths', that allowed us to learn from experience (Grotstein, 2007). If we can find a way, or can be helped to find a way, to bear the emotional pain of loss and the resulting anxieties in this confrontation with life experience, if we can integrate the various elements of this experience – the thoughts, feelings, memories and dreams – then we can continue to both hold the lost person in our mind but also be able to relate to, help and love others.

Continuing bonds

Loss, both actual and perceived, is manifest in different kinds of intimate relationships, at different times and around different events. The experience of loss can be mediated by the relational legacy of the past, as much as by our experiences in current relationships. It is also shaped by our internal working models of relationships and our expectations of ourselves and others, which in turn shape how we are able to utilise the resources we hold. In emphasising that loss is a process rather than an event, we here suggest that, although the relationship may change dramatically, we nevertheless continue to have a relationship with the person who has died or from whom we have separated. In the case of the ending of a relationship, such as through divorce, we continue to relate both physically in most cases but also in the conversations and imagined interactions that we may still have with the person. This of course is apart from the frequent situation where communication needs to continue in order to be able to parent our shared children. Also, many people describe how the previous relationship can continually impact on new relationships in terms of 'corrective scripts', for example as they desperately attempt to avoid the patterns, conflicts and disappointments of the previous relationship.

Even when the person we are attached to has died, we continue to have a relationship with them in our minds. We continue to relate and do not stop relating (Neimeyer, 2006). Grief is, in many ways, a process of meaning making – and when we lose our sense of purpose and experience a rupture in our personal beliefs, it can take a long time to pick up the threads once more. In fact, attachment theory may be especially helpful here in clarifying the different kinds of relationships that people may hold. For example, people with a dismissive style may very well attempt to push away memories – images, conversations and sensual memories of the loved one – since these are too painful to tolerate. Alternatively, those with a preoccupied style may be saturated and continually overwhelmed with such memories and these may also shape and disrupt interactions with new friends and potential partners. A secure strategy may help find a balance between continuing to be able to experience the memories as sources of joy and being able to tolerate the pain of the loss. As relationships are held in mind, there is a balance between staying connected with the feelings and finding some space when necessary to continue with other activities. This process has been described as the 'dual process' of grieving – an ability to stay connected and hold memories of the lost person in mind but also an ability to engage with other activities necessary to continue one's own life and safety.

This theoretical connection between attachment style and grief following the death of a spouse was explored in a research study with 77 widows and widowers (Waskowic and Chartier, 2003). Self-reports from people who had been classified as 'securely attached' as opposed to 'insecurely attached' were less likely to feature anger following the death, with fewer accounts of being socially isolated, fewer feelings of guilt, less despair, less death anxiety, less depersonalisation, and fewer examples of somatic symptoms and rumination. People classified as 'securely attached' were also found to be more likely to reminisce about their loved one and more likely to continue to interchange with their loved one.

Representational systems and internal working models

In the context of therapeutic work with couples, families and carers, and with residential groups, it is helpful to think about grief in terms of our representational systems: our images of grief; our beliefs and cognitions of grief; our stories of grief, held both individually and collectively; our actions and rituals around grief; and our ability to reflect on our grief experience and integrate thought, feeling and action over time. Our therapeutic responses may be governed initially by family members' ease and willingness to respond in one representational system over another. For example, some people cope essentially semantically by using words and concepts to manage their loss – I try not to think about it too much; we have to move on; he would want me to get on with my life; and so on. Others continue to be flooded with images and powerful sensations, reminding them constantly of the loss to such an extent that they are not able to make sense or find ways of managing the practicalities of their life. Central to our ANT framework is providing opportunities to explore the different representational systems preferred by family members. This can be part of an attempt to agree with them the tasks and goals of therapy, including whether they want to address their grief responses now, or perhaps in the future. In many respects we may say that it is the perceived *relational consequences* of loss and grief that we consider in therapy, rather than grief and mourning *per se*.

In this chapter we shall make some distinctions between loss through death of a parent, of a child, or of a grandchild, and the loss of a partner/spouse. We looked at losses arising through the process of separation, divorce and stepfamily formation in Chapter 3. In many respects these experiences of loss are hidden within groups and within the community. The attachment narrative therapy (ANT) framework tries to consider how narratives of loss are developed and expressed, and where possible, made sense of, and how interpersonal difficulties might be resolved in complex circumstances, such as when some family members may be mourning while others in the group may be celebrating, as is often found with early stepfamily formation, for example.

Grief as process

It has long been acknowledged that grieving is a process: embodied, representational, relational and developmental (Hare Mustin, 1979; Bowlby-West, 1983; Raphael, 1984; Murray Parkes, 1996). This section takes a developmental perspective on grief awareness and responsiveness across the life span to foster a reflective systemic approach to the scaffolding of therapeutic conversations around the experience of loss.

Children and bereavement

The research and theoretical literature hosts conflicting views about children's capacity to grieve and mourn, and about the possible longer-term consequences of early bereavement. We have found ourselves repeatedly returning to Bowlby's (1988) views as they fit well with our own observations and practice experience. We shall now summarise the development of death awareness and emotional responsiveness in children.

Evidence for the precursors of grief and mourning in young infants is unclear, beyond the observation of non-specific distress to the absence of a carer. The later interpretation of death may give it meaning. With older infants we see a response to death in terms of separation: protest, despair and detachment (Bowlby, 1980). The separation response will persist unless a consistent caring person takes over the care of the child. Care could be less than adequate if adults think that the infant is too young to be affected by death. Thus, the beginnings of grief and mourning are seen, even though the infant is unable to conceptualise the permanence of death. Young children's capacity for language and symbolic representation is still basic, so grief will be expressed more through actions and somatic states, and then visually. Parents, carers, older siblings and others play an important role in helping the child to express and integrate these different levels of experience and to offer comfort and soothing, when the child may seem inconsolable however their grief is expressed. This developmental task, scaffolded by others, helps the child to ascribe meaning to their experiences. This meaning is both culturally attuned and mediated through the perspectives and values of the household group.

In turn, by helping younger children process their emotional responses to bereavement and other losses, others themselves are helped to manage and process their own grief responses. Of course, all of the above presupposes that family members are able to express their feelings clearly, sensitively and in a relatively straightforward manner. Not all family groups communicate emotional states and responses in this way. One of the tasks of therapy is often to explore how more straightforward communication can be achieved and supported in a way that is congruent with the family members' values and needs.

There are few systematic studies of young children's response to death, but it would appear that as a child's relationships become more varied and they experience more separations and reunions, they learn to trust that parents will return. They learn to understand the permanence of death usually through experiences with birds and animals, and the projection of death can be seen in children's play. Their understanding is concrete, but it may be complicated if adults want to protect them from the knowledge of death, even excluding them from funeral rites. If a parent dies, the child's experience may be of a distressed and emotionally unavailable surviving parent, with strangers in the house, an absence of the dead parent, and perhaps the shock of being sent away to be cared for by others.

If a sibling has died, the child's reactions are likely to be influenced by the quality of the relationship that they had. Younger children may have a limited capacity to put their feelings and memories into words, but their grief and mourning needs a safe adult response, such as clear and realistic information, comfort and recognition of the importance of transitional objects, and tolerance of the child's needy questions, yearnings and searching behaviour. The child might experience a more general sense of anxiety and/or anger because their basic security has been disrupted. The adult's response creates the context within which the child begins to attach meaning to their experiences.

These experiences are invested with emotional meaning that may change with subsequent maturity and reflection. The ANT framework would suggest a careful exploration of how comfort and soothing is given and received, and asked for and reciprocated in the context of loss and grief, and over time, and of how a child's view of themselves as worthy and deserving of care can be shaped by others' responsiveness to them. Similarly, others in the family can find meaning and purpose in giving care. Caring for others at times of bereavement, as well as being a necessary part of life, can provide a focus and temporary welcome distraction from one's own feelings of sadness and hopelessness. This process, however, can become difficult. For example, in one family the father – a fireman – had died unexpectedly of a heart attack. The focus for the whole family became the seven-year-old daughter's responses and a process of selective family attention ensued where, for example, many aspects of curiosity about death common in children at that age became seen as yet further signs of the girl's 'abnormal' distress. It seemed to us that this focus on the girl functioned as a distraction for the enormity of the unbearable distress that the mother, mother-in-law and other family members were experiencing. Thus, the child's needs for comfort and care and the parent's/carer's needs for comfort and care, and to care for others, can become complementary, intertwined and patterned over time. The difficult question is always how family members think they balance out their needs for autonomy and connection, and how that might change in the context of bereavement. We always enquire to what extent family members think that their social compassion and competence have been enhanced and to what extent they may have felt emotionally burdened by shouldering responsibility for the care of others.

School-aged children have broader social networks, and are able to use both words and symbols to organise their memories. By the age of eight, most children understand death as adults do: it is not reversible, it can happen to anyone, including them, and it is the product of a natural process. They have developed a conscience and experience feelings of guilt and sometimes see their own behaviour as causative in death. Denial may be used as a defence. This can result in others believing them to be unaffected by their loss and they may not be comforted nor their need to mourn be properly understood. They may think they have to hide their tears; gender socialisation may pose a problem for boys in expressing sadness. The tendency to inhibit grief alongside a strong need to be cared for may develop into a pattern of compulsive care-giving and self-reliance. Processes of idealisation and identification can be seen as attempts to recover the lost person, mainly through comfort-seeking behaviours, such as wearing the clothes of the dead person, preferring places of special significance, talking to the dead parent, feeling their presence, looking at photographs and so on. At school, bereaved children may be seen to have a changed identity because of the death. Fears about the vulnerability of the other parent can develop, and need to be understood, explored and processed.

Children in the pre-teen years have a greater understanding of what the loss may mean in the future. Their understanding of death is similar to that of an adult, as are their emotional reactions of shock, numbing, denial, distress and anxiety and their capacity to develop death-related fears. There may be culturally embedded and different expectations of boys' and girls' behaviour and roles at this time. General irritability may be mislabelled as difficult behaviour. Quiet and withdrawn responses to bereavement may not attract as much adult attention as more overtly aggressive responses. Children may not have their grief and mourning recognised, while their grief response is helped and facilitated by seeing the grief of their surviving parent and being able to talk about it. As an example, a ten-year-old girl told us how she tried to show her favourite photograph of her recently deceased father to her paternal grandmother. She said that her grandmother pushed her away and appeared very distressed. Other relatives crowded round the girl and whisked her away. She was left with a strong sense of having done something terribly wrong by upsetting her grandmother in this way. As a result she did not want to speak to the family again – she knew it was not safe for her to do so.

If a sibling dies, the responses can include guilt, self-punishment, withdrawal, accident-prone behaviours and a fearful recognition that children can die. Judith Guest's (1976) book *Ordinary People* explores the impact on one adolescent brother of the recent suicide of the other. Although there is not a clear association between grief and psychosomatic problems in children, we would advocate gently exploring the impact of bereavement and the expression of grief. For example, we met with a nine-year-old girl and her mother, at the request of a paediatrician who was about to refer the girl for exploratory surgery on her knees. Since the death of her father, she had become increasingly unable to walk, to the point where she was not attending school, and her mother was pushing her around in a large stroller buggy. When we met, I was struck by the way she hung her head, and walked in the tiniest 'baby steps'. The paediatrician could not find a reason for her difficulty in walking and did not want to recommend surgery until any contributory psychological aspects, as he put it, had been explored. In talking to the girl's mother on her own, it transpired that the girl's father had killed himself by hanging, and that the girl had not been told the manner of his death. Working on the premise that children often know about such 'secrets' in the family, we supported the mother in talking to her child about the father's death, to find out what she knew, and to bring the memory of their father back into their lives. The emotional energy needed to prevent the girl from finding out, and the concomitant feelings of shame, had led to a shutting down of any shared mourning, for fear the secret would be revealed. It was interesting to observe how the girl's walking became stronger and improved as soon as she and her mother started talking and sharing memories. Photographs reappeared, and she put one of her father by her bedside. The girl straightened her posture, resumed her friendships and, with sensitivity from school staff and her mother, rejoined her peers in school. We are not claiming a direct causal link between unspoken grief, unspoken knowledge and a child 'talking with her body', but we do find it helpful to explore the potential for mourning and expression of grief in the context of family bereavement.

Similarly to children, the literature on adolescent experiences of grief and mourning are mixed and sparse. There seems to be some agreement that impairment in general health does not seem to occur in the same way as it does with adults. Adolescents may be at risk for depression, and for suicidal ideation and behaviour. Clearly, the response of the surviving parent will have an impact on the adolescent's adjustment. We may well see stronger gender effects, with anti-social behaviour masking depression and sadness, and an inability to face the loss and death. Adolescents may be more at risk of needing to step into roles vacated by the death of a parent, to meet the needs of other family members.

Case example

We worked with a man whose father had died suddenly when he was 12 years old. His family had migrated to the UK and so his extended family lived a long way away. He recalled his mother's response to his father's death as 'going under the duvet' for about a year. He responded by looking after his younger brother (seven years old), making sure he was ready for school, had packed lunches, and a clean gym kit etc. As a man, he married a woman who was struggling to overcome alcohol dependence and recover from the effects of earlier childhood sexual abuse. He reported that he had continued his role as a carer throughout his life, and was proud of his helpfulness and competence in this regard. As his wife recovered and became more confident, he demanded that she look after him in return. As she turned towards him, in an effort to reach out to him and to respond in the way he asked, he rejected her. Neither of them could understand this pattern, and their mutual responses puzzled and deeply hurt them. They sought couples counselling at this point.

The therapy articulated the pattern, and slowed the process such that each could walk around in their emotional experience, witnessed by the other, and be held emotionally by the therapeutic relationship and a growing trust in the therapist. They both feared rejection and abandonment by the other, and as the man softened his position, it felt safer for his wife to reach out to him again. This time he responded by reciprocating with some affection, touching and holding her, although this was a slow and painful process. This enabled her to feel that she could get close to him, and that she had the right to get close to him (rather than seeing herself as unworthy and undeserving of him) and most importantly that she had something good and caring to offer him, and that he wanted it! As trust grew between them, they began to take more emotional risks and confided more in each other and without fear of rejection – safe in the repeated experience of being properly listened to, modelled initially in the therapy process. Their sense of achievement and pride in themselves, their relationship and their family life grew apace, such that disappointments and setbacks could be faced and lived through. They ended therapy after 20 sessions, with a few follow-up meetings to help them consolidate their substantial achievements.

Adults and bereavement

Murray Parkes (1996) has estimated that in the first six months following the death of a spouse, surviving spouses have an increased risk of mortality compared to the general population of between 40 and 70 per cent. Clearly, grief poses a risk to health and well-being. Adult grief has been conceptualised as a process of shock, protest, disorganisation and reorganisation in a complex weave of emotion, thought and action, which may be beyond words and time (Worden, 2003). If people do experience shock it may be felt as numbness, or a stoical calm, that may last minutes, or for much longer, and not uncommonly for at least a year following bereavement (Murray Parkes, 1996). Family members often tell us that emotional numbness is protective, like being 'on automatic pilot', and enables them to arrange a funeral, get on with the daily tasks of living, look after children, go back to school and so on. However, such numbness can be punctuated by times of acute distress and protest, with a sense of unreality and disbelief about what has happened.

Defensive and distorting processes

Denial as an emotional defence can be both helpful and unhelpful, in titrating a process of slow adjustment. Anger, guilt, anxiety and extreme sadness can be felt throughout these times. People may appear disorganised and have difficulty in concentrating and making plans. Behaviour can be searching and restless, with some difficulty in sleeping and eating regularly. Irritability is common as a result. It could be said that a process of adjustment to loss can be seen to occur as the slow reduction in frequency and intensity of peak periods of distress begins. Sleeping and appetite may improve slowly. New roles, new relationships and new behaviours can sometimes develop as part of the process of reorganisation.

Complex or complicated grief

We note in our practice some clear similarities in the way in which people respond in the early stages of bereavement and following other traumatic events, such as experiencing an uncontrollable swinging from numbness to overwhelming distress. If we conceptualise trauma as a powerful/dangerous experience that overwhelms a child's or an adult's capacity to regulate their emotions, then bereavement can be understood as an emotional crisis and assault on our assumptive frameworks about ourselves, the world and the future. Trauma responses and complex grief responses can look similar, for example with extensive periods of numbing punctuated with acute distress, difficulties with sleep and emotional regulation, irritability and intrusive negative thoughts and memories.

The experience of grief can feel more problematic if a person reflects that their relationship with the dead person was unhappy and complicated in some way – perhaps a partner died while one of the couple was having an affair, or the parent–child relationship was conflictual etc. This can leave them full of regret and recrimination, restlessness, yearning and searching, angry, emotionally shut down, punishing of self and others and with feelings of survivor guilt. Research with those who are bereaved shows us that although these responses can be felt by all of us from time to time in the process of grieving, what characterises a more complicated pattern of grief is both the extent and the duration of the grief response relative to the bereaved person's or family and community's expectations around mourning and grief (Murray Parkes, 2006). Grief that is complicated could result in a prolonged and continued difficulty with caring for children, or in maintaining and even establishing intimacy with others, or in a prolonged and diminished ability to survive economically and to care for oneself. These complexities also may make it difficult for the family as a group to grieve in a coherent and connected way, for example when there are open secrets about affairs, and when ambivalent and mixed feelings in the group may prohibit expression of grief and the giving and receiving of solace and comfort.

Other complications may include a sort of displaced grief (Crittenden, 1995) as an extreme form of a distancing and emotionally deactivating strategy, such as seeing the sadness in another family member. For example, one woman told us: 'when Dad died, my brother was really upset for ages'. One man told us that he had got over the 'passing' of his father, but could not bear to speak or to hear the words 'dead' or 'death' – if those words were spoken he would experience a rush of anger, which he could not understand. Further exploration eventually enabled him to experience the anxiety and the loss that he felt on the speaking of the words 'dead' and 'death'. Anger had long masked these more painful responses, and although the anger had been protective for him, it had held him in a timeless moment, so to speak, such that when we met him 12 years after the death of his father he still had not processed his enormous sense of loss. Alternatively, the process can become very preoccupying with an aggravated and obsessive focus on the details and circumstances of the death, such that the person is constantly overwhelmed by graphic visual and sensory images, that similarly have not been emotionally processed. Here we can see how our comfort and reliance on certain representational systems when under emotional threat, such as an attachment threat, may govern our initial response to loss, and if the opportunity for emotional processing is neither forthcoming nor enabled, a person may get stuck, so to speak, in a pattern of responding that may have been protective initially, but subsequently serves only to make it harder to establish future secure and trusting relationships.

It is not difficult to see potential overlaps with trauma responses more generally. In Chapter 6 we discussed how trauma and loss can be seen in terms of two different but related processes: one a dismissing attempt to cut off from the emotions of the loss and the other a continual preoccupation and inability to gain any emotional distance from the experience. So, initial responses as they become entrenched can become distorted, with excessive and continuing denial of the importance and impact of loss, minimisation and avoidance of all reminders of the loved one, amnesia and a gradual removal from life and other relationships. In contrast, for some, there may be a constant entanglement with the deceased with continuous and distressing intrusions, such as unpleasant and preoccupying thoughts, images and sensory experiences. Neither of these patterns is more or less effective, and we are not attempting to offer judgements. People cope in various and complex ways and it is likely that a combination of dismissing and preoccupied strategies is necessary. People may employ a dismissing strategy to be able to get on with their everyday lives and a secure or preoccupied one to help them remember aspects of the relationship, warm experiences, places they were together and so on, which helps to integrate and shape narratives that help to maintain the relationship. How people achieve this balance of strategies, the balance between them, when one predominates, and for how long, varies and is unique for each person.

Positive and transformative processes

It could be said that a process of adjustment and learning to live with loss can be seen to occur as the reduction in intensity of peak periods of distress slowly begins. Sleeping and appetite may improve slowly. As energy returns, new roles, new relationships and new behaviours can develop as part of a process of reorganisation of life and living in the aftermath of loss. Supporting and developing the capacity to learn from experience and to rework unhappy events into growth-promoting opportunities can be influenced by childhood and adult attachments but do not need to be constrained by them. An ANT framework can help create a context for exploring and illuminating both helpful and unhelpful tendencies towards interpersonal trust and security. For example, promoting narratives of healing and recovery and supporting pleasure in remembering in turn shape our capacity to look back and reflect etc. Thus, the capacity to make sense of our emotional experiences and those of others is key. For example, as a bereaved parent, we can experience a profound sense of loss for ourselves while, at the same time, we are still able to observe the grief of others such as a sibling, a partner or a grandparent. Thus, the capacity to comfort and support others, when we ourselves feel inconsolable, is at the heart of our ability to give spoken or narrative expression to grief and the enacted and embodied experiences of healing. These narratives may well be tentative, if not unvoiced at first, but repeated experience of reflection and accompanying action, with the support of others, helps the narrative threads of loss and life to re-emerge. This is where therapeutic support can be so crucial – in helping piece together fragments of memory, in gently challenging a tendency to dwell solely on remorse and regret, in normalising feelings of despair and protest, and in giving expression to difficult thoughts and feelings in a way that illuminates the process, makes it explicable, helps take advantage of good energy days and puts the experience within a culturally appropriate framework of the ebb and flow of life. At times, in the process of grief, some family members may struggle to continue with a sense of purpose in their lives, and so it is very helpful for people to have structure and routine imposed by work commitments, responsibilities to children and so on – but what we want to stress here is that, in articulating these reasons 'for going on', it not only validates a re-emerging sense of purpose, it also helps tell the story of recovery and healing. Murray Parkes (1996), in his pioneering study of widows found that, with hindsight, widows described this process as taking between two and five years. It is not difficult to see, therefore, how mental health practitioners and others, such as family members, may overlook or misinterpret the longer-term effects of bereavement and responses to loss in its many forms. In addition, we may overlook the impact on other family members as they resonate to a person's grief, and even the possibility of other family members experiencing a traumatic process through the other person's loss.

Bereavement, systemic therapy and attachment narratives

An ANT formulation

From an attachment perspective, illuminating the emotional experience of grief is governed by whether the bereaved person is more inclined to a preoccupied or to a dismissing approach to their experience. For the preoccupied person, helping them to structure their experiences, to develop a framework of meaning (perhaps using the stages of grief model), to regulate their emotional responses, to soothe themselves and to work in their semantic memory system to make cognitive sense of their memories, are likely to be helpful. For a person with a more dismissing style, creating a safe context for the exploration and expansion of emotional responses both for themselves and with others, that enables more direct communication of thoughts and feelings, is likely to be helpful, for example, by raising to consciousness the suppressed visual and sensory memories that are being blocked but may intrude unexpectedly.

This approach is predicated on the assumption that if grief is not enabled, with time, to be expressed in a straightforward way, however that might look for the person/s concerned, it will find expression in indirect ways. Such indirect expression can leave the person vulnerable to being misunderstood and unhelpfully labelled.

In the move towards remembering with pleasure, where the pain of sorrow is more often replaced with a smile or with joy, or sorrow and joy can be experienced in the family simultaneously, gratitude can play a part. In our view it is a higher emotional context marker for recovery following loss. Empirical research on gratitude is in its early stages, and there is not agreement on whether it is an emotional or a dispositional state, or perhaps both. However, early research suggests that much of the gratitude felt in a given situation might be determined by attributions regarding the value of the help given, how costly it was to provide and whether it was altruistically intended. It is speculated that people who feel more gratitude in their life may have better social relationships, with greater closeness in their connections and more reciprocity in their social support. This is based on the premise that, if we receive help with gratitude, we are more likely to respond in kind, creating mutual cycles of positive influence (Wood *et al.*, 2007).

In our therapeutic work with bereaved people, we notice that sorrow and gratitude can co-exist, that even in the most harrowing of moments, people can still speak of their gratitude for having known the loved and lost person, for their emotional and interpersonal legacy, such as helping them to become content with themselves – a process of liberation and actualisation. Bereaved family members value the time they spent together and what that meant, despite the acute sorrow of missing them all the time. Early research suggests that, overall, those who feel more gratitude are much more likely to have higher levels of happiness and lower levels of stress and depression (Watkins *et al.*, 2003; McCullough *et al.*, 2004). Importantly for us, gratitude seems to have the strongest links with mental health and life satisfaction than any other personality variable. And gratitude might be related to attachment, in that we need to be relatively 'free' to think about the loss and not just push it away to get anywhere near any sense of gratitude for what was, and the continuing legacy. For example, with a sustained dismissive response, and a deactivating tendency, the continuing bond with the deceased might not even emerge onto the relational and narrative map. A powerful emotional response of this nature in an influential family member could set the scene for what it is possible to share, illuminate, process and re-process within a family group. Recently we were asked to talk with a group of residential workers for people with intellectual disabilities, where three adult residents in the household had died with age-related illnesses. The request came after a long and protracted negotiation between the staff team and the manager and the local mental health services. The manager had thought it would be unhelpful for the staff to collectively share their grief and wanted staff to resume their duties without such an explicit recognition of their distress. As often happens in situations like this, the perspectives rapidly polarised and created another level of distress and anxiety. We were asked to consult, and we were not surprised to meet, an angered staff team and a somewhat defensive and distressed house manager. We met people separately at first, and then collectively. The outcome of the series of meetings was a commitment to a memorial service, to a dedicated park bench in the grounds and to putting more photographs of residents and staff around the home.

A broader issue, which runs through the other chapters in this book, is that attachment processes are not simply or predominantly personal or even family matters. Grief is proscribed by a variety of cultural norms, religious beliefs, rituals and ceremonies. Discourses about what it is appropriate to feel, how we should show our feelings, how long we should grieve for and so on shape our emotional and attachment processes. These ideas may clash with our basic attachment strategies, such that a dismissive or preoccupied response may be viewed by others as inappropriate, dysfunctional and so on. Likewise, for the bereaved person they may be confusing thoughts and communications from others about what they should be feeling. Hence, throughout the book we emphasise a multi-level formulation that recognises this complex interplay between individual, family and cultural levels.

ANT: creating a secure base

In the early months of grief, the bereaved person is more likely to 'walk with the dead'. This represents a profound phenomenological difference to those potentially supportive others, such as friends, family and colleagues, who walk with the living. We should not underestimate the loneliness, the sometimes intolerable sadness, and the wish for comfort and something or someone to take away the emotional pain. An important ingredient in fostering the therapeutic relationship can be an acknowledgement of both the uniqueness of the grief for that person but also a recognition of commonalities of the pain and distress that the person is feeling. Perhaps above all it can be helpful to emphasise that both the dismissing and the preoccupied patterns are important and that our role as therapists is not to make judgements about what is or is not appropriate. Perhaps by validating the potentially positive aspects of both patterns can help people to feel less compelled to 'get over it' or that they are cold and uncaring because they are not showing and feeling grief enough. This also connects with the 'dual-process' models of grief, which emphasise the need to attend to both these aspects of grief.

While offers of practical support are often welcomed in the early days of bereavement, they may not be needed subsequently. People ask, wishing to be helpful, if there is anything they can do, and often feeling helpless as they know they cannot bring the dead person back, and their availability and accessibility sometimes appears to evaporate. Often, others can be helped to appreciate that all they need to do is to be there – to listen if wished, and if not, to accept the process the bereaved person is in. Learning to tolerate and bear the emotional distress of a loved one is a key life skill and needs to be developed throughout life. Similarly, this capacity to tolerate others' extreme and sometimes sustained distress needs to be addressed regularly in training programmes for mental health practitioners, and in regular supervision and consultation. Attachment thinking highlights the importance of our beliefs in our own loveability and deservingness of others' care and attention, and our perception of others as emotionally accessible and available to us. This is where intervention can be at its most helpful. A well-managed therapeutic alliance has enormous healing potential (Bachelor and Horvath, 1999) both to illuminate the intersubjective nature of grief and loss and to provide stepping stones back to routine and a sense of purpose. This need not amount to disloyalty to the memory of the dead person, sometimes feared by bereaved people, and expressed as: if I am happy and spontaneously forget, does this mean that our love has become less important or has my loved-one assumed less importance? If therapeutic work is going to illuminate and expand such meanings and their associated feelings, a secure trusting relationship with the therapist is central.

ANT: exploring narratives and attachments within a systemic framework

> I hold it true, whate'er befall;
> I feel it, when I sorrow most;
> 'Tis better to have loved and lost
> Than never to have loved at all.
>   Alfred Tennyson (1850)
>   *In Memorium*:
>   *A. H. H. Prologue*

Exploring narratives and family processes

This involves an attempt to map the understanding, beliefs and explanation that people hold about loss and their experience of it. Sometimes discussion of what happened when other family members died, for example how people responded when their grandmother died and what was helpful to them, can illuminate ideas that people hold about what it is appropriate to feel or not feel, and how they should act.

Death is both an immensely personal experience but also one that is circumscribed by rituals, beliefs, religious principles, family traditions and so on and these may shape what people think is appropriate and also what they feel they can expect in terms of support from other family members, friends and so on. Related to this we also see that there are culturally shared ideas about, for example, the 'appropriate period of mourning' – How long is it appropriate to grieve for? What is too short (disrespectful) or too long (obsessed)? How long before it is legitimate to think about, or be attracted to, other potential partners? Left unstated and unexplored, these expectations can cause distress, confusion, self-blame and antagonism between family members. Perhaps a not uncommon pattern of relatives being in conflict over possession, wills and so on relates to disagreements and disapproval about whether people are seen to be acting appropriately or not.

In such discussions with families they can often identify the duality of grief – that is, acknowledging the loss and sorrow, but also that life can and does go on, and that may even have been the wish of the deceased person. The beliefs and stories they hold about the deceased person relate to what stories might develop about possibilities in their future lives. Beliefs and communication in families impact on successful adaptation following a bereavement. Death may be a taboo subject in the family, predicated on whether the family emotional style is more 'closed' than 'open' (Bowlby, 1980; Bretherton, 1995), and as such, rooted in emotionally avoidant relationships, or shame and uncertainty attendant on the death, or the manner of the death, such as suicide. In some senses, family members may experience their grief as disenfranchised, or as grief that may not be spoken about.

Beliefs may have been handed down through the generations that constrain openness and sharing of feelings, such as 'things must go on as before'; 'loss means chaos'; or 'we must do the right thing'. It may not be possible to challenge these beliefs, which may be more or less rigidly expressed as if they were family rules, for fear of causing hurt or risking rejection within the group. Intervention can provide the context for safe exploration of these family 'rules' around grief and mourning. For example: How did they originate? Do they have intergenerational significance? Who can challenge these rules? Who were they devised to protect? What would happen if they were challenged? What would the future look like for the family if the rule was changed in some way?

Resilience in family groups is influenced by the interaction of many factors, internal and external to the family group. The causes and circumstances of the death will affect family members' adjustment, and for children what they are told, and what opportunities are given subsequently to ask about what has happened, and what it will mean for the future. The patterns of relationships within the family prior to the loss will affect family relationships after the loss, particularly the quality of the relationship between the parents and between the parents and children.

Case example

We worked with a stepfamily, consisting of a mother and father, with two children from their relationship and two older children from the mother's first marriage. One of the younger children died suddenly, of a fast-moving disease process. Both parents blamed themselves for not realising that anything was wrong with their son, even though medical personnel had tried to reassure them that no signs would have been visible. Their sadness was imbued with the knowledge that their son would not have a future – they felt it was snatched from him unfairly and that they should have gone instead of him. Their grief began to affect their marriage. Their sense of comfort and trust in one another suffered as they found it harder to give and receive soothing and understanding, partly because they felt they did not deserve it under the circumstances. Previous difficulties in their relationship began to surface as recrimination at a time when they both felt vulnerable.

The therapeutic work concentrated on helping them reconnect as a couple, and stay connected, even though their style and approach to grieving caused them to be out of step with each other on occasion. This focus on their couple intimacy was interwoven with support for them as parents to work together in co-parenting their other children, who struggled to find meaning in recent events and mourned both the loss of their brother and the immediate loss of their parents' attention.

ANT: considering alternatives

We see from the discussion above that any attempt to challenge current beliefs and practices as a prelude to considering alternatives, needs to be grounded in a secure therapeutic base, where accessibility and responsiveness have been established or re-established following the loss.

As parents and lovers, when we love and our loved ones die, we do not stop loving them. It is how, in sorrowing, we can draw on our love and our memories to sustain us and help us endure the acute distress and long sadness of grief. As Caitlin Thomas, the widow of Dylan Thomas, wrote, 'you may get over the death, but you never get over the man' (*The Guardian*, 8 November, 2005). Preferred ways of coping may help and sustain people at these times, but encouragement may be needed to adapt and explore alternative ways of coping. The attachment concept of having a continuing bond with the deceased echoes the systemic notion of calling up the 'spirit' of ancestors and loved ones at times of emotional crisis, when it can be helpful to explore legacies as sources of support and emotional nourishment. For example: What would my grandmother have said or done if she knew I was despairing in the face of loss? What would my father have advised me if I was struggling to comfort my son over the death of his own father? Thinking about 'continuing bonds' in this way enables people to work, rework, and work again their responses to loss while developing a more balanced sense of their relationship with their loved one, such that other relationships in the future do not need to be precluded. Attachment thinking suggests that preferred attachment responses under conditions of emotional threat, that is, actual loss, and with feelings of helplessness, could predict the kind of relationship the living attempt to maintain with the dead. So, for example, a more anxious style might lead a bereaved spouse to feel preoccupied with living with the relationship as it is/was and this may lead to some unhelpful inflexibility in future responding and thinking. Or a more avoidant style might lead the bereaved spouse to minimise the emotional significance of the attachment, to try to push memories and feelings into the background. The ANT framework supports exploration of alternatives: alternative ways of thinking and feeling that can lead to the development of different narrative versions of the self-in-relationship.

Alongside this more direct form of emotional holding, there is an important process of indirect holding, provided by structure and routine in daily life.

Often, a bereaved person will speak of how unmotivated they feel to continue with their tasks of daily living. If the bereaved have responsibilities and care for others, for example in families, these duties provide routine and structure, a sort of external motivation, if you like, when it is hard to motivate oneself to keep going. Similarly, employment provides this kind of structure, with schedules, duties and colleagues with whom to interact. However, at times, intervention may most helpfully take the form of helping the bereaved person put structure back into their lives, which, although it may not provide meaning and purpose as such, initially, it does provide a form of emotional containment that allows a person to continue with their life.

Friends and colleagues can be advised to be straightforward with the bereaved person, checking how they would prefer to manage the bereavement process, for example talking about the dead person, or asking them how they are feeling, rather than avoiding both topics for fear of causing more upset. Avoidance on the part of others, no matter how well meaning, can leave bereaved people feeling as though they represent death, always evoking others' atavistic fears.

ANT: the future – continuing and consolidating

Part of the work with family members may also involve a discussion of how they will continue the relationship with the deceased. For example, some people might hold a belief that one gets over the grief, and that's it!, or that the sadness will continue but also a new life will run side by side. These beliefs may also in part mirror how the relationship is continued with the therapist, for example, whether the work ends, or there is a period of increasing the length of time between meetings, or whether reviews and follow-up meetings are scheduled for the future.

Grief needs to be understood in context. In writing this chapter, we reflected on the fundamental inadequacy of language to convey the variety of experiences described as love and grief. Although language has power to help illuminate and expand understanding, and conversation both supports and *is* lived experience, it cannot capture the profound nature of grief. For example, Neimeyer (2006) writes that the widely held assumption that 'letting go' is required as part of grief is being challenged by his recent work. His view is that the work of grief is to foster a constructive and continuing bond with the dead person. This is another example of how culturally shared assumptions, in part emanating from popular psychology, shape what we think it is appropriate to feel and how our attachments should change. Arguably, this concept of letting go in attachment theory terms belongs to an essentially dismissive discourse that underpins much of 'scientific' thinking in psychology, which has sought to be a rational as opposed to a passionate 'discipline'.

Neimeyer's constructivist view is somewhat similar to our attachment-oriented view, in that we are both arguing for an emphasis on fostering constructive, continuing bonds through remembering good times, creating and continuing an internal dialogue with our loved ones, thinking of them regularly, and imagining their reactions and responses to significant daily events. Empowerment is thought to come from fully experiencing the process of grief – so, much like trauma, the only way out is through.

Chapter 8

Problems of addiction

Alcohol dependency and eating distress

Working with dependence on alcohol

'I drink to forget. Drink anaesthetises me – it takes away the emotional pain. You can trust the bottle – it is always there. When the going gets tough – I reach for the bottle. . . .' And so it goes on. . . .

'Drowning our sorrows' is a common phrase and loaded with meanings as a Western and European cultural discourse. The circumstances under which we turn to alcohol or other activities for comfort and solace rather than depending on our loved ones to provide emotional support is the focus of this chapter. First we will consider problems with alcohol and then eating disorders.

There are, of course, many reasons why people drink alcohol – for pleasure, for courage, to help manage stress and social anxiety, to avoid difficult responsibilities, lack of parental supervision as a child, or perhaps it is part of expected social and peer group behaviour. However, the reasons why we start drinking alcohol regularly, may not be the reasons why we continue to drink. Where we can say that an emotional dependence on alcohol takes precedence over other people, and when the problem drinker or their partner and other family members want to change the quality of their lived emotional experience, we shall explore here how an integration of attachment thinking and systemic practice can both address and help bridge issues of trust and intimacy as a means of forging new emotional connections.

Attachment theory does not pathologise emotional dependency – rather the opposite. It asserts that we all need positive connections to other people to ensure our continued well-being across the life span. So what happens when alcohol is a more trusted companion than other people? When drinking or other substance misuse is the preferred way of coping with unmanageable and unbearable feelings? How does this come to pass? And how can we work in an emotion-focused way, when people may be saying that they neither trust human connection nor wish to seek it. Attachment thinking posits that our wish for connection is still there, even it if is buried, metaphorically speaking, or in some senses transformed as a result of earlier interpersonally neglectful, unsupportive or abusive experiences. Problem drinking can show up in therapeutic work in all mental health services. While in some cases it may be advisable to make a referral to specialist addiction services, we write this chapter to both aid formulation and intervention when working with individuals, couples and families across a range of mental health services.

Clearly, an initial assessment needs to enquire around current substance use and the extent of use, in whatever setting in which we work. If alcohol use is reported, we need to understand how much, how often, and when; how it is paid for, and what purpose it might serve. An understanding of how alcohol is used as a way of coping opens the way for discussion about other ways of meeting the person's needs and the needs of others. It is never acceptable to hold a therapeutic meeting while someone is under the influence of alcohol, as they may well say things they would not when sober and make themselves vulnerable in ways for which they are unprepared. But a discussion around why they attended under the influence helps planning for future work, the communicative intent of such behaviour, and a recognition that while alcohol use may have been the solution, it no longer works and causes problems for the people they love as well. In our experience, we can offer ongoing couples and family work while someone is engaged in active substance abuse treatment, as long as they have periods of sobriety, and if they cannot yet put their feelings and needs into words, we can always offer consultation and support to their family members.

The multiple costs of drinking

The UK Department of Health estimates the prevalence of alcohol dependence as 4.7 per cent of the adult population, with about 27 per cent of men drinking more than 21 units of alcohol per week, and about 14 per cent of women drinking more than 14 units per week (DH, 1999). The UK Office for National Statistics estimates that 21 per cent of men and 8 per cent of women regularly drink twice the recommended limits. Heavy drinking is associated with physical health problems, vulnerability to depression, anxiety, suicide, difficulties at work, financial problems, unemployment, public disorder and violence in relationships, among other factors (Orford and Harwin, 1982). The effects of problem drinking on family life, and of parental drinking on children's well-being, have been documented to include:

- disruption to family routines, rituals and celebrations;
- changes and adaptations in family members' roles;
- changes in opportunities for and styles of communication; and
- an impact on social life and finances (Velleman, 1992; Vetere and Henley, 2001).

These effects have profound implications for family members' lived emotional experiences and intimate relating, and form both the context and the vehicle for children's learning about safety and dependency in relationships. For example: Do children always know if they will be collected safely from school? Can they bring their friends home? What can be talked about when a parent is drunk or afterwards when they are sober? What do they learn about managing emotional arousal? How do they understand processes of shame and shaming in the wider family and community? Are family and cultural rituals spoiled by alcohol?

When working with people with drinking problems in either adult mental health or community alcohol services, the focus of the preferred therapeutic intervention may inadvertently neglect parental issues and responsibilities around the emotional care of children even though child protection issues are addressed. Cognitive behavioural approaches and motivational interviewing can be adapted to incorporate a stronger emotion focus, for example by paying attention to whether the misuse is stable, or chaotic, with swings between states of intoxication and periods of withdrawal and the impact on emotional regulation, the accessibility of the parent for the child, and the impact on the child's emotional safety and learning about emotional dependency and consistency in relationships. If alcohol use is accompanied by psychological disorder, such as depression and anxiety, tracking the impact on the parent's emotional state and judgements around the child can helpfully inform child protection decision making.

Case example

Susan was a 30-year-old white British woman, trying to look after her five children. Each child had a different father and, at times, each father would have lived in the household, and held duties and responsibilities as a stepfather to the other children. The social worker had been trying to support Susan as a mother, but the team was very concerned that the children were neglected, and were witnesses to violence against their mother from the fathers. The fathers were in many respects invisible within the professional system, and never held to account for their violence to Susan, for the impact on the children of witnessing the violence or for not noticing and taking action around the cumulative effects of neglect on the children's well-being. Susan herself was held accountable within the professional system for the impact of emotional abuse on her children's functioning and development. Eventually the children were removed from Susan's care and placed with substitute families. Susan appeared to use alcohol to help herself cope with the stress and distress of frequent physical assaults, which in turn led to more violence against her. At the time we met Susan, she was overwhelmed with fear and anxiety and, not surprisingly, seemed unable to think straight. She appeared unable to understand the needs of her children with any degree of consistency, she could not manage her money or food, and she was unable to sleep or wake regularly with her children. She said she felt persecuted and paradoxically only felt safe in the house, the scene of many assaults on her. We felt that her narratives about her ability to cope with her drinking indicated a distortion consistent with her dismissive and avoidant attachment strategy that had developed during her abusive childhood and in her dangerous and unsafe adult intimate relationships. She had to face the fact that she could not look after her children and acknowledge that she had held an inflated and unrealistic belief that she could control her alcohol use on her own.

Susan herself had been raised in a children's home, following earlier adverse experiences in her family of origin. She had been separated from her siblings and grew up without knowing them. In an attempt to rework these experiences, she had developed a corrective script in which she promised herself that she would instil in her children the wish to always be close and supportive of one another. She understood the lifelong importance of sibling relationships, and in that she had succeeded well.

We worked with Susan over two years to help her recover herself, and her sense of self-worth, and to remain abstinent from alcohol. We developed a series of collaborative questions with Susan that promoted her competence, assertiveness, self-esteem and authoritative parenting. The questions were designed to both support and challenge her, in unpicking her view of herself as a failure and in reworking her sense of herself as a competent woman. Examples include:

- emphasising her right to safety;
- acknowledging her need for change and challenging her feelings of failure by enquiring how she had managed to achieve such a sense of family for her sons, and their consequent feelings of brotherhood;
- asking her about her relationships with her children and what she wanted for them in the future;

- emphasising and supporting her right to safety in close relationships;
- encouraging her to talk about relational aspects of herself, as opposed to her overwhelming sense of individual responsibility;
- asking her to talk legitimately about her relationships with her partners, how these relationships developed and what decisions were made together;
- our refusing to accept the invisibility of her partners and expecting them to have shown responsibility towards her and her sons;
- helping her differentiate between her ideas and emotions about being both a victim and a survivor; and
- stressing the importance of her cooperation and her developing competence in working with social services and the different carers of her children (Cooper and Vetere, 2005).

Susan maintained strong connections with her children, and although no longer their primary carer, developed good working relationships with their carers and, as the children got older, was able to take a more prominent role in their lives. Susan subsequently formed an intimate relationship with a man who treated her well and who respected her resilience and strength.

Links between alcohol use and physical aggression

In Chapter 4 we discussed how to adapt and make safe an emotion-focused approach when working therapeutically with couples who have agreed to a no-violence contract in the aftermath of violent assault. Here we review briefly the research on the links between alcohol use and physical aggression in intimate partner relationships. Although there are many reasons why physical aggression may be used against a partner, the use of alcohol at the time of an assault more strongly implicates the causal role of alcohol. In community samples, it has been found that binge drinking is more associated with physical aggression against a partner, rather than the absolute volume of alcohol consumed in a week or month. The British Crime Survey (1996, 2000) reported that 30 per cent of violent crime was domestic assault, and within one third of all reported incidents, alcohol use was involved. The Children In Need Census conducted in Cheshire, UK, found that in 41 per cent of all social services department cases, domestic violence was a factor (DCFS and DIUS, 2006). The children were twice as likely to experience mental health problems themselves and to live in households where their parents/carers struggled with mental health problems. Of particular note here was the finding that the children were also five times more likely to live in households where psycho-active substances were misused.

Thus, a careful risk assessment that enquires around instances of violent behaviour and explores safety, of self and others, should be at the centre of all mental health practice, when working with children, adolescents and adults. (See Cooper and Vetere (2005) for a detailed discussion of how to establish a platform for safe mental health practice when working with individuals, couples and families where violence is of concern.)

Family involvement in treatment

'Human hibernation' is a metaphor that captures the sense of retreat and emotional disengagement from others that can occur when a family member develops over time a strong psychological dependence on alcohol. Other family members are key. In some senses they may have become part of the problem, or the problem-determined system, but they are most helpfully seen as part of the solution. Outcome research shows that family members can be crucial, for example in motivating the person with the drinking problem into alcohol treatment programmes, that family-involved treatments are margin-ally more effective than individual treatment and that moderate benefits are found when families are involved in relapse prevention (Edwards and Steinglass, 1995). Three factors may mediate these treatment effects:

- the gender of the person who has the drinking problem – most of the research has been conducted with men as the focus, and so for this rea-son, we shall consider here the impact of problem drinking for women and their relationships also;
- the family members' emotional investment in their relationships – here we see the significance of emotional connection and the wish for connec-tion as both the context for support and the vehicle for change; and
- the drinking partner's perception of support from the non-drinking partner for abstinence from alcohol as a goal – this echoes the research on the importance of social support networks for continued well-being across the life span, and that it is the *perception* of relationships as sup-portive that is crucial, even though relationships may not actually be supportive (Brown and Harris, 1989).

Engagement

We have worked in a variety of mental health service settings, in the National Health Service (NHS), social services, voluntary and private sector, but alco-hol treatment services are unique in our experience in needing to provide a prolonged period for engagement in treatment. There are many reasons for this, not least the reliance on alcohol for comfort and soothing, and the regulation of emotional arousal. In asking someone to engage with treatment services, and with a particular keyworker, we are asking them to take risks – to risk trusting others. And as soon as we ask people to take risks, they remember all the reasons why they should not! In dynamic terms, the primary relationship or attachment is with alcohol. So, forming a working alliance with an alcohol keyworker is often a crucial first step in reconnecting to people, and the necessary bridge for exploring a referral for systemic couples and family work (Vetere and Henley, 2001).

Systemic consultation provides a less emotionally arousing context for a tentative exploration around engagement, for both the drinker and their family members, who often approach treatment with the view that the drinker is the problem, or that once abstinence is achieved, family life will resume as normal. In our experience, stopping the drinking often takes a couple to the edge, where they decide whether to stay together and develop a more secure relationship, or to part. Whatever their decision, we work with them, to create a more emotionally secure and satisfying bond, or to help them understand why their relationship did not last, with an eye on future relationships, and/or to help them achieve cooperative parenting post separation.

Partners and relatives can be helpful in confronting the drinker and their drinking, but if engagement with couples and family work is to be successful, they too need to be able to reflect on the adaptations and adjustments they have made, both while drinking was an issue, and with drinking as a legacy. For example, during drinking, the non-drinking partner may have become a skilled detective, hunting down hidden alcohol in the house and garden, pouring it down the sink, and perhaps shaming the drinker around their lack of control, the associated adverse reflection on the family in the community and so on. The non-drinking partner may report strong feelings of fear at any suggestion that the drinker might resume drinking, say during a social invitation where alcohol is served, many months, even years, after drinking has stopped. Such fear may be fear of rejection and abandonment often felt and reported when the partner is emotionally unavailable when inebriated. The fear might underlie the anger and indignation expressed so rapidly at the suggestion the drinker might relapse. If addiction is seen as a pattern of behaviour to be understood and explored, it is helpful to enquire around the times they have turned to alcohol, or wanted to, and did not. For example, is it used as a way of withdrawing when they feel criticised, emotionally overwhelmed, or a disappointment to their partner? Equally complex are patterns between couples where moderate drinking facilitates positive emotional expression and feelings of affection and sexuality, desired by both, but complicated by further drinking, which then spoils the feelings of closeness, and perhaps is intended to regulate and manage an emotional distance that begins to feel too close and overwhelming, as may happen with more fearful patterns of attachment relating.

Equally dangerous are patterns where the non-drinking partner drinks alongside the drinker in an attempt to pace and try to control the amount of alcohol consumed. However these patterns may evolve, they are often underpinned by strong attachment emotions and wishes, which may be couched within a sense of moral entitlement to criticise and try to control the behaviour of the drinking partner. A sense of moral entitlement may make it harder for the non-drinking partner to engage in a reflective manner on their mutual adjustments as a couple, to explore underlying attachment fears and anxieties and to explore the adaptations needed to help them live with the impact of drinking on their relationship and their style of emotional communication.

Consultation creates opportunities to 'externalise' the problem with drink, to explore and validate family members' resources, solutions and wishes, to reframe attempts to control drinking as attempts to problem solve and give credit to people for trying, and to explore available treatment approaches. We find that family members will often see problem drinking as both irresponsible behaviour and an illness, which may or may not be controllable. Using consultation as a context to slowly and carefully track the effects of drinking on relationships and the impact of styles and patterns of relating, both historically and currently, on drinking, creates an opportunity to discuss these patterns of behaviour and views of drinking in such a way that helps family members not feel blamed for 'causing' the drinking. This paves the way for family members to begin to talk about how they have become caught up in the drinking and how their responses, although recognised to be unhelpful, are often repeated again and again as they cannot see alternatives.

Consultation also allows opportunities to explore the implications of engaging in couple and family work. We as therapists ask questions like: Whose idea was it to talk with us? Who most welcomed/most feared the idea? How did they decide to meet us? What have they noticed since deciding to come and meet with us? What are they hoping for from the meeting? How will they decide to meet with us again? Social attraction theory (Zajonc, 1968) suggests that the development of a therapeutic alliance is facilitated by proximity, that is, the more we see of a person, the more our positive attitudes towards them will be enhanced. This repeated and gentle exposure creates the context in which we can start to agree on goals and the means of achieving them. This develops the intersubjective experience of empathy, where we can show that we will try to understand their feelings and their distress, by standing in their shoes as best we can.

Thus, we do not pursue a therapeutic contract, rather we offer systemic consultation and provide multiple opportunities for people to meet with us before taking the risk of committing to an emotionally engaging and arousing therapeutic experience with us. Therapy can be threatening as we focus on the less than optimum relationships within the family, and while we support and encourage resilience and resourcefulness and the wish for change, we need to be mindful of the implicit tensions within this dilemma. The therapeutic triangle created between ourselves as systemic therapists, the couple and/or family members and the alcohol keyworker is crucial for creating a sense of safety so that people can begin to take emotional risks again, and challenge often deeply embedded ideas about themselves as unloveable or unworthy of others' comfort and care, and/or ideas about others as unresponsive, unavailable and ultimately untrustworthy. The emotional leap involved in moving from a primary relationship with alcohol to working with couple and family issues is so great that the drinker needs to have had some success with abstinence in order to cope with the demands of the transition. The alcohol keyworker acts as our 'stable third', helping to manage and understand the anxiety and fear evoked by the suggestion that we move from consultation to therapy.

Failed attempts at engagement

If we accept the central role of the therapeutic alliance in the change process, then failed attempts at engagement may contribute to early termination of therapeutic work. It would seem that there is more variation in outcome between therapists using the same therapeutic approach, than across therapy outcomes in different treatment modalities (Duncan and Miller, 2000). This might suggest that it is more important who the therapist is, and the relational fit between the client/s and the therapist, than which approach is used. Research in the alcohol treatment field on the development of the therapeutic alliance suggests that the communication of subtle and complementary forms of hostility and/or attempts at control may be linked to poor outcome or a weaker/less committed therapy alliance. Motivational interviewing tries to engage the drinker in a collaborative attempt to identify the reasons for change in a way that avoids direct and unhelpful confrontation (Miller and Rollnick, 1991).

We have discussed elsewhere in this book the role of consultation and supervision for therapists when working in an emotion-focused way, not only as a good practice requirement, but also as a prerequisite for exploring and illuminating our own emotional responsiveness when faced with criticism, hostility and subtle threats to our self-esteem. For our clients, defensiveness and emotional avoidance may be well rehearsed ways of protecting themselves when they are afraid, for example when they are afraid of others' potential to reject them, to find them wanting, to be disappointed in them and so forth. The absence of a negative interpersonal process in therapy is not sufficient for therapeutic change, but it would seem that the presence of low levels of negative therapist behaviour may be sufficient to prevent change. Clients report lower levels of therapeutic hope and commitment to engagement when they perceive their therapist to be critical of them, not interested in them, and unwilling to provide information. Trauma theory suggests that fear slows down information processing, and our capacity to process emotionally laden material (Meichenbaum, 1994). Hence, differences in therapist effectiveness may be linked to our capacity to maintain a facilitative stance when confronted with defensiveness and/or hostility from the person with the drinking problem and/or their family members, such that we can slowly encourage people to walk around in their own emotional responses, expanding their options and reflecting on the construction of emotional engagement moment to moment. Similarly, though, fear can slow down therapists' capacity to be helpful, and if we emotionally resonate with our client's interpersonal fears we may become unhelpfully aroused, and thus less facilitative as a result.

We as therapists work in pairs, and use in-room consultation as the vehicle for reflective practice (Vetere and Henley, 2001). Sometimes we notice that it is helpful for the in-room consultant to raise challenging issues, or comment helpfully on the developing therapy process in a way that protects and preserves the emergent therapeutic alliance. This then allows the lead therapist and client/s to comment from the observer position themselves, such that if an idea is raised too soon, the pacing can be adjusted accordingly. Group analytic theory suggests that mirroring processes may occur in families, with family members acting as distorting mirrors, or harsh mirrors (Pines, 1982). Reflecting processes may offer a kinder or less distorting mirror that may make it easier for family members to express and listen to previously unexpressed thoughts and feelings.

We find an example of a failed attempt at engagement in our work with Kate and Bob, a couple in their mid-sixties who were retired. Bob had held a high-ranking management position for much of his paid working life, and had looked forward to his retirement as a time to travel and enjoy his family and his grandchildren. Kate had been a home maker for most of her working life, raising their three children. In her fifties she took up paid employment as a librarian, and said that she discovered feminism as a result. She told us that she wanted to engage Bob in a discussion around power and control in their relationship, but that he did not wish to have this conversation. Kate had been drinking alcohol for much of her adult life. What had started as social drinking had escalated to a dependence that left her inebriated for days at a time, and had reached the point where her three grown-up children and their partners had told her she was no longer fit to be around their children/her grandchildren. It was this ultimatum from her children that had prompted Kate to seek out the community alcohol service. With the support of her alcohol keyworker, she sought a referral to the family therapy team for couples work. Bob told us he was attending only to help Kate sort out her alcohol problems. We offered them four consultation sessions, to include a review. Kate told us that she wished to engage Bob in a discussion around their relationship and how they might work to improve it. Bob described himself as a jovial, approachable and friendly person, much liked socially, while he described Kate as a loner, with few friends. It was interesting for us to note that we warmed to Kate and found Bob to be the more emotionally dismissive in his style of communicating. A few minutes before the start of our third consultation meeting, the lead therapist (AV) was called away on a family crisis. The in-room consultant decided, with AV's agreement, to offer Kate and Bob the consultation meeting, if they so wished, as it was too late to cancel the meeting. The meeting appeared to go well. At the start of the fourth meeting, before we had settled in our seats, Kate announced that she found the in-room consultant to be a much better therapist than AV. It may well be that this was the case, but we formulated this in attachment terms. Possibly we had underestimated the strength of Kate's bond with AV and her feeling of disappointment to be placed second after AV's family, that is, that AV had left her place of work to attend to her own family, thus reinforcing Kate's sense that others cannot be trusted and will always let her down and abandon her, and in this case it seemed that Kate felt a keen sense of rejection.

Kate told us during this meeting that she had decided not to continue with any further meetings, and withdrew completely from the alcohol service. She promised to write us a letter. Subsequently, she explained that it was too painful for her to attend meetings with Bob, that our approach raised her hopes that she and Bob might be able to work on their relationship together, only to find that he was not available and emotionally accessible to her. She could not afford to give us the time to work together to see if her hopes had a chance of being realised.

Communication and relationship issues

A weave of attachment thinking and systemic therapy provides a framework for exploring the intersect between longstanding patterns of drinking and patterns in communication, in relationships, and over time, in the context of an intergenerational understanding of family culture, particularly around attitudes to alcohol use (Vetere and Henley, 2001). Replicative and corrective scripts across the generations around alcohol use and the impact of long-term drinking are contextualised by social and religious attitudes to drinking, which in turn form part of a community response.

Relationships and relationship-making skills may have deteriorated because of the way a drinker behaves in order to maintain a supply of alcohol. When a drinker becomes preoccupied by alcohol and the need to obtain alcohol, everything else risks becoming secondary to this need. Telling lies to hide the whereabouts of alcohol, or to deny drinking, may have become common-place. Systemic therapy is directed towards helping family members 'talk straight' and communicate clearly and effectively about their needs, actions, wishes and fears. Rules around what it is possible to say, and when and how it is said, may have been established during times of drinking, and times of abstinence. The exploration of communication, and any differences in behaviour under conditions of drinking and abstinence, need to be understood and illuminated. For example, a wife's refusal to talk with her husband at all when he is drinking, or a husband's wish for emotional closeness through sex when drinking and his avoidance of intimacy during sobriety may confuse, trouble and preoccupy his partner, leading to a cycle of critical pursuit and emotional withdrawal. Social penetration theory suggests that we hold a multi-layered sense of self, in which we choose to show others aspects of ourselves that vary from the commonplace and easily known and exposed, to the more deeply felt and often hidden fears, hurts and wishes that we hold (Taylor and Altman, 1987). This sense of vulnerability may be concealed from ourselves, and from others, by using drinking as a coping strategy, and the long-term effects for the couple may be to restrict dramatically what it is safe to talk about. When we meet couples and families, where drinking and the response to drinking has organised family interaction over time, and sometimes in intergenerational patterns of behaviour, we carefully, and with constant checking, and explaining why we are asking, explore the layered sense of what it is possible to know, to speak about and to reveal, in an interactional context, which in itself also creates the possibility for new descriptions, definitions of self and others, and the accompanying felt experience. The de-escalation of negative interaction patterns and support for what is going well creates a sense of trust and hopefulness that change is possible, and precedes the development and strengthening of more positive and bonding interactional exchanges.

Systemic thinking understands the emotion of shame to be both a noun and a verb – to be a description of the whole person, and as something we do to people in families and communities. Shame is a many-layered emotional experience that conveys information about a person's status and standing in the family and community. It is both exacerbated and relieved within our close and significant relationships. The non-drinking partner may well know when their partner is not drinking, but because they find it hard to trust that they will not drink again, this too can impede the development of openness and honesty in their communication. For example, if the drinking partner has a tendency to hide alcohol around the house, or to try to conceal their drinking, we work hard to help them be open about their intentions and behaviour, as a basis for rebuilding trust in what is said. Systemic reflecting processes can be very helpful in addressing these sensitive process issues in a non-blaming way.

In our work with couples and families, where problem drinking is our focus, we rarely see intimate relationships that can be described as predominantly providing security of attachment, and rarely do we see couple relationships that can be described in systemic terms as reciprocal (Bateson, 1972; Vetere and Dallos, 2003). Rather, we tend to see relationships characterised by overt complementary patterns, with covert patterns of symmetrical escalation, or frankly symmetrical relationships, where partners are in competition for power and influence, expressed, for example, as who gets the last word, or who knows best, or whose description of reality prevails.

When the woman partner/mother is the one with the drinking problem, we sometimes find that her early attempts to assert her wishes, needs and intentions are experienced as aggressive by other family members. This in turn is sometimes used against her in ways that serve to reinforce her sense of shame as being a 'bad mother/wife', and that continue a pattern of blame and counter-blame. Asking people to take emotional and interpersonal risks is fraught, but therapy can create a safe-enough context for people to take these risks, going beyond their known and accepted parameters of responding, to step outside constraining patterns and to forge new experiences together, often recapturing what they once had, or knew they always wanted. We often open up these conversations by exploring the future as one where drinking might continue and drinking might not continue. A solution-focused approach, taken tentatively, can encourage people to take a step back to reflect on their view of drinking as organising family life (Miller and Berg, 1995). Talking to people in role sometimes helps to reduce defensiveness, and connects them to their strong positive wishes for their children's future well-being. Questions can include: As a mother/father, what do you hope for your children in five years' time? What do you want your children to learn from you about self-soothing and seeking comfort safely? What do you think you might be teaching your children about how to manage themselves in intimate relationships? We find that when the woman can become more assertive around her own wishes and needs and more clearly asks for what she wants from others, the man agrees to work towards a more reciprocal relationship that offers both partners a different sense of felt security. Most of our experience has been in working with opposite-sex partners, yet we find these patterns similarly inform our thinking when working with same-sex couples, although we try to contextualise their relationship issues within a larger frame of openness or secrecy, depending on their relative positions within their kin and community networks.

Systemic attachment-informed work can make a contribution to the management of relapse by offering support and encouragement in the face of disappointment, slowing down rapid responsiveness and helping to de-escalate unhelpful emotional arousal, while thoughtfully considering the impact of relapse on family members and their relationships. Other methods of addressing and coping with sources of stress and unhappiness are not always easily developed. We seek to help promote a range of adaptive responses and to reduce reliance on alcohol as the primary attachment in the context of more positive bonding exchanges between family members. We support what is going well, help to identify and expand resilient responses and reframe attempts to cope with unbearable emotion as just that – attempts to cope.

Case example

Mark and Sheila illustrate how alcohol can be used as a means of coping with relationship dissatisfaction and distress, and how alternative, more constructive ways of coping can be developed, by rebuilding a sense of trust in one's own worth and in others to be accessible and supportive. Mark and Sheila have been married over 30 years. They have three grown-up children, one of whom lives at home while attending a local college. Sheila has worked in the home, looking after the children, and Mark has a job in a company that requires him to entertain other staff and colleagues from other companies. In some sense we might describe Sheila as a corporate wife, in that decisions about where the family live and the pressure on her to entertain Mark's colleagues and attend social functions have been visibly present in her life (Carter and McGoldrick, 1988). Both Mark and Sheila described themselves as heavy social drinkers in the early stages of their marriage. While Mark reduced his drinking as the years went by, Sheila increased hers. Sheila told us that she responded to the pressure to attend Mark's social functions by drinking too much, which resulted in strong feelings of embarrassment for both of them, and much recrimination between them. Despite this, Mark never gave up his wish 'to have his wife by his side'. Sheila's drinking increased to the point where she was rarely sober. Mark tried with desperation to control his wife's drinking. Sheila told us how she had always felt that Mark treated her as a child. Mark struggled to understand this, telling her he had always tried to involve her in family decision making.

Sheila had been sexually abused as a young girl by her stepfather on a number of occasions. She said that the abuse stopped when she threatened to tell her mother. She has never told her mother. She told Mark when they met and married, and she gave him credit for trying to be sensitive and understanding about the effects on her, but she said she never wanted nor enjoyed sex. Prior to meeting them as a couple, Sheila had been working with an alcohol keyworker for about five years, during which time she had managed to stay sober for periods of about three months at a time, before resuming drinking again, much to their disappointment. It was hard for Sheila to take credit for her periods of sobriety because she felt that her 'relapse' was a sign of weakness and showed a lack of self-control. Thus, we see how popular constructions of drinking can feed back into a person's view of themselves and inform their judgements about how others might see them. During these periods of sobriety, Mark observed that Sheila was warm and affectionate towards him, but when she resumed drinking, he found her distant and unresponsive. He said that he stayed hopeful during periods of drinking by comforting himself with the knowledge that when she stopped, she would be warm and close with him again. But his desperation showed in his attempts to control her drinking, by watching her constantly, scouring the house for drink and disposing of alcohol. These actions both infuriated and suffocated Sheila. They both recognised these patterns of power and control and worked hard to illuminate and understand the relational and emotional consequences of drinking and living with imbalances of power and control.

The couple's therapy addressed the following issues:

- Mark's attempts to control Sheila's drinking;
- Sheila's wish to take personal responsibility for her needs and her behaviour;
- Mark's wish for affection and physical intimacy, and acknowledging the impact of his possessiveness and his felt insecurity in their relationship;
- the impact of sexual abuse, secrecy and shame on Sheila's sense of her own worth, and her entitlement to care and comfort;
- financial decision making at home;
- developing their commitment to clear and straightforward communication about their wishes and hopes for their relationship, and on occasion with their adult children, and the impact of Sheila's drinking on them and their relationship with their parents;
- helping the couple develop more satisfying and bonding interactions, in the context of a developing and shared narrative of how they both contributed to healing in their relationship. The healing narrative included shared elements of emotional vulnerability that had been acknowledged, listened to and deeply understood, each of the other; and of how they had both worked hard to develop the capacity to tolerate each other's distress and to support each other's efforts and achievements in reaching out and taking emotional risks – this led to the beginning of a new sense of trust and felt security that enabled more satisfying and increasingly emotionally intimate encounters between them.

Life-cycle transitions and the impact of life events may help us explain the turn to drink in the first place, and the subsequent reaching out for help, albeit often provoked by an ultimatum from a family member in a crisis. We saw in the example above, with Kate and Bob, how their joint retirement triggered a different level of concern around her drinking. His wish to spend their retirement with their grandchildren had been thwarted by his own children's refusal to have their children see their grandmother drunk, or risk leaving them in their care. Living at home full time meant he could no longer ignore the extent of her reliance on alcohol, and for Kate, she could not so easily escape her dissatisfactions with their relationship. Careful exploration of the interaction between life-cycle demands and tasks, the impact of life events and the crisis around drinking provided an opportunity for all of us to reflect on how family life had been organised around the drinker and the drinking. These moments also constituted a challenge to their preferred attachment strategies in their relationship with each other, so that having to spend more time together created the crisis of whether to become closer or end their relationship.

Walking on egg shells, is how some family members describe the felt experience of living in an intimate problem-determined system (Anderson *et al.*, 1986). Behaviours designed to protect others from the effects of drinking, or to minimise or deny the effects of drinking, both inside and outside the family, or to ostracise the drinker, may have become habitual over time. Thus, the crisis around drinking offers an opportunity to track and unpack these problem-determined patterns, in a non-blaming way, by supporting good intentions, and reframing aspects of family members' motivations and behaviour as attempts to protect and cope. Within the ANT framework we help elaborate their narratives by employing Byng-Hall's (1995) idea of corrective and generative scripts and by drawing out the positive intentions underlying their narrative accounts of themselves and their relationships. In these moments when feelings of shame may be running high, we often find it helpful to recruit supportive ideas and feelings from the family's immediate culture, from current positive relationships and from positive relationships in the past, to support the wish for change.

Concluding remarks

In summary, we suggest that therapeutic progress is more likely to occur if (a) the non-drinking partner can reconnect positively and with a growing sense of trust to other people, and lose their primary attachment to alcohol; and (b) if the non-drinking partner can give up their belief – the dominant narrative – that happiness will be attained as soon as their partner ceases to drink, and embraces the idea, however tentatively at first, that they too need to make changes. Attachment theory informs the direction of therapeutic change from a de-escalation of negative and hostile exchanges, which only serve to promote attachment insecurity, towards an expansion of more positive and bonding interactions, which help re-establish trust and safety of emotional expression. Helping couples and family members create new narratives of how they pulled together to heal their relationships, gives all the credit where it is due!

Drinking comes between couples. Sometimes with abstinence achieved, they decide to part. Our task is to help them do so safely, and if they have children, to be mindful of the continuous impact on their children. Sometimes the drinking partner resumes drinking after a prolonged period of abstinence, or never really manages to control their drinking, and family separation is almost inevitable. In the face of disappointment, our commitment to attachment-based thinking means that we always carry hope that change is possible, in the belief that we all hold a wish for connection, no matter how estranged we may feel at times, and no matter that we may not quite know what felt security could look like.

Eating distress and addictions

Eating disorders may seem in some ways to be radically different from problems with alcohol. However, there are some immediate similarities. Both involve issues to do with taking in substances to the body. Both involve a considerable sense of loss of control or being taken over by the problem. Throughout this book the point has been made that central to attachment theory is the question of how we manage, coordinate and control our feelings. Central to this is how we comfort others and ourselves – what have learnt from how this was done for us, which we have internalised to help us to look after and comfort ourself. As infants our parents help us with this process to a very great extent, but this gradually changes such that we need eventually to be able to do it for ourselves. Mikulincer and Shaver (2007) point out that we learn this emotional self-control through various processes that involve observation of our parents with us and also how we see them managing their own feelings. We internalise, for example, both how they talk to themselves but also how they talk with us.

In attachment theory the fundamental difference is between strategies where, on the one hand, we have learnt that we cannot and should not turn to others when we need comfort – we should predominantly if not solely look to ourselves at points of crisis, anxiety, fear, loss and the various other forms of emotional pain – and where, on the other hand, we have learnt that it is not our responsibility to assert control over our feelings but that others are responsible, should, must help us with this and even that our feelings are not solely or predominantly our responsibility – 'look how angry you have made me'! Secure attachment experiences arguably allow us to use versions of both these strategies where appropriate: we can sort things out for ourselves but also invite others to assist us and comfort us.

We have considered the use of alcohol as a way of attempting to manage and direct our feelings. Arguably, excessive drinking has effects of not simply containing difficult feelings but also causing them to escalate, spill out of control and lead to actions that have negative consequences – embarrassing ourself, family and friends, and hurting others and ourself. Although the processes are perhaps less clear we can also see eating disorders, for example anorexia nervosa, as producing altered states of consciousness, changing emotions so as to act as ways of coping with difficult feelings. However, we all know that alcohol produces a warm glow of positive feeling that helps sooth away problems, at least for a while, but the physiological effects of starvation are less clear at first sight. People suffering with the condition, though, report feelings not dissimilar to a sense of intoxication as an effect of starvation. At the same time, both conditions involve pain, for example the alcoholic hangover, sickness, cramps etc. and the unpleasantness of hunger, cramps, aches, skin problems, sores and other side-effects of starvation. Another way of seeing this is that perhaps self-inflicted pain is one of the best distracters from deep emotional pain regarding our attachment needs.

In our early relationships with our parents when we are frightened or anxious we seek their help and reassurance. But from this we learn not only whether they are available but also what ability to influence others we have. We develop a sense of influence regarding others and also of ways in which we can assert such influence. It seems that children who repeatedly experience that their parents will not reassure them learn to give up and abandon ideas that they can influence others to help them. At one extreme, this can become a depressive position where they come to assume that nothing they do can really influence others to love and care for them. They also learn that it is only their self that they can and should control. At the other extreme, they might learn that they cannot control their self but can influence others by continually and relentlessly urging, pleading and coercing others to look after their needs – to help them, to do as they want and to fulfil their needs.

Rather than thinking of how the addictive disorders fall into one or other of these two main insecure attachment styles we might consider instead how each of the attachment styles can in different ways incorporate the use of alcohol or an eating disorder as a strategy that then may become increasingly resilient to change. There have been various studies that have attempted to link eating disorders to attachment styles (e.g. Ward et al., 2000; Ringer and Crittenden, 2006). One proposition is that the restrictive eating disorders are essentially an avoidant strategy whereby the person attempts to distance themselves from the negative feelings about the lack of emotional availability of their parents by distracting themselves with a focus on their body, weight, food, diet, calorie intake and so on. Clearly, many people with a diagnosis of anorexia appear to spend a substantial amount of their lives preoccupied with calculations about the calorific content of food and with their weight, not to mention the feelings of starvation that they are experiencing. Arguably, these are powerful ways of driving away or driving down their distressing attachment feelings and fears.

On the other hand, these eating disorders have also been conceptualised as an anxious–avoidant attachment style in that the disorder causes the young person to be entangled with their parents, in need of care, attention, medical intervention and support. In effect it can be seen as a form of implicit coercion of care and attention from the parents. However, we have often also seen more explicit blaming, accusation and emotional entanglement with the parents, which are characteristic of the anxious–ambivalent attachment styles.

A study by Ringer and Crittenden (2006) found that for anorexia the predominant attachment strategy was a mixed one whereby the person displays aspects of both strategies: an attempt to withdraw emotionally and also an anxious emotional pre-occupation, including angry blaming, accusation and demands made of the parents. Importantly this study also suggested that the young person's attachment strategies were also complicated by unresolved traumas and losses. In many cases these were found to be 'complex' traumas, for example an accumulation of anxiety resulting from imagined or anticipated dangers or threats in the family or elsewhere. In our own research with eating disorders we have found patterns that connect with the Ringer and Crittenden (2006) study. In interviews with young people with a diagnosis of anorexia and members of their families, we have observed mixed attachment patterns of withdrawal and also anxious/angry emotional involvement (Dallos and Denford, 2008). We interviewed families using a version of the Adult Attachment Interview (AAI) with added questions about the experience of mealtimes across the generations, patterns of comforting and specifically the role of food as a source of comfort and pleasure. Most importantly, in the interviews with the parents we saw transgenerational patterns whereby the parents reported attachments with their own parents as cold, uncaring, angry, distant or emotionally unavailable. Specifically in relation to food, many parents described mealtimes as unpleasant, unrewarding or even quite abusive experiences. For example, one father described how his own father used to ritually humiliate him at mealtimes. A mother described how her own mother had embarrassed her at mealtimes by pointing out and even squeezing her spot on her face in front of the rest of the family.

Hence, the parents in our research study seemed to have had little experience themselves of being comforted, helped in regulating their own needs and feelings or generally being emotionally attended to in an attuned way. These negative, shaming and even traumatic experiences appeared to have intruded into their relationships with their own children. In many cases, we also saw examples of powerful 'corrective' scripts (Byng-Hall, 1995; Dallos,

2006a) whereby the parents desired a warmer more emotionally connected relationship with their own children. However, they often lacked the emotional experiences from their own childhoods to be able to offer this to their own children. The difficulties in many cases appeared to have accelerated at adolescence when their children started to show more challenging emotional behaviours and also started to display the typical ambivalent processes of both striving for independence from their parents and focusing on peer relationships as well as remaining connected to and in need of support from their parents. Their parents' own lack of experience of emotional support and containment through these stages in their own childhoods appeared to make it harder for them to help contain and support their own children through these difficult emotional demands of adolescence.

One particular configuration we have seen from both our research and our clinical work with families with eating disorders is that the parents' actions are shaped by a combination of attempted 'corrective scripts' to offer a better attachment relationship for their own children than they had with their own parents. However, unresolved difficulties and traumatic memories from their own childhood intrude and possibly lead to a more rigid, inflexible application of the corrective scripts with their own children. For example, in one family therapy session, as the parents were describing their resolve to be more emotionally aware, sensitive and emotionally attuned to their own children than their own parents had been with them, we realised that we were all ignoring their daughter's distress, tears and protestation about wanting to end the session. Moreover, the parents attempted to retreat to similar patterns of angry confrontation and tearful disengagement with their own daughter (in the session) that they had just described about their own relationship with how their own parents had reacted angrily or withdrawn from them. Figure 8.1 summarises the core dynamic we have seen in many families with a member with a diagnosis of anorexia.

Finally, we have also observed that the children may occupy a particularly significant emotional position in the family. In some cases this can be seen as a triangulated role whereby the child's behaviour serves to help regulate difficult, conflictual feelings and dynamics in the parents' relationship (Byng-Hall, 2008a). This immersion and entanglement into the attachment relationship between the parents may make it all the more difficult for the child to learn effective ways of managing their own feelings and needs. It is possible that the widely documented feature of 'over control' in anorexia may be related to the child's attempts to exert some control in the triangulated emotional system to which they have been inadvertently conscripted by their parents.

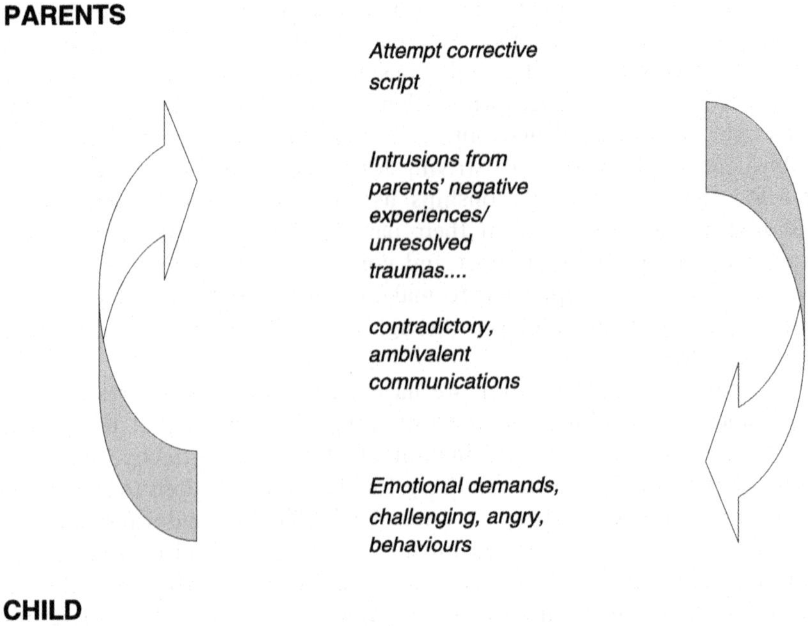

PARENTS

*Attempt corrective
script*

*Intrusions from
parents' negative
experiences/
unresolved
traumas....*

*contradictory,
ambivalent
communications*

*Emotional demands,
challenging, angry,
behaviours*

CHILD

Figure 8.1 Cycle of corrective scripts and unresolved transgenerational patterns.

Case example: Julie and her family

Julie had been suffering with anorexia for a period of over three years. She lived with her mother (Mary), father (Albert) and younger brother (David). Julie had suffered with a severe form of diagnosed anorexia nervosa and had been placed in an in-patient specialist eating disorders unit. RD saw Julie and her family for therapy and also conducted a research interview with Julie and both of her parents.

Formulation and interventions

Julie and her family appeared to embody many of the key elements of our discussion of eating disorders.

ATTACHMENT TRIANGULATION

Julie poignantly described in her individual interview and therapy with RD her sense of being caught between her parents and her role of being an emotional regulator for her parents' relationship. She revealed that she got on better with her father than her mother and had made plans to live in a flat with her father when the day came that her mother and father eventually separated. The parents disagreed in how best to respond to Julie's problems: Albert took to keeping detailed records and adopted a sort of expert medical perspective whereas Mary felt that there were problems between them and that her husband was unavailable emotionally apart from these excessive intrusive reactions to 'helping' Julie. Albert seemed very preoccupied with Julie's well-being and he visited the in-patient eating disorders unit where Julie was resident more frequently than her mother.

As the family therapy sessions progressed, the marital difficulties were more overtly expressed in the sessions, with Mary saying that she was contemplating leaving the relationship. We suggested to Julie's parents that we could see them for some sessions as a couple. They agreed to this and in a number of the sessions they were able to discuss their early relationship and their difficulties. We included in the session an exploration of their attachments through the family genogram (see Chapter 9 – Formats for exploration) whereby they explored their family attachments and relationships. From this we were surprised to discover that in contrast to our assumption that Mary's background had been somewhat privileged, she instead described an extremely financially and emotionally deprived background. Her childhood had been extremely chaotic and unsettled, with her mother having had seven children from three different relationships and she described how they had been rather like feral children left to fend for themselves. Albert also described a childhood where he had experienced very little care and attention and had also been left to fend for himself. Albert described both his parents as distant and that he had left home as early as possible and had kept up very little contact with his parents.

Thus, both Mary and Albert had experienced difficult relationships with their parents and neither had witnessed any positive and warm relationships between their own parents. When their own relationship deteriorated they seemed to find it difficult to know how to negotiate and discuss this. It appeared that Julie came to play an important role in their relationship and Albert described the past period in his marital relationship with Mary when Julie was born. He said that Mary was so happy to have the daughter that she had so long wished for and had wanted to be a much better mother for her than her own mother had been for her. This suggested that Julie played an extremely important role not just in meeting Mary's needs but in meeting the emotional needs of her parents' relationship. Currently it seemed that Julie was also seeing her role as needing to emotionally look after her father. In relation to this her father's extremely intimate knowledge of her body and details of her illness caused us some unease. We wondered whether given the emotional distance in the marital relationship Julie was potentially becoming drawn into fulfilling not only some of her father's emotional but also his sexual needs. Possibly an entry into an eating disorder unit provided some escape for her from the very complex emotional context of her family.

Throughout this period Julie continued to receive individual therapeutic input from a clinical psychologist and it was clear that she really appreciated that her parents were engaged on working on their own problems and felt she was able to become more emotionally and physically independent as a result.

COMPLEX ATTACHMENT PATTERNS ACROSS THE GENERATIONS

During the course of family therapy, Julie demonstrated a pattern of, on the one hand, attempting to withdraw emotionally, for example she described a wish to withdraw from her mother but also an over-involvement with her parent's relationship, for example her wish to look after her father; While, on the other hand, she sometimes became drawn into some escalating accusations with her mother. These demands on her to take sides appeared to make it difficult for her to consistently use an avoidant/dismissing style or pattern of relating in emotionally tense and difficult moments. The preoccupying thoughts about her parent's relationship may have contributed to anxious intrusions of feelings and images that disrupted her attempts to self-regulate her feelings and calm herself.

We discussed some of the key family relationships across the generations and attempted to make connections with the current family patterns of relating. For example, Mary was able to describe how her own mother had been unavailable to her throughout her childhood. She had been distracted by her various relationships and affairs with men, and Mary felt that her mother was irresponsible, promiscuous and had felt ashamed of her throughout her childhood. Albert for his part had also described a childhood in which his family had been emotionally distant.

He said his own mother had been distant, not really caring about him and his siblings and he remembered her making inedible, and frequently burnt food for them, not really caring about their welfare. Neither parent had experienced close relationships and care from their parents and we discussed in what ways that may have impacted on their abilities and confidence to respond to their own children and to manage their own marital relationship.

CORRECTIVE SCRIPTS

Related to this discussion of Mary and Albert's own childhood experiences they also described a wish to have a better relationship with their own children and in their marriage. Mary described that she both wished to be a better mother for her children and to be more responsible and committed to her marital relationship. She had wanted to have a closer relationship with Julie than had been possible with her own mother. Likewise, Albert described that his own father had been a distant figure, and at times angry and frightening. Consequently, he had wanted to be a less severe and intimating father than his father had been to him. However, neither Albert nor Mary appeared to have been able to reflect on and integrate their early emotional experiences and instead these appeared to intrude into their relationship with Julie. At times, Albert appeared to repeat some of the angry, dismissing reactions of his father. Similarly, Mary would at times act in a withdrawn and critical way, implying that Albert was not emotionally aware and in some ways perhaps repeating some aspects of the pattern of her mother in rejecting the men in her life. We were able to discuss with the family how they were attempting to do things differently and the positive intentions they had for their relationship with Julie. In these discussions Julie was at points able to validate how her mother had tried to make things better, because at times Mary was able to reflect on why mealtimes and being an 'excellent' mother was so important to her. She considered that this may have made her particularly sensitive and anxious about mealtimes, which may have served to convey a tense atmosphere. Albert for his part could see that his withdrawal was very painful for Mary since having a 'nice family' meant so much to her and he could see that he was repeating the scripts from his own father and may have been unaware of and insensitive to Mary's needs. They came to consider the possibility that these unresolved tensions and conflicts had been spilling out at their mealtimes, loading these occasions with anxiety, which might have contributed to the eating problems. The focus of these discussions stayed on the parents' positive intentions rather than digressing into what was not working currently or repeated attempts to 'fix' Julie's anorexia. Gradually, both Mary and Albert were able to identify some aspects of how their intentions had been positive and could be developed further.

COMFORT AND THE ROLE OF FOOD

Both in the parents' families of origin and in the current family, comfort and comforting was a difficult issue:

> My mother was just not around . . . we were left to fend for ourselves. I can remember times when there was no food at all in the house and we didn't know when the next meal was coming. She was too busy chasing her men than thinking about us . . . I never wanted my family to be like that. . . .
>
> (Mary)

Albert similarly described a pattern of not being comforted since his mother was emotionally unavailable and his father was a frightening man at times. Interestingly, both of them also found that mealtimes similarly embodied this sense of a lack of warmth and emotional support in their families: both parents had negative memories of mealtimes and a broad sense of a lack of comfort in their childhoods. Specifically, in relation to food they had little experience of food being used in their past or the current family as a source of comfort, warmth or pleasure.

In our discussion we were able to make connections between comfort, their own histories and the role of food. As part of these discussions, the therapist (RD) was able to comment on and share aspects of his own childhood experiences in order to help make connections with the family and help reduce a sense of blame or inadequacy.

With Julie and her family and with other families with eating disorders we have found it helpful to discuss with them the role of food in relation to broader issues of comfort. This has allowed us to both include a focus on the eating problems as well create some freedom to move away from what can become a relentless and often unhelpful focus on the eating problems. In our experience the young people presenting with the eating disorder often wish to move away from an excessive focus on food whereas the parents are anxious that the problems with eating are not sidelined in the sessions.

In this chapter we have attempted to consider both problems with alcohol and eating disorders as examples of broader problems that have been called addictive disorders. In our framework these are related to both difficult attachment issues and, in particular, problems with regulating feelings and managing arousal. The ability to manage feelings moves through childhood from something that we rely totally on our parents to assist us with, to a position in adulthood where we need to have developed ways of doing this for ourselves. However, we have argued in this chapter that it is a mistake to assume that this means that we need to become totally self-sufficient; rather, we need to learn how to ask for help when we need it and alongside this to be able to offer help to others. Frequently, we see that children who struggle to manage this process can go on to develop problems of emotional regulation and difficulties with intimate interpersonal relating. In these two conditions people may have had very difficult experiences about learning this self-regulation. Most significantly, we have suggested that this is in a large part due to the problems that their own parents have faced, which made it difficult for them to offer an emotionally attuned and empathic attachment context for their own children that then allows them to develop this twin ability to self-regulate and to enlist others to help them to do so. Instead, their feelings oscillate and require either the application of alcohol or other drugs to manage their feelings or the use of distraction through hunger and self-denial.

Chapter 9

Formats for exploration

In this chapter we want to bring together a number of formats or templates for ways of engaging in an attachment narrative way of working with individuals, couples and families. We have called these 'formats for exploration' to capture the idea that they involve us working alongside family members to explore both the *content* of attachment narratives, patterns of relating and themes across the generations and also the *process* of attachment narratives in terms of ways of attempting to facilitate the ability of family members to construct, develop and elaborate their narratives. The formats also take an overarching view of attempting to assist in developing narratives in terms of selecting and elaborating material from the various representational memory systems. As with most forms of therapy the formats also contain the central idea of attempting to help people develop more integrated, and reflexive, narratives about themselves and others, and their relationships. We see this as an interactive process in that the formats help to elicit information in the various representational systems and in turn this helps to provide material to build people's ability to develop integrated, coherent and reflexive narratives. As this reflective ability develops they may in turn be able to generate further information from their memory systems, which had hitherto been hidden, submerged or defended. Above all, the formats are intended to provide an underlying sense of safe exploration and contribute to the creation and maintenance of a secure base for therapeutic work with family members.

To start with we offer a format that is central to any therapeutic process and involves a clarification of the aims, goals and methods of the therapeutic work. It might be called the therapeutic contract and emphasises our commitment to openness in work with people and their families.

I Getting started: working with family relationships, attachments and narratives

When we meet with people and their families they are often curious and sometimes anxious about what the therapy will involve. The following can form the basis of an information leaflet, a letter or a conversation with a family to clarify the way we would like to work with them. In particular it makes transparent that we will engage in a way of working that involves looking at their relationships, their attachment to each other and their explanations and narratives that bind these together. The information leaflet below can be employed at the outset of therapy or at some time during other forms of therapy to signal our intention to attempt an integrated way of working with them.

Working with relationships, attachments and narratives – a guideline

You will have had some general information about family therapy and here we would like to outline more fully for you what we think might be some helpful ways for us to work together on the difficulties that you are facing at present. As you know there are many different types and styles of therapy and it can be very confusing to choose between them. We offer some information for you below about a way of working that focuses on family relationships, feelings and attachments. We will discuss these suggestions with you further if you decide that you are happy to explore this way of working for a while. However, in order to be able to decide properly whether you think it is helpful or not, it is usually necessary to try the approach for a while. We want to emphasise that working this way can be seen as an 'exploration' and if you do agree to try it you can later, at any point, decide not to continue this way of working.

The following are some of the main features of the approach we would like to pursue with you and your family. We would like to:

- explore with you what has gone well in your family and how you can work together to assist, comfort and reassure each other in the future;
- explore with you the feelings and explanations you hold about the difficulties that you are currently facing;
- consider the relationships between members of your family and how these both influence, and are in turn influenced by, the problems you are facing;
- look with you at the attachments – the emotional connections – that you have with each other and how these have changed over time and in relation to the problems;
- explore with you the patterns across the generations, for example in terms of what people have learnt about dealing with problems and difficult feelings and how people relate to each other;
- look at your *'family scripts'* – what people want to repeat or change about aspects of their own relationships with their parents or their parents' relationships with each other;
- consider with you patterns of comfort – how family members care for,

look after and reassure each other during times of difficulty, anxiety, crises or illness;

- explore your patterns of communication, for example in what ways people are able to show their feelings to each other in terms of how they feel and what they need;
- look with you at how in tune people feel they are with each other's feelings and whether you think a little more emotional space as opposed to more intimacy is what you need at the moment.

We want to emphasise the following about how we would like to work with you:

- You will be able to direct the pace at which we will explore these issues.
- You will be able to change direction and to discuss other matters if you wish.
- We will change the focus of the work whenever you want.
- At no point will our intention be to blame anyone or criticise members of your current or past families.

2 Exploring attachment narratives through the family genogram

Exploring the parents' attachments

Draw up a family genogram with the family. This can be conducted with the children present and requested to listen and participate. Children may be invited to draw the family tree on a large piece of paper and add drawings, colour etc. At times the children spontaneously make comments or ask questions but may also be invited to comment or elaborate on the questions. Following the interview with the parents, the children can be asked to comment on what they understand about the parents' stories and, for example, how it makes sense of how their parents are with each other and them. Have they heard anything new today? And of course, we acknowledge the multiple ways we can be looked after as children with our parents and carers: step-parents, foster parents, kinship care, adoptive parents and so on.

Some related areas of questions might include the following:

Exploring the emotional atmosphere in the parents' family

- How would you describe the emotional atmosphere in your family – for example, cold, warm, distant, predictable, safe?

- How physical was your family – what do you remember about touching, hugs and kisses?
- How was distress, pain, sadness and disappointment dealt with?

Exploring the nature of the parents' attachments to the grandparents

- How would you describe your relationship with your mother/father?
- Who were you closest to, your mother or your father?
- Did your closeness change as you grew older?
- Can you give some examples of being close or distant?

Exploring the relationship between the grandparents

Questions about the grandparents' relationship can bring out stories about the parents' childhood experiences and prompt a consideration of how their own children experience their relationship (mother and father).

- How would you describe your parents' relationship – cold, warm, distant, passionate, conflictual, safe?
- What differences do you see between the relationships between your mother's parents versus your father's parents?
- In what ways are either of your parents' relationships similar to your own?

Exploring the influence on the parents' relationship with their own children

Questions that invite the parents to consider how their own experiences have consciously or unconsciously influenced and shaped their relationships with their children can be helpful.

- How do you see your relationship (mother and father in turn) with your children?
- How are you different with your children from how your parents/carers were with you?
- Do you think you are closer or more distant to your children than your parents were with you?

3 Scaffolding conversations about feelings and attachments

This activity is built on the idea (Vygotsky, 1986; Bruner, 1990; White, 2006) that forming narratives about our emotional and attachment experiences with others is a complex, developmental task that may require support from the therapist and from other family members. Family members, especially children, may require some support and encouragement from the therapist/s to be able to discuss difficult feelings and further to be able to build these into coherent narratives. Vygotsky (1986) has described children's learning in terms of taking place within their *zone of proximal development*. This is a range that is not too easy or familiar nor too difficult or unfamiliar. As an example, in helping a young infant to learn to walk we might scaffold their learning by placing the child one step away and encouraging them to come to us – perhaps at first just letting them fall safely in our arms. Once this is achieved we might place them two steps away and so on, gradually increasing the distance. This is very similar to behavioural reinforcement, and the idea of building on success. Likewise, in conversations in therapy we may need to ask questions or make suggestions that are not too distant from the family's understanding but neither too familiar to suggest little challenge or difference. Bateson (1972) expressed this as the not too different and the not too similar.

Conversations can be seen within such a scaffolding framework whereby we help family members to build increasingly more complex, elaborate, reflective and integrative accounts or stories that may help them better to anticipate and solve future events and problems. Scaffolding can be described as a series of steps (adapted from Hayward, 2006) and although these are listed below, they are not hierarchical – the order may vary with progression upwards and downwards during a session/s:

- *Naming feelings:* a description of the problems or symptoms along with a request to identify and name the feelings that people are having, for example: How does it feel to have anorexia as a problem in your family? For example, this might be a feeling of powerlessness or sadness in relation to 'the anorexia', or frustration and a sense of loss and sadness in relation to 'the depression'.
- *Considering alternative names and contrasts:* an attempt to elaborate feelings and bring forth other feelings that have been masked by the dominant response, e.g. So do you think that what we have been discussing as anger is perhaps a bit more like . . . frustration, loneliness, feeling overwhelmed, confused that he cannot get close to others and feels misunderstood? It can also involve considering feelings in terms of contrasts, for example that anger can be the other side of sadness: Does anger sometimes turn into something else – sadness, regret, doubt . . .?
- *Exceptions or unique outcomes/feelings:* a consideration of exceptions or 'unique outcomes' e.g. I guess this may be difficult to do right now, since you are feeling desperate, upset . . . but I wonder whether you might be able to remember a time when James was not angry in the morning before school, but relaxed, happy, cheerful? or building on an exception offered by the family, e.g. that James can be quite sensitive rather than angry.

- *Standing in each other's emotional shoes:* invitations to 'stand in each other's emotional shoes', e.g. I know that this might be difficult for you to consider at the moment but I am wondering how do you think James sees things at the moment? How do you think he feels ... angry with himself, frustrated that people don't listen to him, worried about what is happening in the family, sad that his father has left? Offering a choice of emotional terms that family members can utilise or use as contrasts to select their preferred terms or inviting some new elaborations can be helpful. You have said James can be quite sensitive, how do you think he feels about you seeing him as that sort of young man, son, person?
- *Integrating emotions and relationships:* an attempt to connect the feelings with relationships, e.g. How do you think James' difficulties are influenced by how he is getting on with other people, family members? Do you think he feels worse when he feels insecure or lonely? Do you think he acts differently if he feels he can be open with you about how he feels? What do you think others can do to help him feel better about himself? How does he respond when other people are upset or not getting on with each other?
- *Future action and choice:* developing stories about self and identity leads to considerations of what implications these hold for making choices and future actions, e.g. Looking back over the events so far, what have you learnt and feel from what has happened? What do you want to feel and do that is the same or different in the future? One can ask how family members may be able to turn to each other for support, comfort and affection in the future e.g. James, how do you think you may be able to ask for help when you need it? What reassurance or comfort do you think James might need from other people in the future to help him stay on track and become the sort of person he wants to be?

4 Emotional sculpting

Sculpting can be a powerful way of illustrating family relationships and feelings between family members. We can consider two variations on sculpting that perhaps can stimulate different effects:

- *Sculpting with the family members* – in this the family position themselves with the therapist's assistance in terms of their perceptions of their relationships by physically standing, leaning, crouching, touching or holding on to each other. The sculpt can be carried out by different family members in turn, leaving enough time for each to be reflected upon. This can generate powerful emotional responses and may be particularly useful for families who are somewhat shut down in their emotional expression. Being 'inside' the sculpt it is harder to gain a conceptual view of their relationship and instead may produce a more immediate sense of what their own position feels like. The prompts here may be to help trigger feelings and awareness of attachments:

- How does it feel to be at the centre, on the edge, between your parents?
- Now that John and Phil are closer, how does that make you feel?
- If you were to get closer to Peter, what would that feel like?
- How do you think Mary feels being that distant from John?

- *Sculpting with objects* – buttons, coins, stones etc. Here family members pick an object to represent themselves and then they position the objects physically to express their differences between each other, their family patterns, any observed changes over time, e.g. before and after the start of the problems, transitions – family entrances and exits – and so on. This version allows more of a 'bird's eye' view in that family members can see a little more clearly the overall family patterns as they shift over time, and not just their own position. This can be helpful for families who are more preoccupied and anxious, or 'fired up' emotionally, and who may benefit from a more cognitive focus and distancing from their emotional connectedness. The questions here may focus more on understandings and cognitions:

- What changes can you see in the family patterns through what has happened in the family? What patterns do you think will continue in the future?
- How do you think John understands what it is like for Peter to be between his mum and dad?
- When Peter and Mary get close, what happens to John's relationship with them?

5 Exploring patterns of communication

Communication between family members may be patterned in various ways in line with the family's dominant attachment styles:

- Avoidant/dismissive family patterns – expression of feelings may be discouraged in a variety of implicit or even explicit ways.
- Preoccupied/anxious/ambivalent family patterns – may show escalating expressions of feelings, involving expressions of tears, fear or anger.

The following therapeutic work and questions invite consideration of communication in families, which we may wish to adapt when we use a particular question according to the style of family attachment patterns and the current emotional state of the family.

Talk about talk

It can be helpful and containing for families and the therapeutic process to discuss how we should all communicate in the session. This conversation can also reveal the family's preferred style of communication and their attachment styles and we can adjust how we communicate with them accordingly, for example gradually promoting more communication about feelings if they show a dismissive style, as opposed to encouraging reflective communication about when and why things happen for families where the style is very emotionally escalating.

The conversation can include questions such as: How will the therapist/family members know if someone is getting upset, agitated, angry? What shall we do about this – stop, have a break, change the subject? What happens at home, does someone get upset, leave, sulk, change the topic? Shall we do the same here? What rules shall we set about talking? Take it in turns to talk? All talk together?

Rules of conversation with the therapist

Inviting reflection on the communication between the family and the therapist can implicitly raise thoughts about how feelings are detected and responded to in the family, e.g. Can you tell me if the conversation is too difficult or upsetting for anyone? Who recognises this first? Who will tell me if I have 'put my foot in it' and asked something too upsetting? What shall we do if someone is becoming upset? Pause, ignore it, reflect on why it has happened? How can the person who has become upset be comforted, reassured? Who will do this here? Who does it at home?

Exploring the family's communicational style

This consists of exploring how open or closed the family style might be and also differences in the modes of communication:

*   As a family, how would you describe your style of communicating – open, closed, argumentative, emotional, logical, immediate, bottle feelings up? How do people differ in their style of communication? Who is most/least expressive, likely to bottle things up, be secretive, rational?
*   Has your communicational style changed? What causes it to change? How do you see it changing in the future?
*   How would you describe the modes of communication in your family? How much do people communicate through showing feelings, their posture, gestures, visually, through words and concepts, through stories?

- Who is the most/least tactile, visual, sensory, logical, a story teller?
- What ways of communicating do you think work best for you as a family? Showing your feelings? Being rational?
- What ways do you solve problems as a family? Try to be calm and rational? Show your feelings? Argue and shout? Withdraw and let time sort things out?
- What ways of communicating to try to solve problems do you think work most/least well? How do you think your style could be different/ improved?

6 Corrective and replicative scripts

This utilises ideas from Byng-Hall (1995) that we as families make comparisons across the generations in terms of similarities and differences between how our own parents were with each other and us (the children) and how this is repeated or altered in the next generation. Importantly, it allows us to work in a positive frame with the family in that we can construe the *intentions* of the parents positively, i.e. they have tried to repeat what was good and/or correct what they felt was bad about their own experiences. This can then lead to a discussion of whether these attempts have been successful or not, and possibly how they might be altered, strengthened, elaborated and so on.

- What are your thoughts about how similar to or different from your relationship with each other and your children is to your parents'/carers' (grandparents') relationships?
- What have you tried to make similar or different to either of these relationships?
- What do you value versus feel critical about in either of your parent's relationships?
- Does what you have tried to repeat/change work? Is there anything that you want to alter, strengthen, abandon about what you have been trying to repeat or change?

7 Exploring patterns of comforting

The following questions can be employed in work with individuals, couples or families. In the case of couples, the conversation is with one person while the other listens. For some people remembering, incidents can be difficult and they may need reassurance. For some people listening, they may need to be supported in their listening. In some cases the questions may need to become more hypothetical, e.g. What do you imagine happened? What would you have liked to have happened? How do you think you might have felt if you had been comforted, had been held, supported and so on? The questions can then move on to become more integrative, for example regarding what has been learnt from the experiences, what sense has been made of the events and also to the present in terms of the relevance to current relationships, why they think their parents acted as they did etc. With younger children the exploration can include use of drawing, toys and puppets to demonstrate how comfort was or could be given.

- When you were upset or frightened as a child, what happened?
- How did you get to feel better? Who helped you to feel better? How did they do this?
- How do you imagine it might have felt to have been comforted? How could this have been done for you? How does it feel, thinking about this now? How have you learned to comfort and soothe yourself?
- What have you learnt about comforting and being comforted in your childhood?
- How do people comfort each other in your own family/relationship?
- What do you want to do the same or differently now in your own family, with your children, with your partner?
- How do you comfort your children?
- How do they comfort you?

8 Reflecting team discussion: attachment narratives

These have the usual format of reflecting teams as outlined by Tom Andersen and others (Andersen, 1990). However, they have the added the focus of picking up on attachment themes and emotional processes in the family. This can include questions and reflections regarding current attachment processes, transgenerational patterns, patterns of comforting, attachment disruptions and 'injuries', future-oriented conversations about how attachments may evolve and change in the future and integrative conversations. A few examples of the kinds of questions and conversations that this might trigger are as follows:

- I wonder how the parents feel they have been able to do things differently or the same as their parents did? What have they discovered from thinking about this? Has it helped them to think, act, feel differently?
- If they were able to change how they comfort each other, what changes would they make? What could help this to happen? How might this change in the future?
- How do the family members feel about this (the therapy situation)? How has this changed? What helps them to be able to trust us and what gets in the way of that?
- What have they discovered about the attachments patterns in the past?

Do they think that history needs to repeat itself? What could help to alter history repeating itself?

- Looking back over the events in past, how do they think it has made them the family that they are?
- In what ways will the children do things differently in the future? Do they want their family, when and if they have one, to be more cuddly? More independent and self-sufficient?

9 Structured reflective conversation

The aim is to help family members or a couple to be able to listen to each other without interruptions or patterns of accusation, counter-accusation and blaming. For a couple there are two therapists in the room. One of the therapists sits with one of the couples, usually in a same-sex pairing. The other therapist has a conversation with the other partner. The conversation can, for example, be structured around a transgenerational interview, exploring patterns of comfort or instances of attachment breakdown or injury. Following a conversation, usually between five and fifteen minutes, the other therapist and partner have a conversation on the same themes. Following this, each partner reflects (with the help of the therapist if appropriate) on what they have heard. Finally, there is an open discussion on what has been triggered by the conversations.

Variations can be carried out with families, for example parents as one group and children as another, in terms of gender groupings and so on, and can involve the following (see also Figure 9.1):

- family or couple;
- co-therapists;
- discussion with the family about the potential value of a reflective conversation;

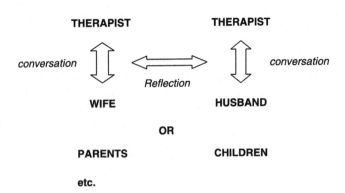

Figure 9.1 Structured reflective conversation.

- two sets of conversation: group A talks – B listens; group B talks – A listens;
- reflective conversation across the two groups.

10 Exploring attachment injury

This format draws on the work of Sue Johnson (2004) and her development of emotion-focused therapy. Johnson conceptualises an attachment injury as a perceived betrayal of trust and/or abandonment at a crucial moment of need in an intimate relationship. It is thought to be a form of relationship trauma, and a defining moment in the relationship, as it defines the relationship as insecure. The hurt and lack of trust inherent in this process can be held in mind over many months and years, and if it is not acknowledged and emotionally processed, it can block avenues of therapeutic change and growth. Johnson points out that the attachment significance of the injury is key, not the content, and like any form of trauma, it needs to be processed – as she says, the only way out is through.

Attachment injuries usually become apparent during the middle of therapy and often at times when both families and therapists are in a therapeutic process that feels stuck. The task for the therapist is to help the hurt partner articulate the injury and its continuing impact in their relationship, in terms of trust, beliefs about their partner's accessibility and responsiveness, beliefs about their own entitlement to be looked after and so on. The therapist acknowledges the hurt partner's distress and elaborates the shared understanding of the event, while supporting the other partner in listening. The hurt partner is encouraged to connect their narrative of the event, with their feelings at the time, and now, and to reflect on its attachment significance in their relationship. The other partner may have been unaware of the injury or, while remembering the event, may have had little or no idea of its attachment significance for their partner. The other partner is encouraged to listen, to acknowledge their partner's distress and to stay emotionally attuned and connected. This may take a while to open up, to acknowledge, to explore and to illuminate – it is important that the therapist does not push the process on too quickly for either partner. Constant checking is necessary. As the other partner listens and acknowledges their partner's hurt, the hurt partner is encouraged to reach out for understanding and comfort. The other partner is helped to respond in an emotionally responsive and supportive way. This process enables their relationship to be redefined as a safe haven, and the couple are able to develop a new narrative – a narrative of shared healing.

Stories of injury often emerge spontaneously in the conversations but the following might be helpful when a partner or family member hints at some past hurt, in prompting some initial recognition and discussion of the issues, while following the process outlined above:

- Can you think of a time, a moment, a particular incident where your emotional relationships changed or deteriorated significantly?
- Can you describe a time when you feel that you lost trust, faith in your partner in some important way? Can you try and describe fully what happened, what you felt, thought, did at that time?
- Some people describe such painful events in their relationships as an 'attachment injury'. Finding your own personal name for this event can be helpful – do you have any ideas what we could call this event?
- In what ways has this altered your relationship?
- Can you describe what was happening between you for this to happen?
- Did your partner realise that this event had been particularly significant, important, painful for you?
- What would you like your partner to say about this event, episode between you? What would be helpful, not so helpful?
- It sometimes takes a considerable amount of time before this sense of hurt, disappointment, loss of trust can be healed. What do you think might help this process or get in the way?
- What do you think your relationship could be like if you were able to overcome this 'injury' in your relationship?

Summary

We have provided these formats for exploration as guides for you to use in ways that you find helpful. As such we have not suggested that their usage should follow a particular order. However, there is some obvious sequencing, for example in getting started and clarifying the therapeutic context. We wish to emphasise that it is extremely important to do this and not to rush too quickly into exploring the problems since, without taking time to establish and explore the context, a sense of unsafe uncertainty may remain and this can reduce the impact of work done later. Mason (1993) describes the idea of safety and certainty as central to the therapeutic endeavour and we hope that these formats offer some useful contributions to how we can create a position of safe uncertainty that he sees as key to a constructive therapeutic context.

The formats can be developed, modified and combined and this is left to your judgement. Often, for example, we find that a discussion through a genogram will trigger discussion of transgenerational scripts and also patterns of comforting and emotional regulation in families. However, we also hope that the formats give some points of focus and encourage us to discuss some of these important areas of experience in a little more detail. They can also be used to assist the collaborative nature of the work and families can take copies of them and think about some of the questions, perhaps even use them as a task to bring back their responses to discuss at the next session. They can also be employed to assist families to hold a focus when viewing a recording of their session between sessions. We hope that the potential for creative use of the formats is great and we invite you to share your applications and adaptations with us on our website: www.fahs. surrey.ac.uk/ant/

Chapter 10

Reflections and conclusions

Our own needs

In Chapter 1 we set out of some of our own personal contexts and issues. In the journey of writing this book we have had time to reflect on how the ideas we have described impact on us in both our professional work and our personal lives. For example, a number of ideas have developed as we have progressed. We had initially not intended to offer a separate chapter on attachments across the individual and family life cycle. However, in the process of writing the book we became struck by how the various demands for change and adaptation on individuals and their families embodies fundamental and powerful demands for emotional adaptation and development. Rather than seeing family life-cycle stages as potential points of transition, coping and crisis, we came to see as we were writing that these offer great and often untapped potential for positive change and reorganisation. It also took us back to the very core of the connections we have been attempting to make between systemic, attachment and narrative approaches. In our work with families, transitions are times of great emotional lability and change. Traditionally, though, the language that has been used to describe these changes has tended to focus more on systemic, relational and organisational features, such as tasks, attempted solutions, reorganisation, clarity of roles and boundaries and so on.

This also took us back to our personal experiences. The resonances were many – expected and unexpected. Both RD and AV remember that their first child leaving home was a massive emotional upheaval for both of them, in their separate families, with common mixed feelings of hope and enthusiasm about their sons' new lives, mixed with regrets about the time that had gone and missed opportunities to be close to their sons. Likewise, many memories returned as we wrote the chapters on love and sexuality, trauma and dissociation, and loss, grief and attachment, of how events that we can so easily overlook may play a huge part in shaping our experiences and feelings. For example, RD remembered his own first failed love affair and seeing his own children go through these first heartbreaks. AV's husband had died the year before we started writing this book, and these three chapters in their inception and completion were therapeutic for her, in helping her walk around in her own very strong feelings of loss and sadness. We came to see increasingly that as we wrote these chapters the early systemic ideas of problems arising from a gradual accumulation of unsuccessful attempts to solve the difficulties could be seen further in the light of strongly held attachment needs and emotions. Dealing with a child's difficulties in their first relationship, for example, is not a dispassionate affair. It reminds us of so much of our own childhood, we feel for our own children, and we may be distracted by our own issues and so on. Although from the outset this book is about how emotions, narratives and actions are inextricably interconnected, we have learnt a lot ourselves as we have mapped these connections across the various areas of intimate relating in families. Coherence and integration is as important for us as the families with whom we work!

We decided at the outset to organise the book in terms of attachment themes rather than specifically focusing on types of problems. We feel that the attachment narrative therapy (ANT) perspective that we describe in the book offers some alternative ways of thinking about/formulating various forms of psychological and interpersonal difficulties. Hence, we did not want to follow a usual psychiatric diagnostic model – Diagnostic and Statistical Manual of Mental Disorders (DSM) or the International Classification of Diseases (ICD) – in talking about areas of our therapeutic work. As we say elsewhere in the book, the attraction of attachment thinking, for us, is that it does not pathologise dependency in relationships; rather, it sees dependency and autonomy as different sides of the same attachment coin. This is part of a bigger enterprise and we think that attachment theory has much to contribute to offering an alternative psychological model of formulating problems to the current use of diagnostic systems. However, we also recognise tension here since so much of the clinical literature starts with the standard diagnostic label. Furthermore, we are caught in the major evidence-based zeitgeist that attempts to direct clinicians to follow the 'most effective' forms of treatment for particular disorders according to the research evidence. Most valued in this framework is the evidence that is based on randomised controlled trial (RCT) treatment outcome studies. We do not offer such studies here for our approach, although our systemic practice draws on the considerable evidence base. This is not to say that RCTs might not be valuable or necessary. However, we take the view that new ways of working need to develop out of current practices, and this happens through initial curiosity, exploration and feedback. We also suggest that any research into psychotherapy needs to look carefully at the processes of what happens in the intimate encounter between people – which is what we think therapy is. Elsewhere we have suggested (Vetere and Dallos, 2003; Dallos and Vetere, 2005) that much highly relevant and important research accumulates by 'practice-based' evidence – what practitioners learn through the process of engaging in therapy. We have attempted to present clinical examples of 'practice-based' evidence through-out this book. This was an attempt both to illustrate how we have used these ideas in our own practice but also an offer of a form of evidence that invites, you the reader, to judge whether the approach makes sense and whether the accounts we offer of our work and the quotes from our families are convincing, and that this can be a helpful way of working.

Above all, we have stressed that the approach outlined offers not simply or predominantly a new way of working but also an integrated set of lenses to look at what we already do. Through the ANT lens we have suggested that many techniques shared across different systemic therapies, such as external-isation, re-storying, looking for exceptions/unique outcomes, genograms and enactments, can also be seen in attachment terms. We have suggested repeatedly, for example, that these techniques may owe their usefulness as much to the ways in which they help build trust and develop the therapeutic relationship as to the specific conceptual changes they aim to produce. Accessibility and responsiveness are seen as the building blocks of a felt sense of security in relationships, and facilitate effective problem solving.

Culture and contexts

Although we have not specifically included a chapter dedicated to issues of culture, difference and diversity, we hope that these run through the book. Attachment theory from its inception took a cross-cultural and even a cross-species perspective. John Bowlby (1988) asserted that seeking protection from our parents in times of danger is something that is common not only to all human cultures but also across species. This involves a Darwinian, evolution-ary assumption that this instinct has evolved to help protect and ensure the survival of each species. Where this protective attachment process becomes flawed, ineffective or maladaptive then the species will suffer and could pos-sibly become extinct.

Attachment patterns have been found across all human cultures. As we have described, the earliest attachment observation were across continents – the United States and Africa – and the emphasis on exploring cultural differ-ences has remained in attachment theory. However, it is also possible to accuse attachment theory of a form of naïve pan-culturalism – that it looks for the gross similarities and tends to ignore variation and difference. This criticism may be somewhat unfair since there have been many studies across different cultures and also exploring different attachment configurations, such as communes and the Israeli kibbutz. We take the view that the signifi-cance and meanings around emotional responding in our key relationships and their associated family practices may be subject to within-culture and across-culture variation. Of primary concern also has been whether there are different balances of attachment styles across different cultures. This is of interest but in our view it may be more relevant to look at how different cultures experience periods of danger and instability, require people to adopt different ways of managing their feelings and looking after each other. As an example, as a child RD lived in Stalinist Hungary in the 1950s. There, to hold a trusting, naïve form of secure attachment could have resulted in great danger and people came to keep their feelings, thoughts and opinions to themselves in order to survive. Likewise, in some parts of the world, such as Iraq or Afghanistan at the moment, to be hypervigilant, anxious and aroused may be adaptive in the context of ever-present danger and highly unpredictable acts, such as suicide bombings. As another example, AV's mother was evacuated during the Second World War and her father fought with the British Army during the whole time of war. Her parents were poor and moved to Canada as economic migrants in the early 1950s. It is not surprising that in her childhood importance was placed on surviving, stoical coping and getting on with things.

In this book we have made reference, often through examples of our work with families and couples, of cultural variations in attachments. A significant example in Chapter 5 (on love and sexuality) is an exploration of the issues involved in arranged marriages. This raises interesting questions about how an attachment connection is formed, for example whether the cultural expectation is that it is something that will grow as the couple start to get to know each other, as opposed to Western assumptions that it has to be the prerequisite or base from which the relationship matures. Other examples that can be found in the various chapters include a look at the more specific assumptions in different cultures. For example, there are normative ideas about how long the impact of a loss of a loved person should last for, or how long before a child should get over the divorce of their parents or a traumatic event. These ideas about what is 'normal' or to be expected provide important links between attachment and narrative ideas. The important point that we want to add here is that attachment theory does not pathologise dependency. By this we have suggested throughout the chapters that attachment theory clarifies that as we develop we learn to be able to turn to ourselves in order to soothe, calm and manage our feelings. And importantly, the capacity to turn to others and seek their assistance is a normal and lifelong process. To be dependent on others is adaptive and secures safety and protection – and so many people we work with have learned that they cannot trust, nor depend on others to be there for them, and/or that they themselves are not worthy of care and attention. In this we do not mean that we advocate that people become so anxious and insecure that they cannot function without a total dependency on others. This issue also relates to a much broader one, which has been the tendency, particularly in Western cultures, to over-value self-reliance, control of emotionality, and stoicism. In particular, we are influenced by the feminist writers who have articulated how emotionality has been employed in a pejorative way to position women and also racial minorities, such as black and Asian cultures, as weak, or manipulative, out of control, impulsive and emotionally unreliable (Gilligan, 1982; Dallos, 1996). Attachment theory helps us to think about emotionality and its expression in ways that to us do not marginalise emotions but place them at the heart of human experience and relationships. It also helps to emphasise the role not just of negative or painful emotions but also of the positive ones. Through the sense of being protected and cared for we come to experience pleasure and joy, and the memory can sustain us in the face of loss:

> Many of the most intense emotions arise during the formation, the maintenance, the disruption and the renewal of attachment relationships. The formation of a bond is described as falling in love, maintaining a bond as loving someone, and losing a partner as grieving over someone. Similarly, threat of loss arouses anxiety, and actual loss gives rise to sorrow; whilst each of these situations is likely to arouse anger. The unchallenged maintenance of a bond is experienced as a source of security and the renewal of a bond as source of joy.
>
> (Bowlby, 1980, p. 3)

References

Abbey, C. and Dallos, R. (2004) The experience of the impact of divorce on sibling relationships. *Clinical Child Psychology and Psychiatry*, 4: 241–259.

American Psychiatric Association (2007) *Diagnostic and Statistical Manual of Mental Disorders* (DSM–ivR) (4th edition – revised). Washington, DC: American Psychiatric Association.

Andersen, T. (ed.) (1990) *The Reflecting Team*. New York: Norton.

Anderson, H. Goolishian, H. and Winderman, I. (1986) Problem-determined systems: toward transformation in family therapy. *Journal of Strategic and Family Therapy*, 4: 1–13.

Bachelor, A. and Horvath, A. (1999) The therapeutic relationship. In M. Hubble, B. Duncan and S. Miller (eds) *The Heart and Soul of Change: What Works in Therapy*. Washington, DC: American Psychological Association.

Bateson, G. (1972) *Steps to an Ecology of Mind*. New York: Ballantine.

Bentovim, A. (1992) *Trauma: Organized Systems*. London: Karnac.

Bertrando, P. (2007) *The Dialogical Therapist*. London: Karnac.

Blom, T. and van Dijk, L. (2007) The role of attachment in couple relationships described as social systems. *Journal of Family Therapy*, 29: 69–87.

Blow, K. and Daniel, G. (2002) Frozen narratives? Post-divorce processes and contact disputes. *Journal of Family Therapy*, 24: 85–103.

Bohannan, P. (1970) *Divorce and After: An Analysis of the Emotional and Social Problems of Divorce*. Garden City, NY: Anchor.

Bowlby, J. (1979) *The Making and Breaking of Affectional Bonds*. London: Tavistock.

Bowlby, J. (1980) *Attachment and Loss. Vol 3: Loss*. New York: Basic Books.

Bowlby, J. (1988) *A Secure Base*. New York: Basic Books.

Bowlby-West, L. (1983) The impact of death on the family system. *Journal of Family Therapy*, 5, 279–294.

Bretherton, I. (1995) A communicational perspective on attachmennt relations and internal working models. In E. Waters, B. E. Vaughn, G. Posada and K. Kondo-Ikemura (eds) *Caregiving, Cultural, and Cognitive Perspectives on Secure-Base Behaviour and Working Models: New Growing Points of Attachment Theory and Research* (*Monographs of the Society for Research in Child Development*. (60, Serial No. 244). Chicago, IL: University of Chicago Press.

British Crime Survey (1996) *The 1996 British Crime Survey*. Home Office Statistical Bulletin 19/96. London: Home Office.

British Crime Survey (2000) *The 2000 British Crime Survey*. Home Office Statistical Bulletin 18/00. London: Home Office.

Brown, G. and Harris, T. (1978) *The Social Origins of Depression: A Study of Psychiatric Disorder in Women*. London: Tavistock.

Brown, G. and Harris, T. (1989) *The Social Origins of Depression*. London: Routledge.

Browne, K. and Herbert, M. (1997) *Preventing Family Violence*. Chichester: Wiley.

Bruner, J. (1990) *Act of Meaning*. Cambridge, MA: Harvard University Press.

Byng-Hall, J. (1995) *Rewriting Family Scripts: Improvisations and Systems Change*. New York: Guilford Press.

Byng-Hall, J. (2008a) The significance of children fulfilling parental roles: implications for family therapy. *Journal of Family Therapy*, 30, 147–162.

Byng-Hall, J. (2008b) The crucial roles of attachment in family therapy. *Journal of Family Therapy*, 30, 129–146.

Carter, E. and McGoldrick, M. (1988) *The Changing Family Life Cycle: A Framework for Family Therapy* (2nd edition). New York: Gardner.

Clulow, C. (2001) *Adult Attachment and Couple Psychotherapy: The Secure Base in Practice and Research*. London: Brunner Routledge.

Conners, C. K., Sitarenios, G., James, D. A., Parker, J. and Epstein, H. (1998) The revised Conner's Parent Rating Scale: factor structure, reliability, and criterion validity – CPRS-R. *Journal of Abnormal Child Psychology*, August.

Cooper, J. and Vetere, A. (2005) *Domestic Violence and Family Safety: A Systemic Approach to Working with Violence in Families*. Chichester: Wiley.

Council of Europe (1985) *Violence in the Family*. Recommendation No. R(85)4. Adopted by the Committee of Ministers of the Council of Europe on 26 March. Strasbourg: Council of Europe.

Crittenden, P. M. (1995) Attachment and psychopathology. In S. Goldberg, R. Muir and J. Kerr (eds) *Attachment Theory: Social, Developmental, and Clinical Perspectives*. Hillsdale, NJ: The Analytic Press.

Crittenden, P. (1997) Truth, error, omission, distortion, and deception: an application of attachment theory to the assessment and treatment of psychological disorder. In S. M. Clany Dollinger and L. F. DiLalla (eds) *Assessment and Intervention Issues Across the Life Span*. London: Lawrence Erlbaum Associates, Inc.

Crittenden, P. (2004) Personal communication and unpublished material from the AAI training programme, Miami, FL, USA.

Crittenden, P. (2006) A dynamic–maturational model of attachment. *Australian and New Zealand Journal of Family Therapy*, 27: 105–115.

Dallos, R. (1996) *Interacting Stories, Narratives, Family Beliefs and Therapy*. London: Karnac.

Dallos, R. (2006a) *Attachment Narrative Therapy*. Maidenhead: Open University Press.

Dallos, R. (2006b) Attachment Narrative Therapy: integrating ideas from narrative and attachment theory in systemic family therapy with eating disorders. *Journal of Family Therapy*, 26: 40–66.

Dallos, R. and Denford, S. (2008) A qualitative exploration of relationship and attachment themes in families with an eating disorder. *Clinical Child Psychology and Psychiatry*, 13: 305–322.

Dallos, R. and Draper, R. (2005) *An Introduction to Family Therapy* (2nd edition). Maidenhead: Open University Press/McGraw-Hill.

Dallos, R. and Vetere, A. (2005) *Researching Psychotherapy and Counselling*. Maidenhead: Open University Press/McGraw-Hill.

Dallos, S. and Dallos, R. (1997) *Couples, Sex and Power: The Politics of Desire*. Milton Keynes: Open University Press.

DCFS and DIUS (Department for Children, Families and Schools and Department for Innovation, Universities & Skills) (2006) *Children in Need in England: Results of a Survey of Activity and Expenditure as Reported by Local Authority Social Services' Children and Families Teams for a Survey Week in February 2003: Local Authority Tables and Further National Analysis*. [Online only: http://www.dcsf.gov.uk/rsgateway/DB/VOL/v000647/index.shtml]

DH (Department of Health) (1995) *Children and Young Persons on Child Protection Registers – Year Ending 31 March, 1995, England*. Personal Social Services Local Authority Statistics. London: HMSO.

DH (Department of Health) (1999) *Alcohol Harm Reduction Strategy for England: Implications for the Treatment of Dual Diagnosis*. London: DH.

DH and DfES (Department of Health and Department for Education and Skills) *National Service Framework for Children, Young People and Maternity Services*. London: The Stationery Office.

Dowling, E. and Gorell Barnes, G. (1999) *Working with Children and Parents through Separation and Divorce*. Basingstoke: Macmillan.

Dowling, E., Gersch, I. and Gower, M. (2005) Parenting adult children: a project combining narrative, clinical and empirical methodologies. In A. Vetere and E. Dowling (eds) *Narrative Therapies with Children and their families: A Practitioner's Guide to Concepts and Approaches*. London: Routledge.

Duncan, B. and Miller, S. (2000) *The Heroic Client: Doing Client-Directed, Outcome-Informed Therapy*. San Fransisco, CA: Jossey Bass.

Dutton, D. (2003) *The Abusive Personality: Violence and Control in Intimate Relationships*. New York: Guilford Press.

Edwards, M. and Steinglass, P. (1995) Family therapy treatment outcomes for alcoholism. *Journal of Marital and Family Therapy*, 21: 475–509.

Erikson, E. H. (1980) *Identity and the Life Cycle*. New York: W. W. Norton.

Fairbairn, W. (1952) *Psychoanalytic Studies of the Personality*. London: Hogarth Press.

Falicov, C. (1998) Commentary on Hoffman: from rigid borderlines to fertile borderlands: reconfiguring family therapy. *Journal of Marital and Family Therapy*, 24: 157–163.

Foa, E. and Kozak, M. (1986) Emotional processing of fear: exposure to corrective information. *Psychological Bulletin*, 99, 20–35.

Fonagy, P. (1991) Thinking about thinking: some clinical and theoretical considerations in the treatment of the borderline patient. *International Journal of Psychoanalysis*, 72: 118–127.

Fonagy, P., Steele, M. and Steele, H. (1991a) Maternal representations of attachment during pregnancy predicts the organisation of infant–mother attachment at one year of age. *Child Development*, 62: 880–893.

Fonagy, P., Steele, M., Steele, H., Moran, G. S. and Higgitt, A. C. (1991b) 'The capacity for understanding mental states: the reflective self in parents and child and its significance for security of attachment. *Infant Journal of Mental Health*, 12: 201–215.

Fonagy, P., Leigh, T., Steele, M., Stelle, H., Kennedy, R., Mattoon, G., Target, M. and Gerber, A. (1996) The relation of attachment status, psychiatric classification, and response to psychotherapy. *Journal of Counselling and Clinical Psychology*, 64(1): 22–31.

Foucault, M. (1967) *Madness and Civilisation*. London: Tavistock.

Foucault, M. (1975) *The Archaeology of Knowledge*. London: Tavistock.

Freud, S. (1922) *Introductory Lectures on Psycho-Analysis*. London: Allen and Unwin.

Gilligan, C. (1982) *In a Different Voice: Psychological Theory and Women's Development*. Cambridge, MA: Harvard University Press.

Grotstein, J. (2007) *A Beam of Intense Darkness: Wilfred Bion's Legacy to Psychoanalysis*. London: Karnac.

Guest, J. (1976) *Ordinary People*. Fontana Paperbacks.

Haley, J. (1973) *Uncommon Therapy: The Psychiatric Techniques of M. H. Erickson*. New York: Norton.

Haley, J. (1987) *Problem Solving Therapy* (2nd edition). San Fransisco, CA: Jossey-Bass.

Hare Mustin, R. (1979) Family therapy following the death of a child. *Journal of Marital and Family Therapy*, 2, 51–59.

Harvey, J. H., Orbuch, T. L. and Weber, A. L. (eds) (1992) *Attributions, Accounts and Close Relationships*. London: Springer-Verlag.

Hayward, M. (2006) Using a scaffolding distance map with a young man and his family. *International Journal of Narrative Therapy and Community Work*, 1: 39–51.

Hazan, C. and Shaver, P. (1987) Conceptualising romantic love as an attachment process. *Journal of Personality and Social Psychology*, 52: 511–524.

Herman, J. (1992) *Trauma and Recovery*. London: Basic Books.

Hill, J., Fonagy, P., Safier, E. and Sargent, J. (2003) The ecology of attachment in the family: the theoretical basis for the development of a measure. *Family Process*, 42: 205–221.

Hollway, W. (1989) *Subjectivity and Method in Psychology: Gender, Meaning and Science*. London: Sage Publications.

Home Office (1996, 2000) *The British Crime Survey*, England and Wales. London: HMSO.

Hughes, D. (2007) *Attachment Focused Family Therapy*. New York: Norton.

Jensen, P. S., Arnold, L. E., Swanson, J. M., Vitiello, B., Abikoff, H. B., Greenhill, L. L., Hechtman, L., Hinshaw, S. P., Pelham, W. E., Wells, K. C., Conners, C. K., Elliott, G. R., Epstein, J. N., Hoza, B., March, J. S., Molina, B. S., Newcorn, J. H., Severe, J. B., Wigal, T., Gibbons, R. D. and Hur, K. (2007) 3-year follow-up of the NIMH MTA study. *Journal of the American Academy of Child & Adolescent Psychiatry*, 46: 989–1002.

Johnson, M. and Best, M. (2003) A systemic approach to restructuring adult attachment: the EFT model of couples therapy. In P. Erdman and T. Caffrey (eds) *Attachment and Family Systems*. New York: Brunnner-Routledge.

Johnson, S. (1998) Listening to the music: emotion as a natural part of systems theory. *Journal of Systemic Therapies*, 17: 1–17.

Johnson, S. (2004) *The Practice of Emotionally Focused Marital Therapy: Creating Connections* (2nd edition). New York: Brunner/Mazel.

Johnson, S. (2008) *Hold Me Tight: Seven Conversations for a Lifetime of Love*. Boston, MA: Little, Brown.

Johnson, S., Makinen, J. and Millikin, J. (2001) Attachment injuries in couple relationships: a new perspective on impasses in couple therapy. *Journal of Marital and Family Therapy*, 27: 145–155.

Kiecolt Glaser, J. and Newton, T. (2001) Marriage and health: his and hers. *Psychological Bulletin*, 127: 472–503.

Kobak, R. R. and Cole, H. (1994) Attachment and meta-monitoring: implications for adolescent autonomy and psychopathology. In D. Cichetti and S. C. Toth (eds) *Disorders and Dysfunctions of the Self*. Based on Papers presented at the 5th Annual Rochester Symposium on Developmental Psychopathology, vol 5. Rochester, NY: University of Rochester Press.

Leff, J., Vearnals, S., Brewin, C. R., Wolff, G., Alexander, B., Asen, E., Dayson, D., Jones, E., Chisholm, D. and Everitt, B. (2000) The London Depression Intervention Trial: an RCT of antidepressants versus couple therapy in the treatment and maintenance of depressed people with a partner: clinical outcomes and costs. *British Journal of Psychiatry*, 177: 95–100.

Lewis, C. S. (1961) *A Grief Observed*. London: Faber.

Lewis, E., Dozier, M., Ackerman, J. and Sepulveda, S. (2007) The effect of placement instability on adopted children's inhibitory control abilities and oppositional behaviour. *Developmental Psychology*, 43: 1415–1427.

Lieberman, S. (1979) *Transgenerational Family Therapy*. London: Croom Helm.

Liotti, G. (2004) Trauma, dissociation and disorganised attachments: three strands of a single braid. *Psychotherapy: Theory, Research, Practice and Training*, 41: 472–486.

Lloyd, H. and Dallos, R. (2006) First session solution focussed brief therapy with families who have a child with severe intellectual disabilities: mother's experiences and views. *Journal of Family Therapy*, 30: 5–28.

McCullough, M., Tsang, J. and Eammons, R. (2004) Gratitude in intermediate affective terrain: links of grateful moods with individual differences and daily emotional experience. *Journal of Personality and Social Psychology*, 86, 295–309.

Main, M., Kaplan, N. and Cassidy, J. (1985) Security in infancy, childhood and adulthood: a move to the level of representation. In I. Bretherton and E. Waters (eds) *Growing Points of Attachment Theory and Research* (*Monographs of the Society for Research in Child Development*), (50 (1–2) Serial No. 209). Chicago, IL: University of Chicago Press.

Malan, D. (1979) *Individual Psychotherapy and the Science of Psychodynamics*. London: Butterworths.

Mason, B. (1993) Towards positions of safe uncertainty. *Human Systems*, 4: 189–200.

Meichenbaum, D. (1994) *Treating Post-Traumatic Stress Disorder: A Handbook and Practice Manual for Therapy*. New York: Wiley.

Mikulincer, M. and Shaver, P. R. (2007) *Attachment in Adulthood: Structure, Dynamics and Change*. New York: Guilford Press.

Mikulincer, M. and Sheffi, E. (2000) Adult attachment and cognitive reactions to positive affect: a test of mental categorisation and creative problem-solving. *Motivation and Emotion*, 24: 149–174.

Mikulincer, M., Shaver, P. R. and Pereg, D. (2003) Attachment theory and affect regulation: the dynamic, development, and cognitive consequences of attachment related strategies. *Motivation and Emotion*, 27: 77–102.

Miller, S. and Berg, I. (1995) *The Miracle Method: A Radically New Approach to Problem Drinking*. New York: Norton.

Miller, W. and Rollnick, S. (1991) *Motivational Interviewing: Preparing*

Minuchin, S. (1974) *Families and Family Therapy*. Harvard, MA: Harvard University Press.

Minuchin, S., Rosman, B., and Baker, L. (1978) *Psychosomatic Families: Anorexia Nervosa in Context*. Cambridge, MA: Harvard University Press.

Mitchell, J. (ed.) *The Selected Melanie Klein*. London: Penguin.

Moffit, T. and Caspi, A. (1998) Annotation: implications of violence between intimate partners for child psychologists and psychiatrists. *Journal of Child Psychology and Psychiatry*, 39, 137–144.

Morel, B. A. (1857) *Traité des Degenerescences Physiques, Intellectuelles et Morales de l'espece Humaine*. Paris: Masson.

Murray Parkes, C. (1996) *Bereavement: Studies of Grief in Adult Life* (3rd edition). London: Routledge.

Murray Parkes, C. (2006) *Love and Loss: The Roots of Grief and its Complications*. London: Routledge.

Neimeyer, R. (2006) Complicated grief and the reconstruction of meaning: conceptual and empirical contributions to a cognitive-constructivist model. *Clinical Psychology: Science and Practice*, 13, 141–145.

Neimeyer, R., Baldwin, S. and Gillies, J. (2006) Continuing bonds and reconstructing meaning: mitigating complications in bereavement. *Death Studies*, 30: 715–738.

NICE (National Institute for Health and Clinical Excellence) (2006) *ADHD : Draft Scope for Consultation*. London: NICE. http://www.nice.org.uk

Novaco, R. (1993) Clinicians ought to view anger contextually. *Behaviour Change*, 10. 208–218.

Orford, J. and Harwin, J. (eds) (1982) *Alcohol and the Family*. London: Croom Helm.

Palazzoli, M. S., Cecchin, G., Prata, G. and Boscolo, L. (1978) *Paradox and Counter Paradox*. New York: Jason Aronson.

Patterson, G. R., DeBaryshe, B. D. and Ramsey, E. (1989) A developmental perspective on anti-social behaviour. *American Psychologist*, 44: 329–335.

Pereg, D. (2001) *Mood and cognition: The Moderating Role of Attachment Style*. Unpublished doctoral dissertation, Bar-Ilan University, Israel.

Pines, M. (1982) Reflecting on mirroring. *Group Analysis*, 15: 1–32.

Raphael, B. (1984) *The Anatomy of Bereavement*. New York: Hutchinson.

Ringer, R. and Crittenden, P. M. (2006) Eating disorders and attachment: the effects of hidden family processes on eating disorders. *European Eating Disorders Review*, 14: 1–12.

Roy, P., Rutter, M. and Pickles, A. (2004) Institutional care: association between over-activity and lack of selectivity in social relationships. *Journal of Child Psychology and Psychiatry*, 45: 866–873.

Rutter, M. (1980) *Changing Youth in Changing Society*. Harvard, MA: Harvard University Press.

Rutter, M. (1999) Resilience concepts and findings: implications for family therapy. *Journal of Family Therapy*, 21, 119–144.

Satir, V. (1964) *Conjoint Family Therapy*, Palo Alto, CA: Science and Behaviour Books.

Scharfstein, S. (2006) *Task Force on the Effects of Violence on Children*. Washington, DC: American Psychiatric Association.

Schore, A. (1994) *Affect Regulation and the Origin of the Self*. Hillsdale, NJ: Lawrence Erlbaum Associates, Inc.

Seligman, M. E. P. (1975) *Helplessness: On Depression, Development and Death*. San Fransisco, CA: Freeman.

Shaver, P. and Brennan, K. (1992) Attachment styles and the five big personality traits. *Personality and Social Psychology Bulletin*, 5: 536–545.

Shaver, P. R. and Mikulincer, M. (2002) Attachment-related psychodynamics. *Attachment and Human Development*, 4: 133–161.

Silva, P. and Stanton, W. (eds) (1996) *From Child to Adult: Dunedin Multidisciplinary Health Development Study*. Auckland: Oxford University Press.

Simon, G. (1995) A revisionist rendering of structural family therapy. *Journal of Marital and Family Therapy*, 21: 17–26.

Spatz-Wisdom, C. (2007) Post-traumatic stress disorder in abused and neglected children grown up. *American Journal of Psychiatry*, 156: 1223–1228.

Steele, H. and Fonagy, P. (1995) Associations amongst attachment classifications of mothers, fathers and their infants. *Child Development*, 57, 571–575.

Stern, D. (1985) *The Interpersonal World of the Infant: A View from Psychoanalysis and Developmental Psychology* (1st edition). New York: Basic Books.

Stern, D. (1998) The Interpersonal Life of the Infant: A View from Psychoanalysis and Developmental Psychology (2nd edition). New York: Basic Books.

Swanson, J. M. *et al.* (2007) Effects of stimulant medication on growth rates across 3 years in the MTA follow-up. *Journal of the American Academy of Child & Adolescent Psychiatry*, 46: 1015–1027.

Taylor, D. and Altman, I. (1987) Communication in interpersonal relationships: social penetration processes. In M. Roloff and G. Miller (eds) *Interpersonal Processes: New Directions in Communication Research*. Newbury Park, CA: Sage Publications.

Tennyson, A. (1850) In memorium: A. H. H. Prologue.

Tomm, K. (1988) Interventive interviewing: Part 3. Intending to ask circular, strategic or reflexive questions. *Family Process*, 27: 1–17.

van der Kolk, B., McFarlane, A. and Weisaeth, L. (eds) (1996) *Traumatic Stress: The Effects of Overwhelming Experience on Mind, Body and Society*. New York: Guilford Press.

Velleman, R. (1992) 'Oh my drinking doesn't affect them': families of problem drinkers. *Clinical Psychology Forum*, 48: 6–10.

Vetere, A. and Cooper, J. (2001) Working systemically with family violence: risk, responsibility and collaboration. *Journal of Family Therapy*, 23: 378–396.

Vetere, A. and Cooper, J. (2003) On setting up a domestic violence service: some thoughts and considerations. *Child and Adolescent Mental Health*, 8: 61–67.

Vetere, A. and Cooper, J. (2005) Children who witness violence at home. In A. Vetere and E. Dowling (eds) *Narrative Therapies with Children and Their Families*. London: Routledge.

Vetere, A. and Cooper, J. (2006) The effects of domestic violence on children: trauma, resilience and breaking the cycle of violence. *Journal of Critical Psychology, Counselling and Psychotherapy*, 1: 26–38.

Vetere, A. and Dallos, R. (2003) *Working Systemically with Families: Formulation, Intervention And evaluation*. London: Karnac.

Vetere, A. and Dallos, R. (2006) Attachment narratives and systemic therapy. *Context*, 90: 5–9.

Vetere, A. and Dallos, R. (2008) Systemic therapy and attachment narratives. *Journal of Family Therapy*, 30: 374–385.

Vetere, A. and Dowling, E. (2005) *Narrative Therapies with Children and their Families: A Practitioners Guide: Concepts and Approaches*. London: Routledge.

Vetere, A. and Henley, M. (2001) Integrating couples and family therapy into a community alcohol service: a pan-theoretical approach. *Journal of Family Therapy*, 23: 85–101.

Vetere, A. and Myers, L. (2006) Families, coping styles and health. In D. R. Crane and E. Marshall (eds) *Handbook of Families and Health: Interdisciplinary Perspectives*. Thousand Oaks, CA: Sage Publications.

Visher, E. B. and Visher, J. S. (1985) Stepfamilies are different. *Journal of Family Therapy*, 7: 9–18.

Vygotsky, L. (1962) *Thought and Language*. Cambridge, MA: MIT Press.

Vygotsky, L. (1986) *Thought and Language*. Cambridge, MA: MIT Press.

Ward, A., Ramsay, R. and Treasure, J. (2000) Attachment in eating disorders. *British Journal of Medical Psychology*, 73: 35–51.

Waskowic, T. and Chartier, B. (2003) Attachment and the experience of grief following the loss of a spouse. *Journal of Death and Dying*, 47: 77–91.

Watkins, P., Woodward, K., Stone, T. and Kolts, R. (2003) Gratitude and happiness: development of a measure of gratitude, and relationships with subjective well-being. *Social Behaviour and Personality*, 31: 431–452.

Watzlawick, P., Beavin, J. and Jackson, D. (1967) *Pragmatics of Human Communication*. New York: Norton.

Watzlawick, P., Weakland, J. and Fisch, R. (1974) *Change: Principles of Problem Formation and Problem Resolution*. New York: Norton.

Wave Trust (2005) *The Wave Report 2005: Violence and What To Do About It*. Croydon: Wave Trust.

Weakland, J. (1982) *The Tactics of Change*. San Fransisco, CA: Jossey-Bass.

White, M. (2006) Narrative practice with families with children: externalising conversations revisited. In M. White and A. Morgan (eds) *Narrative Therapy with Children and their Families*. Adelaide, Australia: Dulwich Centre Publications.

White, M. and Epston, D. (1990) *Narrative Means to Therapeutic Ends*. New York: Norton.

Wiener, C. (2007) *Attention Deficit Hyperactive Disorder as a Learned Behaviour Pattern*. Lanham, MD: University Press of America.

Winnicott, D. (1965) *The Maturational Process and the Facilitating Environment*. London: Hogarth Press.

Wood, A., Joseph, S. and Linley, A. (2007) Gratitude – parent of all virtues. *The Psychologist*, 20: 18–21.

Worden, J. (2003) *Grief Counselling and Grief Therapy* (3rd edition). London: Routledge.

Zajonc, R. (1968) Attitudinal effects of mere exposure. *Journal of Personality and Social Psychology*, 9: 1–27.

Index

Locators for headings with subheadings refer to general aspects of that topic.
Locators in **bold** type refer to figures/diagrams.

Lightning Source UK Ltd.
Milton Keynes UK
UKOW05f0429230217

295122UK00005B/36/P